Recollections of Caulaincourt, Duke of Vicenza

Both Volumes in One Special Edition

CAULAINCOURT, DUKE OF VICENZA

Recollections of Caulaincourt, Duke of Vicenza

Soldier, Commander, Diplomat and Aide to
Napoleon

Both Volumes in One Special Edition

Armand-Augustin-Louis Caulaincourt
and
Désormeaux Eilleaux

LEONAUR

Recollections of Caulaincourt, Duke of Vicenza
Soldier, Commander, Diplomat and Aide to Napoleon
Both Volumes in One Special Edition
by Armand-Augustin-Louis Caulaincourt and Désormeaux Eilleaux

First published under the titles
Recollections of Caulincourt, Duke of Vicenza in 2 volumes

Leonaur is an imprint
of Oakpast Ltd

Copyright in this form © 2016 Oakpast Ltd

ISBN: 978-1-78282-527-2(hardcover)
ISBN: 978-1-78282-528-9 (softcover)

http://www.leonaur.com

Publisher's Notes

Contents

CHAPTER 1

Accidental Meeting Between the Authoress and the Duke de Vicenza

On a fine warm morning in September, 1826, I was seated in one of the shadiest recesses of those lovely woodlands which skirt Plombières, on the side near the Stanislas Fountain. I had a book in my hand, but I was not reading: my thoughts were dreamingly wandering back to a glorious period of the past. Numerous pedestrians paced along the little path which intersected the wood, and near which I was sitting; but they did not rouse me from my reverie: they flitted like shadows before my eyes, without in any way fixing my attention.

I sat with my head resting on my hand, and with my eyes cast down, in a state of complete abstraction. My capricious fancy unfolded before me the magnificent basin of Antwerp, the port, and the spacious dockyards. Two fine vessels, gaily decked out, were to be launched that day, the one in the morning, and the other in the evening.

Napoleon was about to present to the people of the Netherlands the grand-niece of their celebrated Christina; and a series of truly regal *fêtes* were to take place in the principal towns of conquered, though not subjugated, Belgium.

The cathedral clock struck four as we alighted from our carriage at the *Tête de Flandre*. We got into a small boat, which landed us at the port of Antwerp, where all was movement and bustle, though the sun had scarcely risen. The sky appeared dull and cloudy. A *commissaire de marine,* in full uniform, who was issuing orders with a busy and important air, looked up, and, observing that the clouds were becoming more and more gloomy, his countenance expressed great anxiety. Addressing himself to an old soldier, who was occupied in tying some cords, he said, "Maringo, the wind is southwest; I am afraid we shall

7

have some rain. That will be confoundedly vexing."

"Pooh!" replied the soldier, with an indescribable air of confidence, "*he* always carries the Sun of Austerlitz in his pocket. What does *he* care for a few clouds!"

"*Monsieur*," said I, addressing the *commissaire*, "at what hour is the first ship to be launched?"

"Their Majesties will be here at six o'clock. Time and tide wait for no one."

"If they should wait for *him*," said the soldier, in a sort of muttering tone, "it would be nothing more than their duty."

We could not repress our laughter at this strange remark.

"There, my good man," said I, presenting to him a five-*franc* piece; "take this, and drink the emperor's health."

"Thank you, *Madame*," said he; "I would drink the emperor's health with all my heart. But the truth is," added he, significantly scratching his ear, "that Maringo—Maringo knows his own railing. If I begin to drink the emperor's health I shall not have done whilst a single *sou* of the five-*franc* piece remains; and that will not do—especially after *he* did me the honour to notice me yesterday: 'What do you do here, my brave fellow?' said *he*. Now, if I were to drink my hundred *sous*, I should certainly be turned to the right about, and marched to the *Salle de Police*. I would not for worlds that our beloved emperor should have the least cause to reproach me."

Napoleon possessed a power of fascination which inspired his brave and devoted soldiers with the singular belief that each of them individually was an object of attention and consideration to their sovereign.

The places assigned to me and my friends were exactly facing the imperial tent. We saw the emperor arrive. His youthful consort, Maria Louisa, was the object of his assiduous attention. Napoleon's countenance beamed with love and happiness; and he seemed to be proud of showing the empress to his subjects. The ceremony of the launch commenced. A thundering discharge of artillery from the fort, together with the guns on board the ships in the river, saluted the new vessel as she majestically glided into the Scheldt. At that moment the emperor, whose countenance appeared to brighten up with increased animation at the firing of the guns, passed his arm round the waist of his trembling wife, and drew her close to him, as if to protect her from a danger which had no existence. Three years later, that wife forsook her husband, and accepted the protection of others. But, thought I,

Maria Louisa is not a Frenchwoman: this reflection soothed my indignant feelings.

I now awoke from my reverie of recollections. I mechanically raised my head, and I observed a gentleman slowly ascending the sloping path near the spot where I was seated, and from time to time stopping to rest himself. As he approached I was struck with his appearance. His figure was slender and pliant, and he had an air of youth, in spite of his premature wrinkles and his pale and attenuated countenance.

A thought, as it were a reflection of the past, suddenly darted across my mind. That person, said I within myself, is like the apparition of one who is still fresh in my recollection. But when last I saw him, he held his bead proudly erect; his figure, which now appears bowed by infirmity, was then upright, and a rich military uniform accorded with his graceful and gallant bearing. His whole aspect denoted energy and courage; his look bespoke the confidence of a man occupying one of those high positions, to fall from which must be almost at the expense of life.

I beheld before me the Grand Equerry of the Empire, the Duke de Vicenza!

As I gazed upon him, a feeling of melancholy took possession of my mind, and tears, which I could not repress, overflowed my eyes.

"*Mademoiselle*," said the duke, addressing my *femme de chambre*, who was sitting at work near me, "does this path lead straight to the Stanislas Fountain?"

"Yes, *Monsieur le Duc*," replied I, rising hastily from my seat; though I was at the time very ill and feeble.

He advanced a few steps towards me, and with that grace of manner for which all will admit he was eminently distinguished, he said—

"*Madame*, have I the honour to be known to you?"

"Yes," I replied; "all the golden dreams of my youth refer to the glories of the Empire. Of late years I have unremittingly deplored its disasters; and the devoted loyalty of the Duke de Vicenza is in my mind inseparably connected with the name of Napoleon!"

We entered cordially into conversation. We revived old recollections. The great actors in the heroic drama had been mutually known to us. Our sympathies reverted warmly and vividly to the past. From that day our; interminable.

When I met the Duke de Vicenza at Plombières, in 1826, he had grown exceedingly thin. His hair was almost entirely grey, and his altered features bore evidence of the poignant mental suffering he had

9

endured. Instead of a few years, it seemed as though half a century had passed over Napoleon's brilliant Equerry. That dreadful and incurable disease, a cancer in the stomach, was rapidly shortening the thread of his existence. Doctor Broussais had advised him to take the waters of Plombières; but the duke made little or no trial of their efficacy. Life was a burden to him. That existence once so radiant with glory and happiness, was now over-clouded by painful recollections. "There is no longer any room for me in France," I have often heard him say.

The two months I passed at Plombières were to me a sort of compensation for one of those intervals of trial in which we sometimes imagine ourselves forsaken by Heaven—in which we ask ourselves what crime we are doomed to expiate by unremitting suffering—when we pray that each succeeding night may be our last, whilst every morning brings a renewal of pain and anguish. In this pitiable condition, Death, which we can neither fly from nor overtake, is ever present in our view.

I had lingered through three long years in a state of languor between life and death. My resignation and fortitude were almost exhausted. My medical attendants ordered me to travel; and I, weary of confinement, and of those monotonous amusements which had for a time afforded some little diversion during lingering nights and days, joyfully availed myself of the permission afforded me, to suffer in other places, to see other objects, and to inhale a change of air. One of my relations, Colonel R——, offered to be my escort. We travelled by short stages, and the journey was so long, that Plombières seemed to me to be at the further extremity of the world. On our arrival we found the town full of company; and I was obliged to take up my abode at the *Tête d'Or*, the hotel at which our postillion stopped,

My feeble condition prevented me from either making or receiving visits; and I lived perfectly tranquil and secluded in the gay and fashionable town. There were at that time six thousand visitors in Plombières. Arrivals and departures succeeded each other continually; and the excitement, bustle, and animation, doubtless afforded agreeable excitement to invalids less afflicted than myself.

Disabled as I was from participating in the amusements of the place, I regarded my unexpected meeting with the Duke de Vicenza as a singular instance of good fortune. The duke also was suffering severely from illness; and Colonel R—— and myself were the only persons with whom he associated. We met regularly every morning at the Crucifix Fountain, and we afterwards made a ramble of a few hours in the outskirts of the town. I used to ride on one of the wretched little horses of the country, whilst the gentlemen accompanied me on foot.

The duke lodged in a house adjoining our hotel. He occupied the apartments in which the Empress Josephine resided when the balcony of the first floor window gave way and the empress and two of her ladies were precipitated into the street.

What remarkable coincidences sometimes fix our attention! Twenty years after the accident to which I have just alluded, the Duke de Vicenza reposed in the same bedchamber which had so often resounded with the name of Napoleon, pronounced by the sweet accents of Josephine's voice.

It was now the month of September; the evenings were beginning to lengthen, and, with some few exceptions, we passed them all in the society of the Duke de Vicenza. He usually came to us about seven o'clock; and often, when the great town clock struck twelve, we expressed our wonder at the rapidity with which the hours had flown.

The duke felt little inclination to sleep, and Colonel R——and myself were never weary of listening to his conversation, which was always replete with interesting facts. My questions, and his complaisance in answering them, were alike inexhaustible.

The Duke de Vicenza had been the confidant and the bosom friend of Napoleon. He had been entrusted with the most important diplomatic functions, and he always corresponded directly with the emperor. There was no intermediary between them. Their correspondence was the communion of thought between man and man—the private instructions of a sovereign to his trustworthy and intelligent friend. The Duke de Vicenza was, of all men, best qualified to describe Napoleon; he possessed a profound knowledge of his character, and was acquainted with all those little shades of feeling which are imperceptible to common observers. To his ministers, his generals, and to all who approached him, the emperor maintained the character of the monarch; to Caulincourt only he was Napoleon. He might be good or ill-humoured, merry or sad, angry or pleased, but he was always sincere, always himself.

The reason was, that the Duke de Vicenza was a man distinguished amidst all the crowd of courtiers. He possessed an intrinsic superiority, a natural dignity,—he was gifted with a certain elegance of manner and language, which elevated him, as it were, above his equals, and commanded the admiration of everyone. The coldness with which I have seen him reproached was inherent in his proud and independent nature. He had a perfect consciousness of his own superiority; but his exquisite good breeding tempered any little asperities to which the gravity of his manner might give birth.

After an animated argument, the emperor once said to the Duke de Vicenza: "You are a bar of iron—an absolute bar of iron; there is no bending you but by thrusting you into the fire."

"Well, Sire, I frankly confess that I am a bar of iron with your Majesty more than with any other person in the world."

"Ah! indeed!"

"It must inevitably be so, Sire; for when I contradict your Majesty, be assured that nothing but the most decided conviction of being in the right could induce me to do so."

I had remarked that the Duke de Vicenza, when speaking of the emperor, never omitted those respectful forms of expression which he had been accustomed to employ when personally addressing his sovereign. There was a delicate feeling of propriety in this observance: it was an homage rendered to illustrious misfortune. I one day mentioned to the duke how sensibly I felt this mark of good taste.

"My recollections," said he, "are a sanctuary in which I have preserved, in all its warmth and purity, the exalted sentiment which has survived death. I rarely speak of the emperor, and never to those who do not understand my feelings."

The Duke de Vicenza cherished ardent but not blind admiration for Napoleon. He was himself gifted with keen, discriminating powers of judgment, and his enthusiasm for the emperor was based on his own knowledge of Napoleon's mental superiority.

"I have known," said he to us, "nearly all the crowned heads of the present age—all our illustrious contemporaries. I have lived with several of those great historical characters on a footing of confidence and intimacy quite distinct from my diplomatic duties. I have had every opportunity of comparing and judging; but it is impossible to institute any comparison between Napoleon and any other man: those who say otherwise did not know him.

"That noble-hearted fellow, Duroc, once said to me, with his characteristic simplicity of manner—'The emperor, my dear Caulincourt, appears to me to be endowed with a variety of mental faculties, any one of which would suffice to distinguish a man from the multitude. For example, he is the greatest captain of the age—a sovereign, whose ministers are merely his clerks—a statesman, who directs the whole business of the country, and superintends every branch of the service; and yet this Colossus of gigantic proportions can descend with wonderful facility to the most trivial details of private life. He can regulate the expenditure of his household, as he regulates the finances of the empire.' Duroc's remarks were just.

"Some persons have applied a silly and incorrect epithet to the devoted friends of the emperor. Napoleon had no *seides*; he had fanatical admirers, but their fanaticism was founded on conviction.

"As to myself, whenever I take a retrospective glance at the past, it seems as though some rays of the meteor diffused a light over my memory.

"On the day of the Battle of Jena, the emperor sent for me about three o'clock in the morning. He had not been in bed. I found him 'irritable and impatient. Some orders which he had dispatched on the preceding evening had not been executed. As yet all the arrangements were in an advanced state of progress; but the apprehension that any delay might ensue rendered the emperor anxious and impatient. Every moment staff-officers were entering with reports of the missions on which they had been sent during the night. They were required to express themselves very laconically, for the emperor could not endure prolixity or hesitation. The Prince of Neufchatel might certainly have spared him the fatigue of receiving these officers; but the emperor always wished to direct the details of his military plans. His movements were so ordered that it would have been difficult for any but himself to form a comprehensive idea of the whole. The fate of battle depended on the intelligence and strict punctuality of those who had orders to execute. The emperor was therefore greatly irritated when his calculations were thwarted by any neglect or omission.

"'Sire,' said I, when I saw him on the morning of the Battle of Bautzen, we shall have a hard day's work. It is now only four o'clock, your Majesty has had no rest . . .'

"—'Impossible, Caulincourt. I have my plan here,' said he, passing his hand lightly across his forehead, 'but there is yet nothing—nothing marked on my maps. Rustan, go and fetch Dalbe. Desire Dalbe to come to me immediately.'

"A map of the ground chosen as the field of battle had been drawn the day before. Leaning on the table on which it was spread out, the emperor traced his plan rapidly, but with the utmost precision.

"'Now that will do—you understand, Caulincourt! You have all my arrangements in your head. Mount a horse—go and inspect the ground, and select for me a spot whence I may command a view of the field of battle. I shall be on the field at six o'clock.'

"He threw himself on his camp bed, and in a few moments he sunk into a profound sleep.

"The action commenced at nine in the morning, and at two in the afternoon the conflict was still maintained with unabated fury. The victory was so obstinately disputed on both sides that it was impossible for any one to foresee the issue of the engagement. The emperor, who, with his staff, was stationed on a height, anxiously watched the movements of the two armies. Suddenly he quitted his position, spurred his horse, and set off at full gallop. Proceeding to the right of the field of battle, he mounted an eminence which was completely uncovered. The ground was furrowed by the enemy's balls. A battalion of grenadiers had been posted there to do the duty of *tirailleurs*.

"'Dalbe! the maps—the maps!' exclaimed the emperor, alighting from his horse.

"The maps were spread upon the ground. He examined them, traced out several evolutions with his finger, then took a telescope and stood for some time gazing on the scene of slaughter around us. On every side the artillery kept up a terrific fire, and the action was hotly maintained at every point. The emperor, whose intrepid calmness did not for a moment forsake him amidst this frightful devastation, alternately examined his maps and surveyed the field of battle. At length, laying down his telescope, he said—'Gentlemen, the battle is gained. In a week we shall sleep at Berlin.'

"These words were truly magical. They were calculated to rouse the coldest imagination. The fact was, that at that moment none of us could have formed an opinion of the probable loss or gain of the battle, the fate of which was not really decided until more than four days after. Victory was ours, but it was purchased at the price of the most heroic efforts.

"I wish," said the Duke de Vicenza, whose countenance at this moment glowed, as it were, with a reflected light of happiness, "I wish I could retrace to you all the details of this simple anecdote, which so well portrays Napoleon's genius. The emperor had no sooner uttered the words, *the battle is gained, in a week we shall sleep at Berlin*, than the soldiers who had gradually approached now gathered round him so closely that he had scarcely room to mount his horse.

"'Fall back! fall back!' exclaimed the officers of the staff.

"'Let them advance! Let them advance!' said the emperor. 'They shall march with me to Berlin; I will not go without them.'

"The air now resounded with joyful and enthusiastic acclamations. The men waved their caps, and shouted '*Vive l'Empereur!*—On to Berlin with the emperor!'* There was not one of these brave fellows who did not wish he had ten lives instead of one to sacrifice for Napoleon.

"It is impossible by description to convey any idea of the grace, I may almost say the coquetry, of Napoleon's manner when he addressed his troops. There was an irresistible charm in the tone of his voice when he wished to please those to whom he spoke; and that was always his wish when he addressed himself to his veteran *moustaches*.

"I remember that on the evening of the Battle of Bautzen he passed an hospital waggon. It was a horrible spectacle:—a mountain of amputated arms and legs presented itself to our eyes. A *cuirassier* of the old guard, stretched on the ground, was struggling with two adjutants who were endeavouring to hold him, whilst Larrey was preparing to amputate the limb of the wounded man, whose thigh bone had been dreadfully shattered by the bursting of a bomb-shell.

"'Be quiet! be quiet! coward!' exclaimed Larrey, impatiently.

"But the poor fellow still resisted; and the tears run down his cheeks, which were blackened by gunpowder.

"'What is the matter?' inquired the emperor, riding up to the spot where the *cuirassier* lay, 'How is this?' continued he; 'surely a brave *moustache* like you are not afraid of a cut?'

"'No, your Majesty, I am not afraid of a cut; but this is a sort of cut that a man may die of—and there is Catherine and her four little ones.—You know the *cantinière* of the 2nd Cuirassiers?'

"'What of her?' said the emperor.

"'She is my wife, your Majesty, and we have four children—and if I should die'—continued he, striving to repress the sobs which almost choked his utterance.

"'Well, and what if you should die, my good fellow? am I not here?'

"'True, your Majesty—I am very foolish.—Well, doctor, if it must be so, cut off my limb. God bless the emperor!'

"'Larrey,' said the emperor, 'perform this operation in the most careful manner; and in a month hence let him be entered at the Hospital of the Invalides, in Paris.'

"'*Vive l'Empereur!*' exclaimed the wounded *cuirassier*, and his brother invalids in the hospital waggon joined in the shout.

"It has been alleged that the emperor was not endowed with much susceptibility of feeling: there is some truth in this, but perhaps it would be more just to say that he had not time to indulge the emotions of his heart. He proceeded straight forward to the object he had in view, without heeding the thorns which were scattered along his path. Thus, in the hundreds of battles in which he lost so many valuable officers, if feelings of regret arose in his heart, he seldom sought, by the expression of them, to console the grief of others."

Here the duke paused, and heaved a deep sigh.

"There is one occasion," observed I, "on which the emperor appeared to me to betray great want of feeling. I allude to an observation he made after the Battle of the Moskowa, where your brother, Auguste de Caulincourt, was killed. To you, duke, I may speak without reserve, and I must say that I was shocked at the words which the emperor addressed to you in reference to the melancholy circumstance. These words are authentically recorded, and hold a place in history. 'Caulincourt,' said he, 'this, you know, is one of the disasters of war.' There was something exceedingly heartless in this. If he really felt no sympathy in the deep grief of a friend, he should have held his tongue, and silence might possibly have been taken for feeling. Alas! how grievous it is to utter a reproach against one whom we so devotedly worship."

The duke fixed his eyes on me, and I could easily perceive that his mind was occupied by a painful recollection, which the hand of time had but faintly soothed. I inwardly blamed my own inadvertence. I perceived that I had unguardedly given utterance to an idea which doubtless the duke had often sought to check when it arose in his own mind. The grave had now closed over all. The generous heart of Caulincourt cherished no feeling but pure and everlasting regret.

I had touched a chord which vibrated painfully, and I stretched out my hand to him in token of my regret. He took it, and pressed it cordially in his.

"How well you enter into my feelings," said he, with a melancholy smile.

"So well," replied I, "that I will be careful to remember the remark you made some time ago, that the emperor must not be judged on the same level with other men."

The redoubt at which General Auguste de Caulincourt fell was watered with the blood of a thousand brave men and three generals: but the redoubt was carried, and the battle won.

General Moreau lost at once his life and his honour at the Battle of Dresden. Never was crime followed by more prompt and signal punishment. The vengeance of Heaven seemed to have fallen on the head of the apostate! When the emperor was informed of Moreau's death, he hastily turned to the Duke de Vicenza, and whispered in his ear—"My star! Caulincourt! My fortunate star! Oh! this event will form one of the most important pages in my history!"

Several times in the course of that same evening he reverted to the subject. According to his ideas of fatalism, the death of Moreau was a favour of fortune—a returning smile of that destiny which had taken Lieutenant Bonaparte by the hand and led him through the path of glory to the highest altitude of worldly greatness—which enabled him to count kings among his vassals, and to hold a court at Tilsit to decide what share of his munificence each sovereign should receive.

That a French cannon ball should have laid Moreau prostrate at the very moment of his appearance in the enemy's camp is one of those extraordinary occurrences which it is difficult to refer to mere chance. Napoleon deduced from the fact a variety of consequences, suggested by his faith in predestination. The words which he whispered in the ear of his friend were characteristic of his feelings—"My star! Caulincourt!"

"I must confess," said the duke to me when we were conversing on this subject, "that Moreau's extraordinary death almost inclined me to share the emperor's impressions. The multitude is marvellously prone to seize on these sinister moral lessons. With the name of General Moreau an awful warning will be for ever associated."

CHAPTER 2

An Excursion to Remiremont

We had arranged with the Duke de Vicenza to make an excursion to Remiremont, a pretty little town, situated about four leagues from Plombières. At seven in the morning we set out in an open carriage. We visited the ruins of the celebrated Abbey of Remiremont. The church alone remains undecayed. In the cloister our attention was attracted by the remnants of a tomb, of the date of the middle ages. An old legend records that the beautiful Isaure de Coulanges, surnamed *l'Astre des nuits*, is interred beneath this monument.

This excursion very much fatigued the duke. He was so ill that he was confined to his room for two or three days. When he was well enough to see us, we called on him. Our conversation happened to turn on his embassy to Russia—on those four brilliant and poetic years of his existence.

"The time I spent in Russia," said the Duke de Vicenza, "is almost the only interval of my life to which I can refer without the fear of conjuring up some painful recollection.

"In 1807, when I was sent as Ambassador to Russia, the Emperor Napoleon had attained the zenith of his political fortune. France had no boundaries save those determined by her sovereign. The French name was a talisman to which the nations of the world rendered homage and obedience. Then, indeed, there was glory and honour in being the representative of France!

"The emperor always entertained a just idea of the noble and the grand. He was economical in his own personal expenses, and a decided foe to extravagance and wastefulness; yet he was munificent in all that related to the dignity of the crown. No sovereign had a nicer perception of what was due to his exalted position. He was desirous that the ambassador of the greatest nation in the world should maintain, with regal splendour, the rank of the country be had the honour to represent. 'I give you a *carte blanche* for the expenses of the embassy,' said he to me. 'We must not appear like citizens grown rich—the court of France must not show itself mean and petty. Our brother of Russia loves pleasure and luxury. Give magnificent *fêtes*—let them have something for their money.'

"He laughed heartily at this allusion. The emperor was rarely gay, but when he was so, his flow of spirits rendered him singularly communicative.

"If, Sire, I might venture to employ a vulgar phrase, but one that is *àpropos* to the subject, I should say—"

"'That they have paid the piper beforehand,' interrupted he, with a renewed burst of laughter; then, with true Italian mobility of spirit, he added:—'Now, Caulincourt, let us talk seriously on cabinet diplomacy. As to the diplomacy of the drawing-room, I feel assured that you will manage that like a true nobleman. Attend to me, Caulincourt bear in mind my instructions; and, above all, bear in mind my political plans and my system. If you do not thoroughly comprehend me, you will not be able to serve me well. In diplomacy, tact and good management are better than cunning. The machinery which used to be set in motion by the diplomatists of past times is now worn out. All their *finesse* is now well known; and after all, when we have it in our power to speak decidedly and downrightly,' continued he, raising his head haughtily, 'why should we resort to cunning? Dissimulation is always a mark of weakness.'

"He then explained to me his policy in reference to the court of Russia, and took a profound and luminous view of its consequences. His plan was gigantic, and was destined to produce incalculable results. Our conversation was long, and every observation that fell from him so completely riveted my attention, that his instructions were indelibly impressed on my mind. My mission was a great and glorious one, and I felt within me the power to execute it worthily. Whether the emperor intended to give me his final decision in this conversation I know not; but it is certain, that in the course of my embassy I frequently reminded him (though, alas, in vain) of the instructions I had received on the eve of my departure from Paris. But enough of this!

"You wish," continued the duke, "that I should introduce you to the brilliant court of Russia, where I found realised all the traditions of the youthful days of Louis XIV. Indeed, the glories of the *Grand Monarque* seemed at that time a fond dream at the court of St. Petersburg. No court ever presented within itself so many elements of pleasure and excitement. Youth, beauty, gaiety, and splendour, were ever grouped round the throne.

"On reception days, the scene which presented itself in the saloons of the palace exceeded all that imagination can picture. It was a realisation of the wonders of the *Arabian Nights*. Women of the most captivating beauty, grace, and elegance, were sparkling in diamonds, and arrayed with a gorgeousness truly Asiatic. Some were intelligent and well educated, others frivolous and ignorant; but all were beautiful, and all devotedly fond of music and dancing. The young men, by the grace of their manners and language, and the elegance and luxury of their dress, completely eclipsed our most approved Parisian models, our Richelieus, Narbonnes, &c. &c.

"Every day brought new *fêtes*, new parties of pleasure. I confess that I found it no very easy matter to maintain my establishment in a style corresponding with Russian notions of munificence. Balls, concerts, plays, and suppers, occupied the evenings; and sledge parties were a favourite day amusement. I will mention one example out of a thousand, to give you an idea of the profuse expenditure of money in Russia.

"At a supper which was given after a ball at the Embassy, a plate of five pears cost 125 *louis*. On another occasion, cherries, which had been, purchased at the price of four *francs* each, were served as abundantly as though they had cost no more than twenty *sous* per pound. You must not imagine that this was an exception worthy of remark, or calculated to excite surprise. On the contrary, any attempt to spare this expense would have appeared shabby and absurd. Rayneval, my principal secretary, a very clever and promising young man, used frequently to join with me in deploring the necessity of this lavish waste of money.

"I must repeat to you a remark made by the emperor on this subject. In my private correspondence with him, I frequently entered into the most minute details of all that was going on. He had desired me to write him gossiping letters. They amused him. When I informed him of the pears at 25 *louis* a piece, he answered, 'When I was a sub-lieutenant I should have thought myself very fortunate if my yearly income had been as much as the price of your plate of Russian pears. Such extravagances are only to be expected in madmen or fools.'

"I am certain," added the duke, smiling, "that the emperor was really angry at this silly profusion. *Though the piper had been paid before-*

hand, yet he found it very difficult to digest, the pears and cherries."

"Truly," observed I, "in a person so temperate and economical as our emperor, such wanton prodigality was well calculated to excite contempt, and even anger."

"During my residence at St. Petersburg," resumed the duke, "I was continually struck by the curious contrasts which presented themselves to my observation. It would be difficult to convey an idea of the surprise which was excited in us Frenchmen on witnessing the absolute despotism of the emperor, and the sort of idolatrous worship rendered to him throughout his dominions. Then, on the other hand, the excessive familiarity which the Emperor Alexander sometimes tolerated on the part of persons of inferior condition exceeds all belief.

"There was a company of French actors at St Petersburg; Mesdemoiselles Georges and Bourgoin, and Duport, of the opera, were among them, and excited great admiration. The comedian, Frogère, a pupil of Dugazon, was a young man of agreeable manners, and possessed considerable talent He had a good stock of that ready wit which is estimated highly in all countries. Frogère amused the emperor, who treated him with wonderful condescension. This encouraged him to draw largely on His Majesty's favour. Frogère was freely admitted into the highest society. There was no file at the palace, at the embassy, or at the residences of the nobility, to which Frogère was not invited. In short, he was quite the rage.

"One evening, at a party given by the empress, Frogère stepped up to the emperor, and, drawing from his pocket an enormous snuffbox filled with *ducats*, he presented it to his Majesty, saying, 'Sire, will you take a pinch?'

"'What is the meaning of this joke?' inquired Alexander, with a good-humoured smile.

"'It means. Sire, that if your Majesty would take a pinch I shall feel much honoured. M. Demidoff, who sent me this snuff-box today, informs me, that if your Majesty would be pleased to confer upon him the dignity of Knight Commander of Malta, which you promised him, he would often send me a supply of this snuff.'

"'Well, well, my dear Frogère, I will take care that you shall often have a pinch of Demidoff's snuff.' Soon after this the wished-for cross was seen on M. Demidoff's breast

"The Emperor Alexander was one day conversing with Frogère on the dramatic art, and the pleasures of an actor's life. In the course of the conversation, Frogère observed—'You have no need to envy anyone, Sire. The truth is, that if I were not the actor Frogère, I should wish to be the Emperor of Russia.'

"The first presentation of Frogère to the Grand Duke Constantine took place one morning at the hour when the duke received his familiar visitors, whilst he was at his *toilette*. His Imperial Highness drew on a pair of yellow leather pantaloons, such as were worn at that time. Having found some fault with them, he drew them off again, and desired his valet to bring him another pair. Constantine, though his countenance was far from handsome, possessed a very fine figure, and he bestowed great attention on his dress. The grand duke, wholly intent on the business of his *toilette*, had not addressed a word to Frogère, when the latter said—

"'*Monseigneur!* I am not your dupe!'

"The grand duke turned round sharply, and, advancing towards Frogère, with an angry look, said—'What do you mean by that?'

"'I mean, your Highness, that I am not your dupe. You wish to show me that you have a handsome leg, and that you have two pairs of pantaloons at your service.'

"Everyone present burst into a fit of laughter, and from that time Frogère became a favourite with the grand duke.

"In France," added the Duke de Vicenza, "we have no taste for extravagances of this sort. Napoleon would have thrown Frogère out of the window."

I felt very curious to know some particulars respecting a certain lady who made a conspicuous figure at the court of St. Petersburg at the period to which the duke's conversation now referred. "Pray, duke," said I, "tell me something about the beautiful Madame N——, with whom the Emperor Alexander was so deeply in love, and whose coquetry so tormented him. I am quite of Napoleon's taste. I dearly love gossip."

"Oh!" replied the duke, smiling, "Alexander's passion for the fascinating Maria-Antona N—— is quite a romance.

"Madame N——, the wife of the emperor's grand huntsman, was allied on her mother's side to the Imperial family. If I were gifted with descriptive talent, I would draw a portrait of such captivating loveliness that it would turn the heads of half the young men in France, and yet it would fall far short of my model. How is it possible to describe grace of manner and the expression of a heavenly countenance? and these were the charms which rendered Madame N—— the most irresistibly fascinating woman I ever beheld. She was beautiful, exquisitely beautiful, clever, lively—an accomplished musician, an excellent singer, and a most desperate *coquette*.

"One day, when I drew her portrait in this way, to herself, she laughed heartily, and told me the likeness was not flattered.

"I feel convinced that if I had had the good fortune, or the ill fortune, to be the lover of that delightful woman, she would have driven me mad.

"A few months after my arrival at St. Petersburg, the Emperor Alexander admitted me to his friendship. He possessed a truly noble and amiable disposition. We were both of the same age. I loved him as a brother; and he, on his part, maintained his intercourse with me on a footing of friendship and equality which he could not have extended even to his own brothers. Sovereigns can only nave subjects. Sentimental people may deny this feet, but it is nevertheless incontrovertible.

"Many times, when the court circle had broken up, and I had returned home—indeed, not un frequently after I had retired to bed, have I seen the Emperor Alexander enter my chamber. He would pass a portion of the night seated at my bedside, and making me the confidant of his sorrows, his anxieties, and jealousies.

"On one of these occasions he said to me, 'Did you remark, my dear duke, how *coquettishly* she conversed this evening with Tol——? She danced three times with him!—with that blockhead Tol——, who looks just like a lackey, always stooping down to pick up a glove, a fan, or a bouquet, and all to obtain a look or a smile. What fools men are! Such conduct really excites contempt'

"But, your Majesty——'

"'Ah, my dear Caulincourt, for the hundredth time let me entreat you not to address me thus. If you are to regard me merely as a sovereign, there must be an end of this confidential and friendly intercourse, which renders me so happy.'

"'Well then, Sire, let me ask you, do you think it extraordinary that other men besides yourself should admire Madame N——?'

"'But they have not commonsense. My dear friend, I assure you that woman renders me the most miserable of men by her insufferable *coquetry*. She knows it, and cares not. When I reproach her for her love of admiration and flattery, she replies—"What else do women live for? What would life be worth if deprived of all that is agreeable and poetic? I love only you, Alexander; but I like the admiration of all!" She'll drive me mad!' sighed the Autocrat of all the Russias, in the most pitiable manner imaginable.

"When he succeeded in forgetting her for a few hours, he was quite elated by his revenge. But in a little time he was more her slave than ever, and she made him pay dearly for his infidelity.

"It was said that the beautiful Mademoiselle G—— for a time seduced Alexander from his allegiance to Madame N——. All the admirers of the latter lady, elated by hope, were immediately at her feet. Madame N—— felt the slight severely; and though it did not perhaps very deeply wound her heart, yet it mortified her pride.

"The handsome Leon N——, the cousin of Madame N——, had long been an ardent though a silent admirer of his captivating relation. The lady now encouraged him by a few kind words, and his long repressed passion burst out without reserve. He was deeply in love, and was no longer able to conceal the sentiment that gained complete mastery over his soul. He was just at that age when a young man will not hesitate to sacrifice glory, fortune, and even life itself, to an absorbing passion. Leon sacrificed all these. Whether he secured happiness I cannot inform you.

"No circumstance that took place at court could be kept secret. The emperor was not disinclined to be faithless himself, but he did not choose that Madame N—— should follow his example. The consequence was, that a furious fit of jealousy took possession of the emperor.

"'These people,' said he to me, 'are sporting with their own lives, or at least with their fortunes and liberty. I have the power to annihilate the audacious N——, and I might use it. But no, that heartless *coquette* shall not induce me to exile a man for her sake. My dear duke, I cannot prevail on myself to commit such an act of severity to avenge a personal injury to myself. And yet I sometimes feel very much inclined to send that coxcomb Leon N—— to make an excursion in Siberia.'

"I endeavoured to soothe him, and to avert the imperial thunder from the head of the unfortunate lover. I urged many arguments in his behalf.

"'I am certain she does not love him,' resumed the emperor; 'she has not the least regard for him. Antona, in fact, loves no one. She is vain and cold-hearted! She thinks by this means to punish me, to drive me to despair; but she shall see that I know how to estimate her. I assure you that she is now entirely an object of indifference to me.'

"I must needs confess, that whilst the emperor uttered these words

24

I found it no easy matter to preserve my gravity; for I could clearly see through the *coquettish* manoeuvre adopted by Madame de N——. Her object merely was to alarm the emperor's jealousy, and she had succeeded beyond her expectations.

"The misunderstanding between the emperor and the lady, which lasted a month, kept the court in a state of commotion; it was the general topic of conversation. A nobleman of high rank, who was admitted to the intimacy of Alexander, was appointed to open negotiations for peace, and diplomatic notes were regularly exchanged. The lady would stoop to no abatement of her high dignity, and the correspondence was maintained with all the forms which would have been observed between two sovereign powers. It was really a most amusing affair. The empress' drawing-room presented a curious field for observation. There the two belligerent powers, the emperor and Madame N——, appeared every evening face to face.

"Surely," said I, "the *amours* of Alexander must have caused great uneasiness to the empress, who, I have understood, was very beautiful."

"The Empress Elizabeth was a beautiful and captivating woman; but she was amiable and resigned, and she never complained of her fate, though her heart was blighted. The crown well became her noble brow; and she well understood the mission of a woman who wears a crown; she suffered, and smiled. Elizabeth concealed, amidst the splendour of her imperial state, that deep sorrow, that mortal anguish, which casts a gloom even over the brightest things. When her melancholy and penetrating glance dwelt on the lovely countenance of Madame N——, she seemed to reproach her for having usurped her happiness. The beautiful, graceful, and accomplished Elizabeth, was neglected by the man to whom she had given all her affection, and whom she loved, not because be was Emperor of all the Russias, but because he was Alexander."

The evening was advancing, and we took leave of the Duke de Vicenza. Next day we met him at the fountain.

CHAPTER 3

Imperial Reviews

In describing the interesting conversations which we had the good fortune to enjoy with the Duke of Vicenza, I am aware that I may incur the reproach of turning suddenly from one subject to another, and totally disregarding the order of dates. My explanation will be brief.

We listened to the revelations of the duke with all the intense interest natural to persons who were being made acquainted with new facts in a marvellous period of history. I every morning made notes of what I had heard during the preceding day; but in so doing, my object was merely to while away some of those tedious hours which always hang heavily on an invalid; and I had no thought of collecting materials for publication.

I copy my notes literally, without any attempt to arrange dates or subjects; these pages, therefore, present a faithful record of the conversations of a man whose statements need not the colouring of fiction to invest them with interest.

We had been greatly amused in listening to the anecdotes of the court of St. Petersburg, related in the foregoing chapter, and I asked the Duke de Vicenza whether his recollections of Russia were exhausted.

"I understand you," replied he; "I know there is more kindness than curiosity in your wish to return with me to St Petersburg because in so doing we must for awhile forsake Napoleon for Alexander. I have brought with me to Plombières all the papers relating to my embassy to Russia. I happen at this moment to have in my pocket a little autograph note of the emperor, which I will show you.

"I have already told you that the Emperor Napoleon was curious to know all that was passing misunderstanding which prevailed for the space of a month between Alexander and the beautiful Madame

N—— was like an armistice which precedes either peace or a decisive battle. The emperor, who was still a young man, in every sense of the term, could turn his thoughts to nothing but the capitulation which the lady was making him wait for,—the victory which she intended to make him purchase dearly. He was quite unable to attend to business; to get him to sign any document, or to discuss any serious affair, would have been impossible. 'The head follows the heart,' said he to me one day; 'suppose, my dear Caulincourt, that we defer this communication till next week; write to your court, and say that I am rather unwell. You will only tell the truth. That woman will drive me mad!'"

"After I had acquainted the Emperor Napoleon with this affair, he wrote me the following note in his own hand. It was appended to a letter containing diplomatic instructions:—

It is not a matter of indifference to me to observe the character of that man, who was born a sovereign. A woman turns the head of the Autocrat of all the Russias! All the women in the world would not make me lose an hour. Continue to acquaint me of everything; let me know the most minute details. The private life of a man is a mirror in which we may see many useful lessons reflected.

"But," pursued the duke, "if Napoleon was eager to know all that was passing in the court of Russia, Alexander was no less curious in his inquiries respecting the Tuileries. When he questioned me closely, you may easily imagine that I protected myself by a due share of diplomatic discretion.

"With the Empress Elizabeth I found it no easy task to maintain my reserve. Her Majesty's questions respecting Napoleon were endless. Whenever I was present in her little drawing-room circle, she subjected me to a minute interrogatory respecting the countenance, the figure, the manners, and the habits, of *my* emperor. Then, with the graceful frivolity of a woman, she would string together endless questions respecting our court receptions, our balls, *fêtes*, and fashions; whether the French ladies were as fascinating as she had heard them represented? What was their court costume? &c &c. As I could answer such questions without the fear of compromising any state secrets, I most willingly resigned my ambassadorial dignity to enjoy the pleasure of chatting with the charming Empress Elizabeth.

"'*Monsieur le Duc*,' said she one day, in that soft sweet voice which I never heard equalled; '*Monsieur le Duc,* how I should like to hide myself in a little corner whence I might get a peep at one of your court balls! How I should like to see your beautiful countrywomen, arrayed in all their grace and elegance! I am told that they are exceedingly captivating.'

"Oh, your Majesty, replied I, there are captivating women in every country.

"'I don't know that, for I have never been out of Russia,' said she, with indescribable archness of manner; 'however, it is very certain that we cannot vie with the Parisian ladies in elegance. Their fashions never reach us until they are quite out of date.' As she uttered these words her pretty countenance assumed an expression of regret.

"Even Napoleon, the Great Captain," continued the duke, "did not think it beneath him sometimes to turn his attention to female dress. Several ladies at the court of the Tuileries knew this by sad experience. One day at Saint Cloud, I heard him say, in a very angry tone, to the wife of a general, '*Madame,* when a lady has a husband with an income of 100,000 *francs per annum,* she may very well afford a new dress every time she has the honour to pay her court to the empress. Endowments, *Madame,* are favours. I do not owe them; and when I give them it is with the view that they should help to maintain that luxury without which commerce cannot thrive.' The poor lady was overwhelmed with confusion; yet it must be admitted that the general shabbiness of her dress fully justified this mark of imperial displeasure.

"But to return to the Empress Elizabeth. I acquainted my redoubtable master with the admiration expressed by the Empress of all the Russias for French fashions.

"In a very short time afterwards four large packages arrived at St. Petersburg, addressed to the empress. They contained a beautiful assortment of millinery, consisting of hats, caps, toques, flowers, ribbons, &c., all in the most exquisite taste. Elizabeth had ordered nothing, and expected nothing, from Paris. All these elegant things came as if they had fallen from the clouds.

"In the evening, at her little drawing-room circle, the empress stepped up to me, and, holding up her finger with a playful air of menace, she said, 'duke, you have been indiscreet; but no matter: when you next write, pray say that I am delighted with the things. They are exquisite, truly exquisite.' The empress then retired to another part of the room, and left me quite mystified. I could form no idea of what she alluded to.

"Next day there was a sledge party. The emperor did me the honour to desire that I would take my seat in the empress' sledge.

"In the course of our drive I said, Will your Majesty be pleased to explain to me how I have been guilty of the indiscretion with which you last night charged me?

"The empress instantly solved the enigma. I assured her that I had not been let into the secret, and that not a line had been written to me on the subject. This was the fact.

"I have no doubt that the orders were given quite secretly in Paris, and that no one had an idea whence they emanated. This act of gallantry was quite in good taste. The present in itself was of no great value. The articles of which it was composed were suited to the taste of a young and elegant woman, but were not sufficiently costly to be presented to the empress.

"I thought it remarkable that the Empress Elizabeth never asked me any questions respecting Josephine. Possibly she thought that *Madame Beauharnois crowned*, was a person below the level of imperial dignity. Napoleon, the sub-lieutenant, passing rapidly through his vast and glorious career, and by the sole aid of his sword ascending the first throne in the world—Napoleon was like a luminous disc to the Empress of all the Russias, herself the daughter of a king."

"I should like," said I to the Duke de Vicenza, "to hear some account of those brilliant reviews. I have heard that Alexander manifested no little vanity in exhibiting these spectacles, in their utmost magnificence, to the eyes of the French ambassador."

"He did so," replied the duke, "and certainly I never beheld anything of the kind equal in magnificence to the imperial reviews at St. Petersburg. The emperor was extremely vain of them, and he one day asked me whether his reviews equalled those of the Tuileries. Sire, replied I, they are both incomparable. He looked at me, and smiled; I think he understood me.

"In the reviews at St. Petersburg there were never less than 20,000, and often as many as 30,000 men assembled on the ground. The troops, it must be confessed, were admirable, both with regard to personal appearance and dress. Each regiment of cavalry had horses of one uniform colour—*viz.*, all black, grey, white, bay, &c. The colonel of each regiment was one of the most distinguished nobleman of the court of Russia; and they all expended vast sums in keeping up the fine appearance of their troops.

"Among the finest troops in the Russian service I may class the corps of horse guards raised by Paul I. In this regiment, every private is a knight of Malta. Their uniform is red, with massive silver *cuirasses*, and they wear the cross of Malta in relief on their breasts, forming a large escutcheon. The officers of this corps are all noblemen of the highest rank. Their uniforms, and the trappings of their horses, glitter with gold lace and jewels. Their Arabian horses, too, are of immense value.

"One of the best regiments of the hussar guards was that commanded by Colonel Scherwertiuskim, the brother of Madame N——. He was one of the most elegant young men I ever saw. His scarlet uniform, richly adorned with gold lace and a profusion of costly fur, set off his tall military figure to the best advantage. He obtained permission to have black horses in his regiment; and the shining jetty skins of these fine animals, contrasted with the brilliant red uniforms of their riders, produced a fine effect. The saddle clothes and trappings of the horses were richly embroidered with gold. Colonel Scherwertiuskim expended on his regiment no less a sum than 50,000 *roubles per annum* over and above the allowance granted by the state. The officers vied with each other in luxury and munificence. Not one of them would mount a horse of less value than 2,000 *roubles*. I have mentioned only two corps, but all were characterized by equal magnificence.

"Nothing could surpass the splendour of the imperial reviews,— for Russian uniform is at once martial and elegant. Both men and uniforms are alike well made, and present a most warlike aspect. The staff officers who surrounded the emperor formed a most dazzling group; and the young sovereign had good reason to be proud of his reviews.

"The military evolutions and manoeuvres were executed with the most perfect precision and effect; and every man engaged in them, even down to the privates and corporals, sought and found, amidst the fairer portion of the spectators, two bright eyes to stimulate his spirit and address.

"At the close of one of these imperial reviews, the emperor alluded to an amusing adventure which was at the time the general topic of conversation.

"Alexander loved to go out unattended and plainly dressed; and in these solitary excursions he frequently wandered as far as three or four leagues from the capital. One day feeling fatigued, he stepped into the first sledge he met. 'Drive to the Imperial Palace at St. Petersburg,' said he, to the *ystwotshilk*, or sledge driver.

"'Very well, officer,' replied the man. 'I will set you down as near to it as I can; but you know the guards will not allow us to approach the gates.'

"On arriving within some distance of the palace, the sledge driver stopped.

"'You must alight here, sir, if you please; I cannot take you further.'

"The emperor got out of the sledge, saying—'Wait there, my good fellow, and I will send you the money.'

"'No, no,' said the man, 'I give no credit. I have lost too much already by you officers: I have trusted many of your comrades, and they always forgot to pay me. You must leave me something as a pledge, or—'

"This greatly amused Alexander, who could not repress a hearty fit of laughter, and unclasping his cloak, he threw it into the sledge.

"On entering his apartments in the palace, he directed his *valet-de-chambre* to give fifty *roubles* to the *ystwotshilk* who had driven him in the sledge, and to bring back his cloak.

"The valet went out, and found about twenty sledges drawn up at a little distance from the palace gates.

"'Which of you drove the emperor?' said he, addressing the drivers.

"To this inquiry no answer was returned.

"'Which of you has a cloak left as security for payment?'

"'An officer left this cloak with me,' replied one of the *ystwotshilks*.

"'Give it to me, and here is your money.' He handed him the fifty *roubles*.

"'Gracious Saint Nicolas!' exclaimed the astonished sledge driver. Without uttering another word, he seized his reins, and, setting his horses at a full gallop, he departed with the swiftness of an arrow, amidst the loud huzzas of his comrades.

"This little incident took place on the evening preceding one of the imperial reviews. It used to be the custom, after the manoeuvres were ended, for the commanders of the different corps to form a group round the emperor.

"'Gentlemen,' said his Majesty, 'I am very well satisfied with you. Your regiments look well, and are altogether in admirable condition; but, gentlemen, I request you will tell your officers from me, that I was yesterday indebted to them for the humiliation of being compelled to leave my cloak in pledge.'

"All stared at one another with amazement.

"'It is so, I assure you,' resumed the emperor. 'The *ystwotshilk* who drove me to the palace last night, refused to give me credit, because, to use his own words, my brother officers often forgot to pay him.'

"Everyone was bewildered in conjecture, and no one could guess to what the emperor alluded. In the evening, at a party given by Madame N——, the emperor solved the mystery by relating his adventure. He told it with such admirable humour, and imitated so perfectly the voice and manner of the sledge driver, that all who heard him were convulsed with laughter.

"I have already mentioned," said the Duke de Vicenza, "the easy familiarity observed by Alexander towards his inferiors. One morning, as the emperor and I were walking on the Perspective, (a spacious and beautiful promenade in St Petersburg,) we met Andrieux, the actor, the husband of Madame Philis.

"'Good morning, Andrieux,' said Alexander, 'how are you?'

"'Very well, Sire; and how are you?'

"'How is your wife?'

"'Very well, Sire. I hope your Majesty's wife and mother are well.'

"This sort of familiarity used to amuse Alexander; and his descriptions of droll scenes of this kind often excited great merriment in the drawing-rooms of St. Petersburg.

"When I was speaking of Frogère the actor," pursued the Duke de Vicenza, "I forgot to relate to you an anecdote which I had from the mouth of the emperor himself.

"Frogère was on a footing of the most perfect intimacy with Prince Alexander before his accession to the throne. But when the death of Paul I. raised the prince to the imperial throne, Frogère was no longer seen at court. Some time afterwards the emperor met him.

"'Ah! Frogère!' said his Majesty, 'how is it I never see you now?'

"'Why Sire, the truth is, I could visit the Imperial Prince just like one of my own comrades,—but now—'

"'But now you will not come to see the emperor?'

"'Precisely, Sire. I confess that I was afraid your good fortune might have rendered you proud. But now, since I find that you are not so, I will come and see you.'

"Instead of being offended at this free and easy style of behaviour, the emperor was highly diverted by it.

"The young noblemen who figured at the court of St. Petersburg were guilty of licences which, though not less reprehensible, were more consistent with courtly breeding. Alexander viewed them with inconceivable indulgence. General Ouwaroff, who enjoyed the friendship and intimacy of the emperor, was a remarkably handsome man. His vanity, his luxury, and expenses, exceeded all imaginable extravagance. He was celebrated for his love intrigues and conquests; and his name was constantly figuring in some affair of gallantry. He was a man of undaunted courage, and his redoubted sword kept all assailants at defiance. He was the fortunate lover of the beautiful Princess S——, whom he suddenly deserted, and avowed an ardent passion for Madame L——. The princess sent back his letters, and his portrait which she had received from him in her days of happiness. She disdained explanations and reproaches; but she was weak enough to love, though conscious of being no longer beloved. In her despair she ended her existence by a dose of poison.

"This event caused a great sensation, and the fate of the princess was universally deplored. Ouwaroff perceived that he could not brave the storm. He solicited his *congé*; it was granted; and he passed several months in travelling. On his return, the emperor read him a severe lecture, and desired him to be more circumspect.

"'Sire, it is my wish to be so—but these women's brains are turned. I cannot say how soon they may draw me into another scrape.'

"This General Ouwaroff, in spite of his vanity and levity, was one of the bravest of the brave. At the interview which took place between the two emperors on the Niemen, after the Battle of Friedland, in 1807, Alexander arrived on the raft, accompanied by the Grand Duke Constantine, the General-in-Chief Benigsen, Prince Lubanoff, and General Ouwaroff. The Emperor Napoleon was attended by Murat, Marshals Berthier and Bessières, General Duroc, and myself.

"There was an indescribable charm in Napoleon's manner when he was intent on pleasing. The interview on the Niemen, within view of the two armies, was invested with a poetic ideality which could not fail to excite the imagination. Napoleon, the conqueror, held in his hands the destinies of two great powers, whom he might have annihilated by a single breath: yet, disdaining to punish, he offered protection and friendship to his vanquished enemies. This is a glorious page in Napoleon's history."

Here the duke paused, and his countenance forcibly expressed the painful feelings which crossed his mind,—feelings naturally excited by a comparison of the glorious past and the miserable present. Alas!

at that moment I felt the justice of the duke's remark, that *there was no longer room for him in France!*

"When the two emperors met," resumed the duke, "on the raft, on the Niemen, they cordially embraced each other several successive times. 'Brother,' said Napoleon, holding one of Alexander's hands in his, 'the fate of arms has proved adverse to you. But your army is valiant and devoted. Your troops have performed prodigies of valour. The Russians are essentially a brave people. Who commanded the cavalry?' continued he, addressing the General-in-Chief, Beningsen.

"As soon as Napoleon asked this question, a very elegant young officer stepped forward, and eagerly answered it by the words '*Je, Sire.*'

"On hearing this, the two emperors could not refrain from smiling. 'General,' said Napoleon to the young officer, 'though you do not speak very good French, you are a brave man and an able commander.'

"The power of fascination which Napoleon exercised over his own soldiery was felt in an equal degree by all who surrounded him. It gave him the ascendancy in all places and in all situations. No words can express—no pencil can portray—the enthusiasm which was excited in all who witnessed the interview on the raft of the Niemen. Alexander possessed the advantages of imperial birth and a noble figure, (he was a foot taller than our Napoleon ;) yet the latter seemed to rise majestically above all who surrounded him, and was the principal personage in the magical scene. At the moment when the two emperors embraced, the troops who covered the banks of the river raised enthusiastic hurras which almost rent the air. That was one of the most glorious hours of my life.

"I need not relate to you the occurrences of Tilsit, all the official details of which are generally known. But only those who were near the person of Napoleon at the time can form an adequate idea of the grace and delicacy he observed in his relations with the sovereigns, and the easy and polished dignity with which he maintained his high post of magnanimous protector. He had no vulnerable point for adulation and flattery. In vain did the fascinating Queen of Prussia call into play all the powers of seduction with which beauty and high talents had liberally endowed her. Napoleon did what he had determined to do; and be conceded nothing which be bad resolved to keep. Never was man gifted with such perfect self command. He really appeared superior to human nature.

"In the evening, when he returned to his own apartments, he

would enter into familiar conversation with me. On one of these occasions, he said—'What do you think of us now, *Monsieur le Grand Écuyer?* Are we not a magnificent conqueror?'

"Sire, you do the honours of the country in admirable style to your brothers of Prussia and Russia.

"He laughed and said—'Between ourselves, Caulincourt, I have conquered hearts as well as countries.'

"But I trust that your Majesty will not leave your own heart behind you?

"'Truly,' replied he, 'I have something else to think of than love. No man wins triumphs in that way without forfeiting some palms of glory. I have traced out my plan; and, *ma foi!* the finest eyes in the world (and there are some very fine eyes here, Caulincourt) shall not make me deviate a hair's breadth from it.'

"Your Majesty is then quite inaccessible to seduction?

"'*Ah baste!* The King of Prussia excites my pity, Caulincourt. But no matter! he must be satisfied with the share I have given him. If I were to yield one thing today, another would be asked tomorrow, and something else the day after, till at length I should find that I have been working to serve the King of Prussia. Alexander is an excellent young man. I believe him to be honourable and sincere. We shall come to a right understanding with him.'

"I have no doubt of that, Sire. He is filled with admiration of your Majesty.

"'That is because I am so singular a being, Caulincourt. My fate has been so extraordinary!' As the emperor uttered these words, I could read in his countenance that his thoughts were reverting to Toulon.

"But I am wandering far from the court of St. Petersburg," resumed the Duke de Vicenza, after a short pause.

"In the year 1810, there was collected in St. Petersburg a distinguished conclave of professors of the dramatic and musical arts. Most of our favourite Parisian singers and dancers had solicited *congés* for Russia; and at the Theatre of St. Petersburg we might, without any great stretch of imagination, have supposed ourselves at the Grand Opera in Paris. Besides the actors and actresses whose names I have already mentioned to you, we had Madame Philis Andrieux and her husband, and about ten others of second-rate talent. Boieldieu composed operas, and charming little pieces for private concerts.

"The beautiful Madame Lafont was a distinguished favourite: she sang divinely, and her eyes discoursed, if possible, more eloquently than her voice. Her husband, at that time the first violinist in Europe, collected all the *beau-monde* of St. Petersburg at his morning concerts. Nobody having any pretension to fashion would have been absent without very good cause from Lafont's musical *réunions*. Beukendorf, the brother of Princess Lieven, and then Governor-General of St. Petersburg, would have thought himself lost had any thing occurred to prevent him attending Lafont's concerts, and paying his devoirs to the elegant women whom he was sure to find assembled there.

"M. Narishkim, the Grand Chamberlain, brother to the grand equerry, lived in a style of regal splendour. His palace was the resort of all the best company in St. Petersburg, and was frequently honoured by the presence of the emperor himself. His apartments, profusely decorated with gold, bronze, porphyry, and flowers, gave a fairy-like character to his balls and *fêtes*, of which similar entertainments in Paris can convey no idea.

"A report was current that the emperor intended to confer the dignity of prince on the Grand Chamberlain. At one of his splendid *dejeuners*, I was walking with M. Narishkim, in one of the delicious conservatories adjoining the suite of drawing-rooms. The melodious strains of the music, and the balmy odour of the flowers, threw new spells over the enchanting scene. I could not help expressing to M. Narishkim my admiration of the exquisite beauty and magnificence of his palace; and I added, that the owner of such a residence ought to bear the title of prince.

"'Look round, duke,' replied he, and tell me whether you think any title can add to the splendour of my station? I do not think it worth my while to contradict this absurd report every time I hear it idly repeated; but to you, duke, I will explain the truth, for I do not wish it to be believed at your court that a Narishkim can derive the title of prince from any other than himself. The truth is, that the emperor has expressed a desire to confer that dignity upon me; but when he mentioned the matter, I replied—'Sire, the mother of Peter the Great was a Narishkim; the title of prince, therefore, cannot elevate the dignity of a family which has the honour to be so nearly allied to your Majesty. The Narishkims are no less illustrious than the Emperor of all the Russias.'

"Whether Alexander was displeased at this proud language, I cannot say; at all events he possessed too much magnanimity of feeling to manifest displeasure. The chamberlain continued in favour; but the subject of the principality was never again mentioned to him."

CHAPTER 4

The Battle of the Moskowa

"The Battle of the Moskowa made frightful havoc in the forces of Russia. The natural courage of the Russians, joined to despair and fanaticism, prompted them to dispute the victory to the utmost. On the fate of the battle depended the fate of Moscow; and to the Russians Moscow was the holy city, the favoured of Heaven. The *levée en masse* had been effected with indescribable ardour and enthusiasm. The clergy, who exercise an all-powerful ascendancy over the minds of the peasantry, had summoned them to the defence of the country, blessed them, and predicted their invincibility. The revered Virgin of the Seven Sorrows had been paraded through the city. Every army corps directed against the French had knelt at the feet of the holy statue, sworn to defend Moscow, and to return victorious.

"During the month which the Russian troops occupied in marching through Moscow, the city resounded with cries of 'Death to the French!' A serf, who had been emancipated in the reign of Paul I., and who, at the time to which I am now alluding, was a blind old man of eighty, had thirteen sons or grandsons serving in the Russian army as volunteers. 'Go,' said he, on taking leave of them, 'and do not spare your blood in the defence of your country and your religion. You will return victorious. God is just. But if the heavenly wrath should light upon our city—if it be ordained that foreigners shall profane our capital, I swear that they shall march over my body before they enter it.'

"The Russians lost the Battle of the Moskowa, and the French troops advanced to the ancient capital of the empire. The inhabitants fled, and the city was speedily deserted. Petrowisk, the blind old man, resisted the tears and entreaties of his family, and refused to depart 'This is the soil that gave me birth,' said he, striking the ground with his stick; 'here I have lived for eighty years, and here I am resolved to die.' This old man was inexorable. All the family emigrated, taking with them the little property they could rescue from the pillage of the soldiery. At the moment of departure, four generations on their knees implored the blessing of the revered head of their family. The tall figure of Petrowisk, his white hair and flowing beard, his large dark eyes, open and fixed, imparted a sort of poetic interest to the scene. With uplifted hands, he pronounced these words—'May the blessing of Heaven, and of your aged father, follow you wheresoever you direct your footsteps. We shall meet again in heaven;—to that abode of the righteous the French will never gain entrance.' Then, turning to his eldest son, he said in a low voice, 'You have given me your word, Ivan!' The son replied, in a resolute tone, 'Father, I will keep my promise.'

"The blind man remained in his dwelling. All his family departed, with the exception of one of his grandsons, a youth of sixteen, who had resolved to share the fate of his grandfather. Next day, the French advanced guard defiled on the high road: the head of the column touched the gates of Moscow. At intervals several musket-shots penetrated the ranks. They were evidently fired by a practised hand, and not a single ball missed its aim. Many soldiers were killed and wounded. An officer struck in the head by one of the balls fell dead from his horse. All eyes were turned in the direction whence the shots had been fired. An old man, whose long white beard covered his breast, was seen sitting on the ground, and resting his back against a tree. Our soldiers rushed towards him with their drawn bayonets in their hands. At this moment a young man descended from the tree, and, throwing himself before the old man, fired two pistols which he had in his girdle, and then drew a large poignard to defend himself. But he was speedily overpowered by numbers, and fell bleeding and lifeless at the feet of Petrowisk. 'Now,' exclaimed he, 'kill me, accursed French! That brave youth is my grandson, and it was I, Petrowisk, who armed him.'

"About an hour afterwards, the emperor, attended by his staff, passed the spot where this incident had occurred. 'Ah!' exclaimed he, turning his horse to the opposite side of the road, 'this is a cowardly murder! An old man!' All who beheld the appalling sight turned away from it with horror. The old man was still in a sitting position; his eyes were open and fixed, his white beard was clotted with blood, and his garments were pierced by the swords of his assailants. At the foot of the tree, the lifeless corpse of a young lad lay weltering in a pool of blood.

"The emperor was naturally superstitious, and this horrible spectacle made a profound impression on his mind.

"As he passed through the streets of Moscow, on his way to the Kremlin, he was struck with the aspect of the city. All the houses were closely shut up, and not one of the inhabitants was to be seen. It would be difficult to form an idea of the melancholy effect of this silence and torpor in the midst of a great capital. On first descrying the city our soldiery raised the cry of 'Moscow! Moscow! the promised land!' But their joy was speedily succeeded by depression.

"'This solitude is awful,' said the emperor to me.

"In the evening a man was discovered concealed under the staircase leading to the emperor's apartments. The emperor wished to see and question him, but the man could not speak a word of French, and an interpreter was sent for. The emperor, who was agitated and impatient, paced rapidly up and down the room, and several times spoke to the prisoner, forgetting that he could neither understand nor answer him. At length the interpreter arrived.

"A long colloquy ensued, and it was curious to observe the air of pride and inspiration which sat upon the countenance of the man. He was about fifty years of age, of tall stature, and his features had a fierce expression. 'What does he say? what does he say?' inquired the emperor every moment. We elicited from him that his name was Ivan, and that he was the son of Petrowisk, the blind man. He had solemnly sworn to his father that he would assassinate Napoleon; and to accomplish that purpose he had disguised and concealed himself. He had stripped one of our soldiers, who had been killed on the road, and, disguised in the French uniform, he experienced no difficulty in gaining access to the place where he had been found concealed.

"'Why this furious hatred towards me? How have I injured this Petrowisk personally?' said Napoleon. 'I spare this man's life,' added he; 'let him be conducted out of the city, and I desire that he be not harmed. This matter must rest among ourselves,' he said, addressing himself to the persons present. 'I desire it may not be mentioned.'

"'Caulincourt,' said he to me, when we were alone together, 'my entrance into Moscow has been marked by gloomy presages. Diabolical machinations have been set on foot here. Religious fanaticism has been called into action. It is a powerful and a successful engine when exercised over an uncivilized people. In France, if we were to resort to such jugglery, we should be laughed at. In Russia, it raises up devoted assassins. This war resembles no other. At Eylau, at Friedland, we had to contend only with soldiers; here we have to conquer a whole nation.'

"After his interview with the Russian assassin," said the Duke de

Vicenza, "Napoleon was thoughtful and downcast. His eyes, usually so bright and animated, appeared dim and languid, and an indescribable expression of uneasiness was depicted in his countenance. I endeavoured to rouse him from this state of nervous depression, which I knew was the result of the restraint he had imposed on himself for the preceding eight-and-forty hours. But unfortunately I was myself at that moment under the influence of the most gloomy presentiments.

"The emperor rose, and walked several times up and down the room, with his arms crossed on his bosom, and his head hanging down; then stopping short, he exclaimed:—'And Murat!—Murat, without awaiting my orders, without seeking any counsel, save that of his own wild brain, has thought fit to take the route to Voladimir! Murat is ardent, brilliant in the field of battle. He possesses dauntless courage; but he is totally devoid of judgment To know when to stop is sometimes the best proof of understanding. Murat has not common sense. This *fanfaronade* has thrown me into a most embarrassing dilemma. I cannot call him back without proclaiming our weakness, and to send him reinforcements would be to recommence the war. I am always ill understood and ill seconded by the members of my own family.' These last words were uttered in a very dissatisfied manner, and he began again to pace up and down the

"I made some remarks on the ardent courage and impetuosity of the King of Naples, and endeavoured to excuse his inconsiderate movement, which at the time threatened the most unfortunate consequences.

"'No, no, Caulincourt,' resumed the emperor, 'his imprudence is unpardonable. The fact is, that he, and some others of my family, know not how to support their high fortune. Their heads are turned; I have done top much for them. But no more of this.'

"He stepped up to a table, and spread out upon it a map of Poland. 'You see, Caulincourt,' said he, 'I could not have remained in Poland. I should speedily have been surrounded on all sides, supposing some defections among my allies. That plan might have been attended with danger—and yet No, it was best to advance—to astonish by the rapidity of my marches and my victories. Now the die is cast. Before six months have elapsed I must be in St. Petersburg—I must! I will establish my winter quarters there. I thought to have stopped here—but I shall merely halt long enough to let the army rest: I must positively be in St. Petersburg by the first of November. I will echelon my troops,' pursued he, and his countenance brightened up as he spoke. 'I shall

40

receive reinforcements from France. My garrisons are provisioned for six months. This is a formidable league. But I will subdue it, with God's help.'

"I was far from sharing the emperor's hopes. Adverse circumstances were multiplying around us. A volcano seemed ready to burst beneath our feet; and," added the Duke de Vicenza, in a tone of deep dejection, "even then I saw no promise in the future. The emperor might possibly be under the influence of illusion; but certainly I was not. The plots which had long been secretly hatched by England, were now ripe for full and complete execution. Russia, by letting loose upon us her barbarous hordes, was employing dangerous resources. She was playing a desperate game. At that time, General Kutusoff, who was the tool of the English Cabinet, possessed such unbounded power, that he was more like the Sovereign of all the Russias than Alexander.

"It was incumbent on Alexander to vanquish Napoleon, under pain of forfeiting his crown and his life. His long refusal to break with France had excited distrust in all classes of his subjects, and rendered him unpopular. In the heart of his dominions there existed a redoubtable party, which was only watching for a favourable opportunity to hurl from the throne the liberal *Czar* who had dared to conceive the generous idea of emancipating the serfs. To Alexander's predilection for Napoleon were attributed the injuries inflicted upon commerce by the continental system: that system, it was affirmed, had proved ruinous to Russia, and favourable only to France, to whom breach of faith was said to be mere matter of sport. These alleged grievances, forcibly represented by a popular military commander, made a ready impression on the multitude. The upper classes, too, joined in the outcry against France; but their complaints were grounded in mere pretext.

"During the few last months of my sojourn in St. Petersburg, how frequently did Alexander make me the confidant of his anxious feelings! England, the implacable enemy of France, maintained secret agents at the Court of Russia for the purpose of stirring up disaffection and discontent around the throne. The English Cabinet was well aware that a propaganda war was impossible as long as Russia should continue allied to France. On this point all the powers agreed; and the consequence was, that all the sovereigns were perjured, one only excepted; he was to be seduced from his allegiance, or doomed to destruction.

"Alexander, at the period to which I am now referring, was no longer a gay, thoughtless young man. The circumstances by which he found himself surrounded had forced a train of serious reflection on his mind, and he seemed perfectly to understand the peculiarity of his personal position. In his private conversations with me he often said many things which he would not have said to his own brothers, and which possibly he could not have said with safety to his ministers. Beneath an exterior air of confidence he concealed the most gloomy apprehensions. In short, matters had reached that point when it would have been very impolitic in the emperor to have renewed those evening visits, in which he was wont to impart to me his love secrets, and to relate the jealous torments inflicted on him by the coquettish Madame N——.

"In the irritated state of feeling which then pervaded the public mind in Russia, Alexander's intimacy with the French ambassador was severely reprehended, and he knew it. We sometimes enjoyed a hearty laugh at finding ourselves compelled to make assignations with as much secrecy as two young lovers. 'My dear Caulincourt,' said Alexander to me one evening, when we were conversing on the balcony of the empress' apartments,—'My dear Caulincourt, in all my vast dominions I have not a single friend to whom I can lay open my heart. I cannot impart my secret inquietudes to the French ambassador: but let me confide them to your honour. Napoleon ought to be made acquainted with the plots that are hatching here against him. I have concealed nothing from you, my dear duke. In my confidence, I have perhaps overstepped the limits of strict propriety. Tell your emperor all that I have revealed to you; tell him all that you have seen and read; tell him that here the earth trembles beneath my feet; that here, in my own empire, he has rendered my position intolerable by his violation of treaties. Transmit to him, from me, this candid and final declaration:—If once the war be fairly entered upon, either he, Napoleon, or I, Alexander, must lose our crown.'

"I fulfilled the mission entrusted to me; I braved anger and reproaches; I combated, at the risk of my own ruin, all the reasons urged as a pretext for the war of 1812. In a warm discussion with Napoleon, in which I had vainly exhausted all my best arguments, being pushed to the extremity by some expressions which fell from him, I replied:— 'Sire, my life is at your service. Dispose of it on the field of battle for the sacred cause of France. But here my conviction is at variance with yours. My conscience and my honour belong only to myself, and I should consider myself dishonoured if, for the sake of pleasing your

Majesty, I were to desert the cause of my country.'

"'What have you to say, sir?' said he, advancing eagerly to me.

"I repeat to your Majesty, whilst there is yet time, that this war must inevitably be attended by results fatal to France; that all the powers of Europe have risen in a mass against one. If you pursue this course, Sire, you are lost; and on you depends the fate of France.'

"Six months after this scene, I again found myself closeted with the emperor, not in the Palace of the Tuileries, but in the ancient Palace of the *Czars*, the Kremlin at Moscow! It was miraculous! Inexplicable fate had impressed a terrible seal on my despised warnings! Whether the emperor then remembered our discussions, and my obstinate resistance to his arguments, I cannot pretend to say, but he knew that he could never lose my attachment—my absolute devotedness, and in the day of misfortune he confidently relied on them. I endeavoured to mitigate the anxiety which preyed upon his mind. I kept up the train of conversation, for I knew Napoleon well: the outpouring of his feelings, when it could be brought about, never failed to produce a soothing effect on his mind.

"But his meditative organization inclined him to suppress his sensations, and he was often reserved on subjects in which his thoughts and feelings were deeply engaged. The student of Brienne and the sub-lieutenant of artillery had acquaintances, bat no friends. Napoleon had never shared any of those intimacies which are almost inseparable from boyhood and youth. His elevated fortune wrought no change in his vigorous and unbending mind, which always retained its character of self-concentration. He was attached to Berthier and Duroc; they were almost the only two men with whom he was familiar; but even with them he was not communicative and intimate. With me, on the contrary, he was not *familiar*, and yet when we were together his conversation was so unreserved that he might be said to think aloud, though I not infrequently ventured to contradict him. When Napoleon could be himself he was invariably sincere and amiable.

"I sought to impress upon the emperor that our late victories afforded us the chance of receiving overtures of peace from Russia. I confess that I had not myself any faith in the probability of such an occurrence; but my object was to restore Napoleon to that tranquillity of mind which was so necessary in our fearful position. 'No, Caulincourt,' replied he, 'neither you nor I can be blind to the fatal consequences of this fanatical and desperate war. The resources which our enemies employ annihilate my conquests with more certainty than fire and sword.'

"Having related to you some details connected with the Battle of Moscow," said the duke, "I will take the opportunity of contradicting an assertion which has recently obtained some degree of credit among that class of people who eagerly seize on every circumstance that can be interpreted to the prejudice of the emperor.

"There is no truth whatever in the statement that Napoleon proposed that I should go on a mission to the Emperor Alexander; and that I declined doing so. In the first place, the emperor never could have conceived the idea of sending one of the officers of the crown as the bearer of a letter to Alexander. If the amicable propositions of Napoleon had been acceded to, there would have been ground for stipulating a treaty of peace; in that case, my services might have been useful, and I should have considered myself honoured in being chosen as negotiator. But circumstances did not admit of an official plenipotentiary being sent from the French camp to St Petersburg.

"My refusal, therefore, has no existence, save in the imaginations of the authors of this fiction. The same may be said of the coolness which it has been alleged I evinced towards the emperor, and the pretended ground for which was my disapproval of the campaign against Russia. I certainly exerted my efforts to prevent it; but this fatal step being once taken, the idea of reproaching him for his error would have been most base, amidst the host of misfortunes that overwhelmed him. That was the moment when every man of honour felt himself bound to repay, by blind and unrestricted devotedness, the benefits Napoleon had heaped on us in the days of his prosperity.

"The bearer of the private letter from Napoleon to Alexander, was General Lauriston. Neither the emperor nor I expected that it would be attended by any favourable result. The fact is, that the emperor, who felt himself responsible for the fate of the army, nobly sacrificed his pride to his conscience. This humiliation was a necessity which he would fain have spared by his own blood. The circumstance, which has been made a subject of reproach, was one of the noblest traits in Napoleon's career.

"But to return to my narrative:—Night was drawing in. The emperor, who continued in a very disturbed state of mind, restlessly paced up and down the room, and now and then threw himself for a few moments into a chair.

"'Go to bed, Caulincourt,' said he, in a tone of mingled grief and kindness.

"No, Sire, said I, I cannot. Permit me to remain with your Majesty.

"He stretched out his hand to me.

"'Be it so, then, my dear Caulincourt. But let us do something to amuse ourselves. (He spread out the plans of his movements.) Look here,' said he, 'in three days I shall have two hundred and fifty thousand men assembled here. They most find quarters. We must look after provisions. But desolation and famine everywhere stare us in the face!'

"At that moment a vivid light flashed across the windows. We rose, and on looking out, observed a red flaming light on the horizon. There was a suffocating heat in the atmosphere. Cries of fire! Fire! were raised in the courts of the Kremlin in which our guards were bivouacked: and with these cries were mingled shouts of *Vive l'Empereur!* The brave fellows were anxious to prove that they were at their posts and watching over the safety of their emperor. On the preceding night there had been some partial fires, which Marshal Mortier, then Governor of Moscow, had attributed to the disorder inseparable from the installation of the troops.

"A staff officer entered and informed us that fires had simultaneously broken out in different quarters of the city, and likewise in several unoccupied buildings within the enclosure of the palace. Several generals successively brought in reports, all coinciding one with another. The truth was no longer doubtful. The destruction of Moscow had been regularly planned and ordered.

"The emperor in a moment summoned all his presence of mind and dignity. In a firm and decided tone he gave orders for rendering assistance on those points which were threatened, but not yet reached, by the flames. 'Prevent the different fires from communicating,' said he, 'and save everything that can be rescued. Be gone, gentlemen, I make each commander of a corps responsible for the execution of my orders. Every one most do his duty. Let my horse be got ready, and acquaint my troops that I shall be amongst them instantly.' He sent for the Prince de Neufchatel:—'Berthier,' said he, 'where are the corn magazines situated? Dispatch an intelligent officer, and direct him to report to me whether the corn magazines are in danger. Let the young guard be sent on this duty. Quick, Berthier! Let no time be lost.'

"When we were again alone, he said to me—'Truly, Caulincourt, this exceeds all belief; they are absolutely waging a war of extermination. These atrocious measures have no precedent in the annals of civilization. The execration of generations to come will light on the perpetrators of this vandalism. To burn their own cities! Good Heaven!' Whilst the emperor uttered these hasty and broken sentences he was in a violent state of excitement; a gloomy lustre kindled in his eyes. 'These Russians,' continued he, 'must be inspired by Satan. What a ferocious crime is here committed.'

"At that hour, I am convinced Napoleon's death-blow was struck! His moral energy was unsubdued, but his physical energies gradually gave way. The first thread of his existence was snapped at the Kremlin; his death-knell was tolled at St. Helena! Such emotions are deadly in their consequences. I know it by fatal experience!

"Next day," continued the duke, "the emperor, as usual, inspected his guards in the Kremlin, and no one could read in his placid countenance any trace of the anxious perturbation he had suffered on the preceding night. The fact is, that Napoleon was eminently endowed with that quality so indispensable to a sovereign—dissimulation. A monarch must smile even when his crown of thorns causes the blood to trickle down the forehead that bears it. He must smile when every golden dream has vanished, and every bright illusion is dispelled. He must smile, because, on the moral confidence of each of his subjects depends the welfare of all. Alas! that smile is one of the hardest conditions attached to the miseries of a throne!

"Attempts have been made to censure or ridicule the reviews which took place amidst the smoking ashes of Moscow, the decrees issued from the Kremlin, &c. This is the very height of absurdity. At the distance of 800 leagues from the capital, it was necessary to prove that the power of the emperor was still predominant. It was necessary to convince the army, that whether near or afar off, he was watching over all, and for all,—that in Moscow our troops were merely in a conquered province, and holding free communication with their homes and their families. This faith helped our brave troops to endure the pangs of hunger, and the mortification of reverses, so bitterly felt by men hitherto acquainted only with victory. The hope of a triumphant return was indispensable to counteract that depression of spirit which, like a hideous leprosy, spares neither the strong nor the brave.

"When in the streets of Moscow, I beheld Napoleon passing between lines of flame, and amidst showers of fire, calmly braving the most imminent danger for the sake of assisting, by his personal efforts, in saving a corn magazine or an hospital, I viewed his intrepidity as an act of high policy. When he thus braved danger and death in the burning streets of Moscow, I have heard the soldiers who accompanied him express their confidence, even in the most perilous situations, that no harm could befall them whilst the emperor was there to extricate them. The truth is, that Napoleon was greater and more magnificent in his reverses than when he astonished the world by his brilliant triumphs.

"During fourteen days and nights which followed the disasters of Moscow, I am enabled to affirm, that never, under any circumstances, did I see him manifest such heroic magnanimity. Seated by my side, in a narrow sledge, exposed to every kind of danger, suffering severely from cold, and often from hunger—for we could not stop anywhere—leaving behind him the scattered wreck of his army, Napoleon's courage never forsook him! Yet his spirit was not buoyed up by any illusory hope. He had sounded the depth of the abyss. His eagle eye had scanned the prospect before him. 'Caulincourt,' said he, 'this is a serious state of things; but rest assured, my courage will not flinch. My star is over-clouded, but all is not lost. The French are essentially a noble and brave people. I will raise national guards. That institution of the national guard is one of the greatest achievements of the Revolution. It is a resource of which I shall successfully avail myself. In three months I shall have on foot a million of armed citizens, and three hundred thousand fine troops of the line.'

"True, Sire, said I, you may rely on France.

"'My allies,' interrupted he, earnestly, 'are numbered in my plans, but that is all. For the last six months, Caulincourt, they have been nothing but an embarrassment to me. Their co-operation is a mere mockery!'

"'But,' he resumed, after a few moments' pause, 'France is still invincible! France presents great resources. The French are the most intellectual people in the world. My twenty-ninth bulletin is not a ball fired at random—it is an act of well-concerted policy. In some circumstances, truth and candour are the best *finesse*. French intelligence will comprehend the position of the nation, and the vast sacrifices which that position demands. I, the emperor, am only a man; but all Frenchmen know that on that man depend the destinies of their country, the destinies of their families, and the safety of their homes. Fools have attempted to give a ridiculous interpretation to a remark of Louis XIV., who said, *l'Etat, c'est moi*. These words convey an undeniable truth; they imply a power of will, without which a king is but a gilded manikin. The state is an assemblage of undisciplined men, who soon become undisciplinable if they be not restrained by a hand of iron. *Monsieur le Russe*,' added he, good-humouredly, 'are you not of my opinion.'

"Your Majesty, replied I, knows how much I am mortified by being addressed by that title.

"'*Ah, baste!*' said he, and changed the subject of conversation.

"Napoleon," continued the duke, "persisted in regarding the constant efforts I had made since 1810 to prevent him from coming to a rupture with Alexander, his most devoted and faithful ally, merely as promoted by a predilection on my part in favour of the Emperor of Russia. In my correspondence, and subsequently in conversation, I explained to him the political circumstances which rendered the Russian alliance the strongest support of France. I owed to the generous confidence of Alexander communications of a nature which plainly indicated the storm that was gathering round us. I had read, with my own eyes, during my mission in Russia, propositions which Alexander daily received from the other powers, even from the Austrian Cabinet, to rise *en masse* against the domination of the *insatiable Corsican*. I told the emperor all this. I offered him proofs of its truth; but he would not listen to me, and he always cut the matter short by saying, '*Monsieur le Russe*, Alexander is an enchanter, who has cast a spell upon you,'

"By throwing himself into Russia with an army of five hundred thousand men, he hoped to take the other powers by surprise. But they had been conspiring for four years previously, and for the space of a year all their measures had been completed. My warnings were vain! In 1811, when I demanded my recall, it was in the hope of being able to avert the storm which then seemed ready to burst over us. In one of my last interviews with the Emperor of Russia, he said to me, 'Tell the Emperor Napoleon that I will not separate from him unless he force me to do so. My friendship for him is so sincere that I cannot withdraw it.' This was absolutely true: Alexander cherished for Napoleon a passionate friendship—an enthusiastic admiration.

"Napoleon was under the influence of a fixed idea, and he would not deviate from the plan he had laid down. He did not place faith in the sincerity of the communication made to me for the purpose of being conveyed to him. Could be not understand the generosity of Alexander? I know not; but his doubts, whether real or dissembled, produced fatal results."

CHAPTER 5

Execution of the Duke d'Enghien

The conversations we enjoyed during our morning drives and walks with the Duke de Vicenza, always turned on subjects less serious than those which we discussed in the evenings. Autumn evenings seem naturally to excite feelings of melancholy and regret—a regret inseparable from the consciousness that the bright days of summer have left us. We usually employed our mornings in exploring the environs of the town. The country about Plombières is veil wooded and picturesquely varied by alternate hill and dale. We continually met gay parties riding or walking. The cavalcade of asses reminded us of Montmorency and its rural amusements. Anguish, whether of mind or body, is temporarily assuaged by the influence of objects which please the eye. The sight of a graceful and smiling landscape lulls the mind to tranquillity and repose.

One day, whilst we were strolling about, we were accosted by a poor crazy female, known in the neighbourhood by the name of *Thérèse la folle*. She served to divert those thoughtless persons who can derive amusement from the most melancholy affliction to which human nature is subject. Poor Thérèse was gentle and inoffensive in her madness. To every person she met she addressed inquiries respecting the empress, and when asked to whom she alluded, she would reply, with a naive air of surprise, "The Empress of Plombières, to be sure." We were informed that one of Thérèse's sons had been inscribed on the conscription list during the time that the Empress Josephine was on a visit to Plombières. Therese implored her Majesty's intercession to get her son exempt from service. This favour, however, exceeded the bounds of the empress' power; it was a point on which Napoleon was inexorable. But though her Majesty could not obtain a soldier's exemption from service, she could purchase a substitute. Josephine, ever kind and generous, gave the money, and the son of Therese remained to comfort his mother. This circumstance occurred several years before Therese was visited by her melancholy affliction; but though bereft of reason, the poor mother retained the remembrance of her benefactress.

"Our *rencontre* with this maniac," said the Duke de Vicenza, "reminds me of a circumstance which occurred at our entrance into Pyrna in 1813. On that occasion we were obliged to remove the patients from the lunatic hospital to make room for our wounded troops. Indispensable as this measure was, yet the emperor reluctantly saw it adopted. He sent to inquire how the unfortunate lunatics had been disposed of. The town was completely filled with our troops, and they were temporarily lodged in one of the churches. Among the lunatics, there was a woman who fancied herself the mother of God. On entering the church she installed herself in the chapel of the Virgin, and did the honours as a lady would in her own drawing-room. 'How happy I am,' said she, 'at finding myself removed to the house of my son. Offer my thanks to Bonaparte, sir,' said she, addressing herself to a French officer. 'Tell him he will be welcome here. My son and I expect a visit from him.'

"Another patient, a very beautiful young lady, connected with a family of rank, had fallen in love with Napoleon during the wars of 1807. She would not answer to any other name than *Napoleonida*. During her removal from the hospital to the church, the sight of the French uniform appeared to make a forcible impression on her, and she expressed an earnest wish to see *her Napoleon*. With her long fair hair dishevelled, her eyes suffused with tears, and her hands joined, she ran about imploring everyone she met to conduct her to Napoleon. She repeated this request with indefatigable perseverance to every officer who visited the church in which the lunatics were lodged. Turenne, the emperor's equerry, related the story of the unfortunate young lady to his Majesty, and asked whether he would be pleased to see her. 'By no means, Turenne,' replied the emperor, smiling. 'I have lunatics enough in France, without troubling my head about those of Bohemia.'

"I accompanied the emperor (I think in 1807) on a visit to the Maison Royale at Charenton. He inspected the establishment in its most minute details, made inquiries into all the remedies that had been tried, and all the cases which presented a probable chance of recovery. He was much interested by this visit, and when he left the Maison Royale he gave particular orders that 'the poor lunatics should be treated kindly.'

"On his return from Charenton, the emperor seemed thought-ful. 'This visit,' said he to me, 'has made me melancholy. Insanity is a frightful degradation of human nature. I shall never go mad, that is certain. My head is of iron (this is an expression which he often employed). Despair, indeed, is another thing! I have fixed ideas upon that subject. Some time or other, Caulincourt, it is possible you may hear that I have deprived myself of life, but never that I have lost my senses.'

"He reminded me of these words," pursued the duke, "in the ter-rible night we spent at Fontainebleau in 1814. 'This idea,' he said, oc-curred to me when I was at Charenton. I then felt convinced that it would be better to die than to become an object of pity.'

"Moscow, Châtillon, Fontainebleau, and the Hundred Days," add-ed the Duke de Vicenza, are nightmares which incessantly haunt my restless couch."

That day the duke appeared unwell and low-spirited, and I pro-posed an excursion to Val-Dajon, which is about a league from Plom-bières. The duke acceded to this proposal, and we set out.

Val-Dajon scarcely deserves the name of a hamlet. It consists mere-ly of a few little houses scattered over the slopes of a chain of hills, the hills themselves being crowned with thickly shaded groves. The Val is all verdure and freshness, and neat little white houses, roofed with varnished tiles, glitter here and there in the sun. The lower meadows, which are intersected by a pellucid stream, afford delightful pasture for numbers of cows, sheep, and goats. Here and there groups of laughing children are seen dancing and playing on the grass; or a young girl, with a jar of water on her head, is seen slowly and cautiously ascend-ing the slope between the stream and the houses. Here a few poor but happy families live and die, circumscribed within the funnel-shaped valley called Val-Dajon.

The Duke de Vicenza, Colonel R——, and myself, took our seats on some wooden benches, which are fixed on the hills overlooking the charming scene; and we began, in philosophic style, to discuss the inexhaustible theme of comparative happiness. As I looked down upon the smiling valley, I thought that in that tranquil spot I might recover my health and pass the remainder of my days without bestow-ing a regret on the noisy pleasures of town life. I forgot that Val-Dajon, then so verdant and smiling, was during eight months of the year enveloped in snow.

"No doubt," said the Duke de Vicenza, whose taste was probably less pastoral than mine, "no doubt these people are happy, but we could not be happy on the same conditions. Theirs is a negative, a purely material, sort of happiness, which would not accord with our tastes and habits, and would fall very far short of our intellectual wants. Enjoyments are relative to the character of the individual, to his tastes, his sensations, his passions—"

At this moment we were joined by M. de N——, who, like ourselves, was a visitor to Plombières. The colonel and M. de N—— went to take a walk together, and I remained in conversation with the duke.

I had observed that he was that day unusually thoughtful and low-spirited, and I had endeavoured, by leading the conversation to other subjects, to divert him from those recollections which invariably tended to increase his melancholy; but he always returned, as it were involuntarily, to the events of the empire.

"There was a period of my life," said he, after a long and meditative pause, "when I felt myself wanting in that sort of moral courage which enables a man to make the greatest of all sacrifices—the sacrifice of those objects which have been the fondest dreams of youthful ambition. In the consciousness of the rectitude of my own conduct, I braved a host of injustice and prejudice which fed the gossip of the Parisian *salons*. When events brought about the downfall of the man to whom I owed my elevation, the odious accusations of which I had been the object were once more revived. I trust, *Madame*, that you do not believe me to be the odious wretch I have been represented?"

I was struck with the hurried and anxious tone in which this interrogation was addressed to me. The too famous mission to Ettenheim was a subject which I should have cautiously refrained from touching on, though I was fully convinced of the injustice of the animosity cherished by a certain party against the Duke de Vicenza. I had heard the affair variously described, and I was naturally curious to hear the details from the duke himself. When he asked me whether I believed the reports circulated against him, the question at first disconcerted me, but soon recovering my presence of mind, I replied—

"I was very young at the time of the Duke d'Enghien's death. I heard the affair spoken of for the first time in 1814. Opinions appeared to me to he divided on the subject. You had accusers, duke, it is true, but at the same time you had honourable and zealous defenders. For my own part, I never could believe you guilty of the iniquity laid to your charge. I judged you by the previous course of your life, which was unsullied by any act of dishonour. I could easily discern that your enemies, in conjuring up this accusation, masked the real motives of the malignity they cherished towards Napoleon's grand equerry. The negotiations of Châtillon, and subsequently of Fontainebleau, your strenuous efforts to preserve the crown for the son of the emperor, were, I verily believe, the real causes of the hatred and malice of which you have been the object. These causes, too, provoked the warm defence made by your friends. General Leval, to whom the dispatches of which you were the bearer were addressed, rendered you signal justice."

"He did; but still he converted only those persons who were just and unbiased."

"Party spirit," observed I, "is blind and prejudiced. Time will render you justice by proving the fallacy of the odious accusation. You have secured to yourself a glorious claim to the sympathy of your country-men by your useful intervention in the affairs of France, and your in-trepid devotedness to Napoleon. The day will come when your name will never be uttered without feelings of respect by both friends and enemies."

"I declare upon my honour," said the duke, proudly rearing his head, "that my conscience is free from all self-reproach. I will acquaint you with the real facts of this unfortunate affair as far as I was person-ally concerned.

"In the year X. I was Colonel of the 2nd Carabineers, and I was appointed *aide-de-camp* to the First Consul. This appointment was conferred without favour, and merely in consideration of seniority of rank, according to the rule then observed. The First Consul, General Bonaparte, as he was called, was a few years older than I, and he was the object of my enthusiastic admiration. I recollect that I thought him very good looking, though I should have been laughed at by my comrades had I expressed that opinion in their hearing, for at that time he was certainly anything but handsome.

"I was devotedly attached to my general, and would have followed him through every privation and danger; I would have laid down my life for him; and yet he had at that time done nothing for me. His manners were not remarkably friendly or social; and he was so rigidly strict in all that regarded military duty, that no one dared venture on the least infraction of his orders; yet I refused the rank of general to re-main attached to his person as colonel *aide-de-camp*. None but military men can understand the full extent of this sacrifice on the part of a colonel of seven-and-twenty. During the Consulate and the Republic, I certainly had no foresight of the miracles of the empire. How am I to account for the pure friendship, the devotedness, I felt for a man who had never even shaken hands with me? We feel, but we cannot explain, the power of attraction.

"The First Consul had never yet distinguished me from my comrades, and in truth I had as yet done nothing that could have justified a preference. One evening, to my surprise, he sent for me. I can fancy I see him now seated at a little wooden desk, painted black, which he was cutting in every direction with his pen-knife. He looked at me for a few moments, and then said—

"'Colonel Caulincourt, you are to set out tonight for Bavaria. On your way you will deliver these dispatches to General Leval, the *commandant* of the Strasburg division. Sit down, and listen attentively to what I have to say. There is a letter to the Elector of Bavaria. You are not to let it out of your possession, but deliver it to the Elector in person. This letter contains certain demands, and you must insist on their being conceded within four-and-twenty hours. You understand, colonel,—within four-and-twenty hours!' As he uttered these words his eyes looked searchingly into mine, as if he wished to read in them the assurance of my determination to execute his orders.

"'I will explain to you,' resumed he, 'the spirit of the dispatches of which you are the bearer. There is at present at the little court of Bavaria, an English *Chargé d'Affaires*, named Drake. I know that this man has been engaged in plots and intrigues against the French government. I also know that there is a certain Baroness von Reich, who has set herself at the head of the French emigrants, and that she and Drake are organising conspiracies against my life. Wherever plots are carried on against France, England has her hirelings at work.

"'I require, first, that the Elector of Bavaria shall dismiss Drake from his court within twenty-four hours after the receipt of my letter; secondly, that the intriguing Baroness von Reich shall be removed from Munich. If my demands are not complied with, I shall find myself compelled immediately to send a military force into the Bavarian territory. Now, Colonel Caulincourt, you perceive the importance of your mission. Do not permit any tergiversation, and accept no compromise. These petty princes of the Rhine must be taught to respect France. Weakness emboldens conspirators. Munich and some other places that I could name are the hot-beds of base machinations against

France. All this must be brought to an end.

"'The dispatch which you will deliver on your way to General Leval contains directions for him to place, troops at your disposal, in case you should be forced to employ them. Ordener will have the command of these troops, he will be on the spot, and you must return immediately to render me an account of what has been done. You understand. Drake must receive his passports four-and-twenty hours after your arrival at Munich. Go, Colonel Caulincourt, fulfil your mission with speed and intelligence.'

"As I was leaving his cabinet he called me back and said— 'Caulincourt, take with you your uniform of colonel *aide-de-camp*. Those people yonder must be taught to respect the French uniform.'

"I was young and ardent," pursued the Duke of Vicenza, "and I was not a little flattered by the mark of confidence conferred on me by the First Consul. Four hours after my interview with him, I was on the road to Germany, seated in a light cabriolet, drawn by two post-horses and preceded by a courier. I had not allowed myself time to bid *adieu* to my family. Just as I was stepping into my cabriolet, I saw one of my friends approaching to speak to me; I asked him to seat himself beside me, that we might chat together as we drove along. I informed him that I had been entrusted with a mission by the First Consul, that I was on my way to Germany, and begged him to communicate the circumstance to my family and our mutual friends.

"The First Consul had not enjoined me to observe secrecy, and I did not conceive that I was guilty of any indiscretion in vaguely mentioning the place of my destination. But fate ordained that these few words, addressed to a friend who happened accidentally to meet me at the moment of departure, should be attended with a fatal result. My absence was remarked in those circles of society in which I was in the habit of mixing. On the night of my departure from Paris, another individual, who was the bearer of dispatches from the war-office, set off on a journey to Germany. On our arrival at Strasburg, which probably we both reached nearly at the same time, we each presented our dispatches to General Leval. Without stopping, I proceeded straight to Offenburg, and the probability is that a few hours afterwards there departed from Strasburg a superior officer, a colonel of *gendarmerie*, and three hundred troops, who effected at Ettenheim the fatal arrest of the Duke d'Enghien.

"When the unfortunate prince reached Strasburg, orders were given that he should be conducted to Paris. General Leval afterwards informed me that he lent some money and clothes to the duke, who was arrested at night, and was not allowed time even to pack a portmanteau. The dispatches from the war-minister enjoined the most absolute secrecy on General Leval, who forwarded his prisoner to Paris, without suspecting that he was sending him to receive sentence of death.

"Chance might have decreed that I should have been the individual entrusted with the dispatches relating to the Duke d'Enghien; and, like the person who had the misfortune to be the bearer of them, I should have delivered the letters in the most perfect ignorance of their contents. But the fact is, they were not consigned to me.

"I reached Munich on the night of the 2nd of March, 1804. At eight on the following morning I wrote to the Elector, requesting the honour of an audience, and stating that I had orders to deliver into his own hands some important dispatches entrusted to me by the First Consul. Several hours elapsed and I received no answer, I was reflecting on what it would be best for me to do, when one of the Elector's chamberlains waited on me. 'Colonel,' said he, 'I am sent by my sovereign with orders to conduct you to the palace.'

"We stepped into a carriage which was waiting at the door. Not a word was exchanged between the chamberlain and myself as we drove along. Having ushered me into a small audience-chamber, my guide bowed and withdrew. I waited alone for about a quarter of an hour. The Elector then entered, attended, by three gentlemen. I presented to him the First Consul's letter. He took it from me, and read it rapidly. I attentively observed his countenance. He turned very red, and the paper trembled in his hands. He glanced it over a second time, and having endeavoured to collect himself, he turned to me, and said, in a voice faltering with emotion—

"'Colonel, you shall have my answer this evening.'

"I bowed and withdrew without uttering a single word. At the door of the audience-chamber I found the chamberlain who had brought me to the palace. We stepped into the carriage; he accompanied me to my abode, and took his leave.

"When I entered my apartment I could not repress a hearty fit of laughter. This German formality and silence appeared to me extremely amusing. I refrained from going out, lest my perambles about the city should give rise to absurd suspicions; and I do not think I was ever so weary of my life as during the interval I remained a prisoner in my hotel at Munich.

"At ten o'clock in the evening the chamberlain again called on me. He observed the same formality and silence as before. I was conducted to the presence of the Elector. He was the very *beau ideal* of phlegmatic German aristocracy. Still, to render him justice, the prince was not wanting in a certain degree of dignity, and I have no doubt that in his social relations he was a kind and amiable man. When I was ushered into his presence I found him alone, and he informed me 'that the *commands* of the First Consul of the French Republic were in their nature very painful to him; that the First Consul had been misinformed; that neither Mr. Drake, the Baroness von Reich, nor any other person in his states, had conspired against the French Republic; that the First Consul, by requiring the immediate removal of the Minister Drake, placed Bavaria in a very unpleasant position in relation to a friendly power, England; that he, the Elector, would ascertain whether there were any grounds for dismissing the English minister, by directing his police to institute inquiries respecting the imputed machinations against France; that those machinations were unjustly imputed to Mr. Drake; and that, finally, if it should be proved that he had conspired against the French Republic, the violent measure required by the First Consul would be justified, *to a certain point*, in the eyes of his ally, England.'

"The Elector spoke slowly and hesitatingly, and he thus gave me time to arrange my answer. I stated that it was not for me to judge of the accuracy of the information received by the First Consul respecting Mr. Drake and the Baroness Reich; that the object of my mission was to obtain complete satisfaction; and that my orders were to see that the demands of my government were complied with within four-and-twenty hours after the delivery of my dispatch.

"'But, Colonel,' resumed the Elector, 'the First Consul can scarcely expect that I should, at so short a notice, obey so arbitrary a demand, and one that sets at defiance the law of nations.'

"I have the honour to observe to the Elector," replied I, "that I cannot comment on the orders of my government, and that it is not in my power to modify the terms of my mission.'

"'The First Consul shall be obeyed, sir,' answered the Elector, drily. He then bowed, and I withdrew.

"I had experienced no little difficulty in maintaining my gravity during this conversation. Every time the poor Elector pronounced the words *French Republic*, they seemed almost to choke him, and he made the most ridiculous grimace imaginable.

"Next day (4th of March, 1804) Mr. Drake was dismissed, the Baroness von Reich left Munich, and I sat out on my return to France. I stopped at Strasburg merely to change horses, and then hurried on to Paris.

"I was elated at my success. This was the first mission on which I had been employed, and I felt a pride in serving General Bonaparte, who knew so well how to enforce respect to France. In my own family I had had to contend against a host of prejudices, and I had experienced no little difficulty in subduing the disapprobation caused by my attachment to *little General Bonaparte*.

"Thus vanity prompted me, on my return, to boast of the success of my mission. I entered Paris at six o'clock in the morning. At that early hour I could not of course present myself at the Tuileries. I drove to the residence of Madame de ————, an old friend of my mother. There I heard of the death of the Duke d'Enghien, who had been arrested at Ettenheim, and shot at Vincennes. I was seized with a thrill of horror. I immediately perceived the interpretation that might be given to my mission to the Rhine. The coincidence was singular, and to me most unfortunate.

"On the night on which I left Strasburg for Offenburg, the officer who was directed to arrest the Duke d'Enghien set off from Strasburg to Ettenheim. He, with the dispatches consigned to his charge, departed from and returned to Paris unperceived; whilst I had incautiously announced my departure in *salons* in which the death of the unfortunate Duke d'Enghien excited cries of horror. I felt that an odious suspicion must light upon me, and I was so overcome by my feelings that I fell senseless on the floor.

"I will not express my opinion on the affair of Ettenheim. My tongue shall never utter a censure on Napoleon. When I cannot praise or admire him, I will be silent. I cannot concur in the opinion of that individual who has said, 'It was worse than a crime, it was a fault.' The execution of the Duke d'Enghien was a two-fold misfortune. It was the specious cause of the first war between France and Russia; the pretence for that war being the violation of the territory of the Grand Duke of Baden, the father-in-law of the Emperor Alexander.

"I had no share in the catastrophe which cost a gloom over what would otherwise have been the happiest period of my life. The only reproach that I can make to myself is, that I did not bow my head beneath the thunder-bolts which were hurled against me.

"By resigning my appointment of *aide-de-camp* to the First Consul, and thus openly avowing my indignation at the affair of Ettenheim, I should have cleared myself of a false and odious imputation. But in so doing I must have renounced the brilliant career which I saw opening before me, and repressed the glowing enthusiasm which animated my heart. I was young and ambitious; conscious that my honour was unsullied, and that I had no cause of self-reproach, I boldly defied my accusers. The high position which I subsequently attained, and the favours which the emperor heaped upon me, all tended to corroborate the malignant imputations.

"My real crime, that for which persons of my own caste will never pardon me, is, that in 1814 I dared to dispute inch by inch the rights of the son of Napoleon; and to wrest from the allied powers a few leagues of sovereignty for the greatest man of modern times—for him who had possessed the world, and whose very name shook to their foundations all the old thrones of Europe. My crime was, that in 1815 I aided and assisted my benefactor by every means in my power.

"In the discharge of my political duties I listened to the dictates of feeling, and for this courtiers will never pardon me. Viewing with disdain the miserable passions of the day, I retired to my estate in the country, and devoted myself to the education of my sons. The death of the Emperor Alexander has destroyed my last dream of future happiness.

"When I was appointed Ambassador to Russia, I wrote to the emperor, to whom I had been personally known since the period of my first mission to St. Petersburg. I knew not what opinion he might have formed of my conduct in reference to the affair of Ettenheim. The emperor's answer was—

"'I made every inquiry of my ministers, who were residing in Germany at the time; and I ascertained that you had no participation whatever in the sad affair. If I entertained the slightest doubt on this subject, there is no power, *celestial* or *terrestrial*, which could induce me to receive you. At the time of your first mission to my court, you and I were both very young; but from the opinion I formed of your character and disposition, I could have vouched that you were incapable of an act of dishonour.'

"I have this letter, written in the Emperor Alexander's own hand. I had written to him without soliciting the permission of the Emperor Napoleon. But his police served him well, and I took no pains to keep the matter secret. Whether it ever reached his knowledge, I cannot say; but he never mentioned it to me. If he had, I should candidly have acknowledged the fact, and I feel assured that he would have understood my motives, and would not have blamed me. It is a remarkable fact, considering the intimate relations existing between us, that the name of the Duke d'Enghien was never mentioned in our conversations. Whatever may have been said or written on the subject, I am convinced that the event left a deep wound in the heart of Napoleon. I am also convinced that the favours with which he overwhelmed me were in a great degree dictated by feelings of justice. He was anxious to repair as far as possible the injury I had suffered through the coincidence of my mission to Munich and the affair of Ettenheim. Certainly he never planned the affair for the sake of compromising me. I was not a person of sufficient importance to make it worth his while to resort to such a scheme.

"In spite of public clamour, I will boldly render homage to the noble character of the Emperor of Russia, not because he treated me kindly, but because his noble nature is a fact which impartial history must acknowledge. Alexander warmly defended me to Louis XVIII. against the aspersions cast upon me in relation to the affair of the Duke d'Enghien; and he did not relinquish the subject until he received the assurance that the king was convinced of my innocence. But it was of little avail. Louis XVIII. was of a sardonic turn, and becoming impatient at the Emperor Alexander's enumeration of my merits, he terminated the conference by saying—

"'I trust that my brother of Russia does not intend proposing that M. Bonaparte's Grand Equerry should fill at my court the post of the Prince de Lambese?'

"Alexander was piqued, and answered carelessly—

"'Oh! by no means! His Majesty the King of France knows as well as the meanest peasant in his dominions, that in making a bargain between two persons, it is necessary that both should agree.'

"Louis XVIII. felt the force of this rebuke, and I believe he never liked me for it.

"I learned these particulars from the Emperor Alexander himself. 'My dear Caulincourt,' added he, with great warmth of manner, 'come and reside at the court of Russia. You shall there find a friend in me; and your sons shall be established in a way which they cannot hope for in France. The Bourbons are convinced of your innocence, but they wish to let suspicion still attach to you—that serves their policy. Besides, they are aware that in the conferences of April 1814, you powerfully defended the interests of your unfortunate master, and

I can assure you it depended on the turn of a straw whether your cause would triumph; theirs was poorly advocated by their *improvised* friends. We naturally esteem and love the devotedness which is rendered to ourselves; whilst we think lightly of that which is exercised in favour of a competitor. The Bourbons know, too, that you will never crouch to them; that your apostasy will not add to the humiliation of Napoleon. In a word, Caulincourt, you are a *man too much* in the kingdom of France. Come, then, to the court of Russia, where there is room for you and yours, and in me you shall find a friend who will never renounce you.'

"I threw myself at the feet of the generous monarch," pursued the Duke de Vicenza, "I formed in my own mind plans of future happiness, which, alas! are buried in Alexander's grave!

"I have now given you a true statement of all that relates to my mission to Germany."

I had listened to this narrative with the deepest interest, and at its conclusion I said, extending my hand to the narrator, "Let me assure you, duke, that at all times, and in all places, my feeble voice will render a tribute of admiration to your noble conduct. Henceforth, when I hear you attacked, I will repeat your justification."

"Do you intend to stay much longer at Plombières?" inquired the duke.

"You," replied I, "possess the power of detaining me here as long as you please. Until you are tired of narrating, I cannot be tired of listening. Then, and not till then, I will order post-horses."

"There are," said the duke, "some curious facts connected with the campaign of 1813, with which, possibly, you may not be acquainted. The scenes at Fontainebleau would also interest you. I will relate to you how, when driven back by the advanced posts of the allies encamped before Paris, I entered the capital, concealed in the carriage of the Grand Duke Constantine; how I remained for four-and-twenty hours undiscovered in the apartments of that most generous of men, the Emperor Alexander. I will describe to you the difficulties and dangers which beset me in the *Hundred Days*, during which interval I may almost say I lived a hundred years, and when you look at my wrinkled brow, sunken eyes, and attenuated form, you will say, they bear convincing testimony of the truth of my statements. At all events, let it be well understood, that whenever I begin to weary you, you order post-horses."

CHAPTER 6

The Battle of Eylau

I reminded the Duke de Vicenza of his promise to continue his narration of the events of the empire.

In the course of conversation I happened to mention the name of Captain Ernest Auzoni, who was killed at the Battle of Eylau. He was a brave young officer, and his death blighted the happiness of a beautiful and accomplished woman whom I numbered among my friends. There was one remarkable circumstance connected with the last moments of poor Ernest Auzoni. The emperor was an eye-witness of his death.

I questioned the Duke de Vicenza on this point.

"It is perfectly true," replied he. "Auzoni, who was a captain in the grenadiers of the guard, was a young officer of the highest promise. He was brave, even among the bravest, and he several times distinguished himself during the Battle of Eylau. His dauntless courage attracted the attention of the Emperor. Auzoni's company, animated by the example of its young and valiant captain, had performed prodigies in the course of the battle.

"I could," pursued the duke, with a melancholy smile, "describe to you in a few words the glorious death of the gallant Auzoni; but in so doing my memory would carry me back to the field of Eylau, where the emperor shone so transcendency. When I cast a retrospective glance on the glorious scene, Napoleon is the engrossing subject of my reflections, and I cannot trace the most feeble sketch of the picture without assigning to him a place in the foreground."

"Duke," said I, "poor Ernest Auzoni is to me an object of secondary interest in comparison with Napoleon. Your details of the emperor's private life have an inexpressible charm to me. History, always dry and barren, gives me facts and dates: but you conduct me, as it were, into Napoleon's presence; whilst listening to you, I can almost fancy that I see him and hear him."

"We passed the night of the 4th of February," resumed the duke, "at Schlitt, a little village situated a few leagues from Eylau. This was a few days preceding the battle. The emperor installed himself in a miserable cottage, which contained no fireplace except that in the kitchen; there the Imperial head quarters were established. I scarcely ever saw Napoleon more good-humoured or in better spirits than on the night on which we bivouacked in that wretched hovel. I recollect that there was only one table, and on that was spread the emperor's supper. He dispatched the meal in five minutes, and then good hu-mouredly throwing his napkin at the head of Constant, his favourite valet, he said:—'Quick, quick, take away the remains of my banquet' (it consisted of only one dish).

"Then advancing to his little camp bedstead, on which his maps had been deposited, he took up his map of Prussia, and spreading it out on the ground, knelt down to examine it. 'Come here, *Grand Ecuyer*,' said be, addressing me, 'and follow me from Schlitt—from this splendid capital, Schlitt, to Paris.' He marked with pins all the places through which we were to pass according to his plan. 'I shall beat them there,' said he, 'here—there again—and in three months the campaign will be ended—Russia must have a lesson. The fair Queen of Prussia shall learn too, at her expense, that advisers sometimes pay dearly for the advice they give. I do not like those women who throw aside their attributes of grace and goodness. A woman to instigate war!—to urge men to cut each others throats! Fie on it! She may run the risk of los-ing her kingdom by playing that game!'

"At this moment some dispatches were delivered to the emperor. He rapidly glanced them over, and exclaimed:—'Bravo! bravo!—we have them now! But surely these dispatches have been a long time on their way! How is this?' continued he, knitting his brow. 'Tell the orderly officer who brought them that I wish to speak with him.'

"'*Monsieur*,' said he, in a severe tone, addressing the officer, 'at what hour were these dispatches placed in your hands?'

"'At eight o'clock in the evening, Sire,'

"'And how many leagues had you to ride?'

"'I do not know precisely, Sire.'

"'But you ought to know. *Monsieur*,' pursued he, drily, fixing his eyes upon the officer, who trembled beneath his glance of displeasure, 'an orderly officer ought to know that, *Monsieur—I* know it: you had nine leagues to ride, and you set off at eight o'clock—look at your watch, sir. What is it o'clock now?'

"The officer was quite disconcerted, and he stood motionless.

"'Tell me what it is o'clock, sir, if you please.'

"'Half-past twelve, Sire. The roads were in a terrible state. In some places the snow obstructed my passage—'

"'Poor excuses, sir. Retire and await my orders,' and as the officer closed the door, he added—'this cool leisurely gentleman wants stimulating; the reprimand I have given him will make him spur his horse another time.—Let me see—my answer must be delivered in two hours hence; I have no time to lose.'

"The dispatches which the emperor had just received were from General Lasalle, who was encamped in the village of Deppen. He informed the emperor that a column of the enemy, amounting, it was presumed, to between fifteen and sixteen thousand men, having been unable to work a passage through the snow, had got separated from the main body of the Prussian Army. This intelligence was of the utmost importance. The emperor's answer was, an order to General Lasalle to attack with his division the column commanded by General Lestocq, and thereby to prevent the junction which the latter was endeavouring to effect with the Russian Army. At the same time, he directed two regiments of dragoons, who had been posted as scouts, at half a league from Deppen, to join Lasalle's division, and to fall simultaneously on the column, which was attacked in front by the troops of General Lasalle.

"He sent for the orderly officer whom he had rebuked a few minutes previously. 'Set off immediately, sir,' said he; these dispatches must be delivered with the utmost speed. General Lasalle must receive my orders by three o'clock—by three o'clock. You understand, sir?'

"'Sire,' replied the young officer, in a most resolute tone, 'by half-past two the general shall have the orders of which I have the honour to be the bearer.'

"'Very well, sir; mount your horse—and, stay—'added he, calling the officer back, 'tell General Lasalle that it will be agreeable to me that you should be the person selected to announce to me the success of these movements.'

"This orderly officer was the son of a senator. The emperor was perfectly aware of this fact; but he was always more strict and severe towards young men who left the military colleges with the rank of officers, than towards those who gained their epaulettes by facing fire and sword. It is but just to acknowledge that the latter rarely needed a reprimand, and when they did, the emperor admonished them with paternal gentleness. Thus he created in all ranks of the army men who would have sacrificed their lives rather than incur his displeasure. It is remarkable, too, that men who performed prodigies of valour, and covered themselves with glory, never looked for any reward. It seemed that the lives of all belonged to one alone, and that to perish in the cause of that one was merely the performance of a sacred duty. The heroic phasis of the empire impressed a noble stamp on the French character.

"At the time to which I was just now referring," continued the duke, "wherever we fought the victory was our own. The intrepid Lasalle, with less than three thousand men, repulsed the enemy's column. General Lestocq, closely and vigorously pursued, owed his safety only to the swiftness of his horse. Three thousand Prussians perished in the conflict; two thousand five hundred prisoners and sixteen pieces of artillery were the trophies of this partial engagement. Its consequences were of vast importance, for the Russian Army was cut off from some of its communications, and awaited in vain the promised reinforcement.

"On learning this news, the emperor was quite transported with joy, and he several times exclaimed, 'Brave General Lasalle!—Admirable troops!—I am now sure of gaining the battle which I am going to fight at Eylau!—This is a good augury!—We will now march forward to Eylau, gentlemen!'

"On the day of the battle the weather was dreadful. The snow, which fell thickly in fine flakes, froze as it reached the surface of the earth. Our clothes, being covered with this sort of hoar frost, were stiff and heavy. The horses could not keep their footing. The sanguinary conflict had been maintained since morning, and when night set in, all was yet undecided. The emperor, in a state of the utmost anxiety and impatience, galloped up and down the field of battle, braving the grape-shot which was showering in every direction. He was always to be seen on those points threatened with the greatest danger, well knowing that his presence would alone work miracles. Meanwhile, the ceasing of the fire on some points indicated that the enemy was falling back.

"At eight o'clock, Napoleon was informed that the important position of the church, which had been obstinately disputed, taken and retaken several times in the course of the day, had again been carried by the enemy. Our troops, whose numbers were infinitely inferior to those of the Russians, retired fighting to the church-yard. At the moment when the orderly arrived with this intelligence, the emperor had dismounted, and was personally directing a formidable battery pointed on the left wing of the Russian Army. He instantly leaped on his horse, galloped off with the rapidity of lightning, and throwing himself into the midst of the battalions, which were beginning to give way, 'What!' he exclaimed, 'a handful of Russians repulse troops of the Grand Army! Hear me, my brave fellows. Let not a Russian escape from the church! Forward with the artillery! We must have the church, my lads!—we must have it!' This address was answered by '*Vive l'Empereur!*'—'Forward! we must have the church!' and all rushed onward, rallying in good order.

"At a few paces from us we espied an old grenadier. His face was blackened by gunpowder, and the blood was streaming down his clothes. His left arm had been carried away by a bomb-shell. The man was hurrying to fall into the ranks. 'Stay, stay, my good fellow,' said the emperor, 'go and get your wound dressed,—go to the *ambulance.*'—'I will,' replied the grenadier, 'when we have taken the church,' and we immediately lost sight of him. I perceived the tears glistening in the emperor's eyes, and he turned aside to conceal them.

"At ten o'clock that night the church was ours. The emperor, who was thoroughly exhausted, tottered with fatigue as he sat on his horse. He ordered the firing to cease; and the army reposed, surrounded by the enemy's bivouacs. Our head quarters were established on the Plateau, behind Eylau, in the midst of the infantry of the guard.

"'All is going on admirably,' said the emperor to me as he entered his tent. 'Those men have fought bravely!' Without undressing, he threw himself on his bed, and in a few instants was sound asleep.

"At four in the morning the emperor was again on his horse. He surveyed the ground, arranged his plans, posted the artillery, harangued the troops, and rode past the front rank of each regiment. At daybreak he gave orders that the attack should commence simultaneously on all points. About eleven o'clock, the snow, which had fallen incessantly during the whole morning, increased with such violence that we could scarcely perceive any object at the distance of ten paces. After the lapse of some little time, a Russian column, amounting to between five and six thousand men, was discerned; during the night this column had received orders to join the main body of the army, and had missed the way. The troops, who were marching forward hesitatingly and without scouts, had strayed to within the distance of a musket shot of our camp.

"The emperor, standing erect, with his feet in the stirrups, and his glass at his eye, was the first to perceive that the black shadows slowly-defiling through the veil of snow must belong to the Russian reserve. He instantly directed towards them two battalions of the grenadiers of the guard, commanded by General Dorsenne. Whilst the grenadiers advanced in silence, the squadron on duty near the emperor turned the column, attacked it in the rear, and drove it forward on our grenadiers, who received it with fixed bayonets. This first shock was terrible to the Russians. But soon comparing their numerical strength with the small number of troops opposed to them, the officers drew their swords, rallied their men, and all defended themselves with great courage.

"At one moment our grenadiers appeared to flag, when a young officer darted forward from the ranks, exclaiming in a loud voice, 'Courage, my brave comrades! follow me, and the Russian colours are ours!' He rushed forward, sword in hand, followed by his company, and penetrated the compact centre of the Russian column. This unexpected assault broke their ranks; and our grenadiers resolutely entered the passage opened to them by the brave Auzoni. The Russians were all sabred or made prisoners. 'This is one of the most glorious achievements of this memorable day,' said the emperor, who had been an eye-witness to the heroic conduct of Auzoni. He summoned him to his presence, and thus addressed him—

"'Captain Auzoni, you well deserve the honour of commanding my veteran *moustaches*. You have most nobly distinguished yourself. You have won an officer's cross and an endowment of 2,000 *francs*. You were made a captain at the opening of the campaign, and I hope you will return to Paris with a still higher rank. A man who earns his honours on the field of battle stands very high in my estimation. I present ten crosses to your company,' he added, turning towards the soldiers.

"Enthusiastic shouts rent the air, and these same men advanced to meet the enemy's fire with a degree of courage and enthusiasm which it is impossible to describe.

"Two hours after the victory was ours. The enemy's forces, routed and dispersed, retreated in the utmost disorder, abandoning their wounded, their baggage, and their parks of artillery.

"But the day's work was not yet ended for the emperor. According to custom, he went over the field of battle to estimate the enemy's loss, and to hurry the removal of the wounded. It was truly horrible to survey the immense extent of ground over which the snow of the preceding day was crimsoned with blood.

"A quarter-master of dragoons, grievously wounded, perceived the emperor passing at a few paces from him. 'Turn your eyes this way, please your Majesty,' said the man. 'I believe I have got my death-wound, and shall soon be in the other world. But no matter for that! *Vive l'Empereur!*'

"'Let this poor fellow be immediately conveyed, to the *ambulance?* said Napoleon. 'Raise him up, and commend him to the care of Larrey.' Large tears rolled down the cheeks of the dragoon when he heard the emperor utter these words. 'I only wish,' said he, 'that I had a thousand lives to lay down for your Majesty.'

"Near a battery which had been abandoned by the enemy we beheld a singular picture, and one of which description can convey but a faint idea. About a hundred and fifty or two hundred French grenadiers were surrounded by a quadruple rank of Prussians. Both parties were weltering in a river of blood, amidst fragments of cannon, muskets, swords, &c. They had evidently fought with the most determined fury, for every corse exhibited numerous and horrible wounds.

"A feeble cry of *Vive l'Empereur!* was heard to emanate from this mountain of the dead, and all eyes were instantly turned to the spot whence the voice proceeded. Half concealed beneath a tattered flag lay a young officer, whose breast was decorated with an order. Though pierced with numerous wounds, he succeeded in raising himself up so as to rest on his elbow. His handsome countenance was overspread with the livid hue of death. He recognised the emperor, and in a feeble, faltering voice, exclaimed, 'God bless your Majesty!—and now—farewell! farewell!—Oh! my poor mother!' He turned a supplicating glance to the emperor, and then uttering the words, 'To dear France—my last sigh!' he fell stiff and cold.

"Napoleon seemed riveted to the spot, which was watered with the blood of these heroes, 'Brave men,' said he: 'brave Auzoni! Excellent young man. Alas! this is a frightful scene. The endowment shall go to his mother. Let the order be presented for my signature as soon as possible.' Then turning to Doctor Ivan, who accompanied him, he said, 'Examine poor Anzoni's wounds and see whether anything can be done for him. This is indeed terrible!'

"The emperor, whose feelings were deeply excited, continued his mournful inspection of the field of battle. On various similar occasions I have seen him powerfully moved. Yet he never expressed by words his regret for the inevitable miseries which follow in the train of war. This was a very characteristic trait in Napoleon. I am certain that his heart was painfully wrung when he beheld his devoted friends and servants stretched lifeless at his feet. But he seldom betrayed any outward manifestation of grief, either because it was not natural to him, or because he was so perfectly master of himself that he could repress the signs of inward emotion.

"Now that I am free from the fascination which his presence exercised over me, I sometimes endeavour coolly to analyse that character, that peculiar organization, which seemed to be made up of so many incongruous shades. Napoleon defies psychological science. His character, doubtless, presented imperfections, but the beautiful and the sublime are predominant, and the more I study the character of Napoleon the more I am impressed with its grandeur.

"I have now told you," said the Duke de Vicenza, "all that I know relative to Captain Auzoni. Whenever my memory reverts to the Battle of Eylau, the aspect of the field on the day after the victory appears, as it were, visibly present to me."

"Were you near the emperor," inquired I, "when the Dukes of Istria and Frioul were killed?"

"I was," replied he; "they fell in the campaign of 1813. From that period we sustained a continuity of reverses which have no precedent in the annals of any other nation. It would seem that after having passed through every grade of human prosperity, Napoleon was destined to suffer every degree of moral misery. From that fatal year commenced my hourly, I may say my momentary, duty of alleviating that bitter anguish—of sharing that silent grief, which the sufferer cannot and will not express, and which he fears to betray either by word or look.

"We left Saint Cloud for Mentz on the 15th of April, 1813, at four in the morning. When the carriage started, the emperor, who had his eyes fixed on the castle, threw himself back, placed his hand on his forehead, and remained for some time in that meditative attitude. At length, rousing himself from his gloomy reverie, he began to trace in glowing colours his plans and projects, the hopes he cherished of the faithful co-operation of Austria, &c., &c. Then he resumed his natural simplicity of manner, and spoke to me with emotion of the regret he felt at leaving his *bonne Louise*, and his lovely child.

"'I envy,' said he, 'the lot of the meanest peasant in my empire. At my age he has discharged his debt to his country, and he may remain at home enjoying the society of his wife and children; whilst I—I must fly to the camp, and engage in the strife of war—such is the mandate of my inexplicable destiny.' He again sunk into his reverie. To divert him from it, I turned the conversation on the scene of the preceding evening, when at the Elysée the empress, in the presence of the princes, grand dignitaries and ministers, had taken the solemn oath in the character of regent. The arch-chancellor (Cambacérès) and the Duke de Cadora were appointed her counsellors. Those were two men of vast ability.

"'*Ma bonne Louise*,' said the emperor to me, 'is gentle and submissive. I can depend on her. *Her love and fidelity will never fail me.* In the current of events there may arise circumstances which decide the fate of an empire. In that case I hope the daughter of the Caesars will be fired by the spirit of her grandmother, Maria Theresa.'

"The emperor," continued the duke, "was mistaken in his idea of the character of the empress. She was endowed with none of that energy which gives birth to great resolutions. She was, it is true, gentle and submissive, and in the every day routine of private life she might have conferred relative happiness on her husband; but that is all. Beneath that envelop of ice, it would have been vain to seek a heart; and like all weak-minded people, she was a dissembler, not from calculation, but from apathy and fear. She was cold and methodical, and utterly incapable of feeling that enthusiasm, that ardour of feeling, which, under certain circumstances, inspire heroic actions and prompt to noble sacrifices.

"Had Maria Louisa been tranquilly seated on the throne of France in ordinary times, she would have passed unobserved—had she owed her importance solely to the reflection of Napoleon's glory, she would have commanded respect, though never admiration. But her contemporaries have been called upon to judge her in her character of empress. History, forced to inscribe her name side by side with that of her immortal consort, must acknowledge that the Austrian arch-duchess proved herself incapable of discharging the duties of wife, mother, or sovereign. Maria Louisa was in fact worse than incapable, for she was below the level of her position.

"The emperor, though an accurate judge of men, knew nothing of women. He had mixed but little in female society. His feelings in reference to women were wholly material, and he did not admit the fascinating power of intelligence and talent in the female sex. He did not like learned or celebrated women, or those who in any way stepped out of the quiet sphere of domestic life. He assigned to women a very low grade in the social order, and thought they ought not to exercise power or influence over the minds of men. A woman was in his eyes merely a graceful being, and nothing more. Endeavours have been made to throw a romantic colouring over his short-lived amours; but the fact is, that Napoleon never formed any of those attachments in which the strongest party is the weakest, and in which the enslaved heart gives more than is demanded of it. 'Love,' said he to me one day, 'is merely a silly infatuation, depend on it.'

"The emperor and I used to have very animated discussions when the fair sex became the subject of his caustic remarks. I was very far from sharing the notions of my honoured master on this subject. I used to assert my opinions with my accustomed frankness, and it is but just to say that he bore with great patience the contradiction of his most firmly-rooted ideas.

"One day, when I was transacting business with him, I proposed the advancement of a person who had filled a situation in the civil administration of the imperial stables. He was a man of integrity and business-like habits, recommendations indispensable to persons employed in public departments under the empire. I was rigid in exacting strict attention to duty; and I always used my influence to forward the interests of those who were most deserving. I spoke to the Emperor of M——, and set forth his good qualities.

"'No, Caulincourt,' he replied, 'M—— is very well where he is. Leave him there.'

"But, Sire, returned I, he is a man of excellent abilities, and most assiduous in his attention to business. The appointment which I request for him is only an act of justice.

"'My dear Caulincourt, I assure you that your *protégé* is a fool.'

"I manifested some surprise on hearing this.

"'Yes, I tell you he is a fool. A husband who suffers himself to be led by his wife always ranks very low in my estimation.'

"But, inquired I, with a smile which I could not repress, how happens it that your Majesty has been made acquainted with circumstances which certainly have no connexion with the service of the imperial stables?

"'Ah! ah! *grand ecuyer*, you see I know what is going on better than you do,' said the emperor, rubbing his hands and laughing. Cagliostro was a poor conjuror in comparison with me.'

"I nevertheless persevered in my suit in behalf of poor M——, and I obtained for him the place to which his merit well entitled him.

"'Well, well,' said the emperor, 'let him have it, but tell him I like a man to be master in his own house.'

"You see," added the Duke de Vicenza, "that my capricious imagination has carried me very far from the road to Mentz, along which the emperor and I were journeying on the 15th of April, 1813. We reached Mentz late on the following night. I will tell you tomorrow the news we learned on our arrival."

CHAPTER 7

A Fatal Day!

"On our arrival at Mentz," resumed the Duke de Vicenza, "we learned that Erfurth and the whole of Westphalia had been thrown into the utmost, alarm by false reports which had been artfully propagated. This was a scheme which had just then been set on foot for the purpose of exciting disaffection. The emperor insisted on proceeding onward without even stopping to rest. The speed at which we journeyed was inconceivable. We were only eight hours in proceeding from Mentz to Erfurth. There, as everywhere, the presence of the emperor operated like a talisman in tranquillizing the public mind. During the whole of our journey through this conquered country, Napoleon was the object of fervent prayers and benedictions.

"On our way through Weimar, the emperor saw the grand duchess, and he made a remark upon her, which was very singular as coming from Napoleon. The remark was, to be sure, made in reference to a crowned bead. 'This Grand Duchess of Weimar,' said the emperor, 'is an extraordinary woman. She has the talent of a clever man.'

"We reached Eckartsberg, and found the place occupied by troops, parks of artillery, &c. The emperor had only two apartments assigned to him, and both looked to the market-place of the town, which was the scene of incessant noise and confusion. The uproar was perfectly intolerable; yet the emperor, seated at his table, with his maps spread before him and his compasses in his hand, seemed as undisturbed as though he had been in his quiet cabinet at the Tuileries. He was wholly absorbed in the plans he was meditating, and quite unconscious of all that was passing around him. I never knew any one gifted with the power of mental abstraction in so great a degree as Napoleon, or who could so easily endure cold, heat, hunger, and the privation of bodily comfort. It seemed as though he had the power of controlling his physical wants. He was a singularly organised being.

"On the 1st of May we reached Lutzen, and the battle was fought on the day following. It was a brief but glorious conflict. By Ave in the afternoon the enemy was completely routed. The firing had ceased; and only a few stray balls, aimed at random, were flying to and fro. Marshal Bessières, wrapped in his cloak, and mounted on a height, was watching, with his telescope at his eye, the retreat of the Russians. A brigadier attached to his escort was killed by the bursting of a bomb shell. 'Bury that brave man,' said he, and in a moment after he had uttered those words he was himself killed by a ball fired from a very considerable distance. The emperor was much attached to Bessières, who had followed him in all his campaigns and had taken part in all his battles. Bessières had passed through almost every grade in the command of the imperial guard. His courage had stood the test of every trial. He was universally esteemed and beloved, and sincerely regretted.

"The emperor was deeply affected by his death. 'This is a great loss,' said he, 'a very great loss—Bessières deserved to die the death of Turenne. Gentlemen, this is an enviable end!' A few weeks subsequently the emperor's feelings sustained a more poignant wound. Grief has its different gradations of pain for the human heart, as the rack has its degrees of bodily torture!

"On the 10th of May we entered Dresden, where the good, the noble-hearted King of Saxony joined the emperor on the following day. The character of that sovereign presented the very *beau ideal* of exalted virtue, and seemed to be uncorrupted by the vice of human nature. Party spirit has sought to chill the admiration naturally inspired by his noble conduct towards Napoleon, by describing the king as a person not above the level of ordinary mediocrity. But these misrepresentations will find no credence among persons of discernment. The King of Saxony was a man of talent, extensive information, and of chivalrous honour. He was not one of those who can make integrity give way to interest; or who regard a promise as a thing to be fulfilled conditionally, according to circumstances. It was the King of Saxony whom I first heard utter a phrase, which has since often been quoted, and which will portray the moral feeling of the man, *viz.*: '*Probity and truth are the best finesses in politics.*' The Emperor Napoleon, who revered the King of Saxony as a father, often repeated the above words, without perhaps placing faith in them, but as a tribute of admiration to a beautiful and noble idea.

"In our conferences with the King of Saxony, we spoke without reserve of our hopes and fears, and of the probable result of the' nego-tiations which had been opened, and which I was entrusted to con-duct with M. Budna, and with the Emperor Alexander. With respect to Austria, I cherished but faint expectations; and on the part of Rus-sia and Prussia, I saw nothing to hope for. You may easily believe that it cost me a painful effort to conceal beneath an outward show of con-fidence, my profound conviction of the inutility of Napoleon's efforts to avert the storm—I saw that it must inevitably and surely break over our heads, even at the very moment when, to the emperor's dictation, I wrote those pages which must ever remain a monument of the sin-cerity of Napoleon's desire to make peace on reasonable conditions.

"But all our sacrifices, all our efforts, were unavailing when op-posed by the machinations of England—England, our implacable and eternal enemy. Five powers were leagued against one! A contingent of two millions of men nullified at once their defeats and our victories! In vain did the sons of France perform prodigies of valour on the field of battle, which they watered with their blood. They but enfeebled the resources of their country, which sooner or later was doomed to succumb in the unequal conflict,

"When we had gained the victory of Lutzen I offered, in the em-peror's name, peace to Russia and Prussia; but the offer was refused. A few days after this we were again victorious at Bautzen, but we sealed our triumph with the bravest blood in the French army. Bruyères, Kir-gener, and Duroc, were among the lamented trophies of the enemy's defeat.

"Presentiments are a sort of instinctive communication—a reflec-tion of the future. On the evening of the 1st of May, just four days before the battle of Bautzen, the emperor had a long conference with M. Budna, who had been sent as envoy from the Emperor Francis to his son-in-law. Whilst M. Budna was closeted with the emperor, Duroc and I walked up and down, conversing together in the apart-ment leading to the Imperial cabinet, to which M. Budna had been introduced at 10 o'clock. The extraordinary length of the interview surprised us: it was quite at variance with Napoleon's custom. The great clock of Dresden struck twelve; and profound silence prevailed throughout the city, in which, during the day, the presence of the troops had kept up incessant noise and movement.

"Our candles were nearly burnt out, and a dim and unsteady light was diffused over the dark hangings of the apartment. Every object around us presented an aspect of gloom. We were discoursing on the events of the campaign, when Duroc suddenly seized my arm, and pressing it convulsively, uttered emphatically these words, which seemed like a mysterious revelation:—'My friend, this has been going on too long!—We shall all be swept off one after another—and he—he too will fall a sacrifice.—An inward voice whispers to me that I shall never again see France!'

"These were the prophetic words of a man whose death was near at hand.

"The emperor informed me that his conference with M. Budna had produced no result. 'Caulincourt,' said he, 'among these men, born kings, the ties of nature are matter of indifference. The interests of his daughter and grandson will not induce Francis to deviate one hair's breadth from the course which the Austrian cabinet may mark out. Oh! it is not blood that flows in the veins of those people, but cold policy.—The Emperor of Austria, by rallying cordially with me, might save all. United to France, Austria would be formidable—Prussia and Russia could no longer maintain the conflict. But Austria is ruled by an ambitious traitor.—I must yet humour him a little ere I can destroy him. Metternich, Caulincourt, will do a great deal of mischief!'

"I could never understand how the emperor bore up under the physical privations and bodily fatigues of that campaign. The days were occupied by battles and rapid movements from place to place. Alternately in the direction of the Elbe and Pyrna the Russians and Prussians presented themselves. Both men and horses were exhausted by marches and counter-marches. The hospitals were crowded by sick and wounded. The emperor, who during the day was incessantly on his horse, usually passed his nights in writing.

"The memorable Battle of Bautzen lasted thirty-four hours, and during the whole of that time the emperor took no rest. On the second day, overcome with lassitude and fatigue, he alighted from his horse, and lay down on the slope of a ravine, surrounded by the batteries of Marshal Marmont's corps, and amidst the roaring of a terrific cannonade. There he fell asleep. I awoke him an hour after, by announcing that the battle was won. 'Ah!' he exclaimed; 'it may truly be said that good comes to us in sleep.' He immediately mounted his horse, for, though the engagement was actually decided, the fighting was partially kept up until fire in the evening.

"That victory was marked by marvellous feats of courage. This army, formed of the wreck of the unfortunate Russian expedition, of raw recruits, and young troops unused to service—this army performed prodigies of valour. During the action, I several times heard the emperor exclaim—'Bravo! these are mere boys—soldiers of yesterday's creation. Oh, there is nothing like French courage!'

"The emperor's tent was pitched on the field of battle, near a solitary inn, which had been the headquarters of the Emperor Alexander during the two preceding days.

"I will now," pursued the Duke de Vicenza, "relate to you a circumstance which is very honourable to a man whom I know you highly respect,—I allude to our excellent Larrey. An immense *ambulance* had been established at a little distance from headquarters. In the evening the emperor visited it, with the view of stimulating, by his presence, the zeal of the surgeons, whose number was very small in proportion to the multitude of wounded. The emperor remarked that many of the young conscripts had lost two fingers of the right hand; and it struck him that they had mutilated themselves purposely, for the sake of evading military service. Larrey decidedly pronounced the suspicion to be unfounded. The emperor, nevertheless, retained his opinion, and, in a tone of great displeasure, declared that every man who might be guilty of such disgraceful cowardice should be shot.

"It was a serious affair; and there could be no doubt of the necessity of checking so dangerous an example by severe punishment Larrey, with his characteristic humanity and generous feeling, took up the defence of his patients; but, unluckily, his defence did not appear to be grounded on convincing proof. The emperor, with his accustomed pertinacity, determined to inquire into the matter, and the result was the confirmation of his belief that the wounds, which were all uniform, were not the result of accident. Larrey suffered the word *injustice* to escape him. The emperor turned pale with anger; but he suppressed all expression of his displeasure. Larrey, as if inspired by a sudden thought, cast his eyes towards some poor creatures who were creeping about the *ambulance*. 'Come hither, conscripts!' said he, in his gruffest tone of voice.

"Even now I can scarcely refrain from laughing, when I think of Larrey turning up his sleeves to his elbows, and armed with his bistoury, running eagerly towards the soldiers, who shrunk back in alarm, exclaiming—'We are not wounded, doctor!' Larrey pursued them, and seizing one of them by the arm, dragged him forward, saying: 'Come this way, blockheads. Now load your muskets and range yourselves in three ranks, the foremost kneeling, and fire. Obey me without delay, or I will cut off your ears. Now, Sire, observe, if you please.' The soldiers fired, and the man who was in the foremost rank cried out he had received a wound in the right hand. 'Well done!' exclaimed Larrey, triumphantly, and then, hurrying to the assistance of the wounded man, he said—Never mind, my lad, never mind. Come with me, I'll dress your wound; it will be healed in a few days. It is nothing at all!'

"The proof was convincing. The uniform wounds observable in the right hands of the soldiers, had all been caused by the hurry and unskilfulness with which the young conscripts discharged their muskets. They held them in too inclined a position, and consequently the balls, frequently struck the hands of the soldiers who were kneeling in the foremost rank,

"'Larrey,' said the emperor, 'you are a clever and an excellent fellow! I am very glad that you have proved me to be in the wrong; but at the same time—'

"'At the same time, Sire,' interrupted Larrey, without ceremony, 'let every man mind his own business.'

"The emperor could not refrain from laughing.

"On the day following that on which the above curious scene took place, the emperor was cut to the heart by the irreparable loss of his dear friend, Duroc. Marshal Duroc was one of those men who seem to be too pure and perfect for this world, and whose excellence helps, to reconcile us to human nature. In the high station to which the emperor had wisely raised him, the grand marshal retained all the qualities of the private citizen. The splendour of his position had not power to dazzle or corrupt him. Duroc remained simple, natural, and independent; a warm and generous friend; a just and honourable man. I pronounce on him this eulogy without fear of contradiction. His death spread grief and consternation through the army and in Paris. The emperor was perfectly overpowered by his affliction. Poor Duroc! my last conversation with him is still vividly fresh in my memory.

"Only those who took part in the disastrous campaign of 1813 can form an accurate idea of our inextricable position. Every day brought a fresh battle, and every battle a fresh victory, but unattended by any advantage. The emperor closely pursued the Russian rearguard, which unceasingly evaded him. Then the Prussians would show themselves—we would drive them back; and the same thing was repeated over and over again. Dresden was our headquarters, our magazine-general, our hospital-general, and we sojourned night and day in the highways.

"On the day on which the grand marshal was killed, he had scarcely left the emperor for a single moment. For the tenth time, perhaps, since the morning, the Russians had eluded our pursuit after we had killed a considerable number of them. This engagement, though it did not deserve the name of a battle, caused great havoc on both sides. Several balls had struck the ground at the emperor's feet He turned sharply to Duroc and me, who were standing beside him. 'How,' said he, 'after all this carnage is there no advantage gained? Surely these Russians rise up and come to life again. Will there never be an end of this?' At that moment a bomb-shell, which burst near the spot where we were standing, overthrew three horsemen, struck an officer of the escort, and threw him under the legs of the emperor's horse. The animal started, and the emperor angrily pulled the bridle.

"'Sire,' said an *aide-de-camp*, who at that moment galloped up to us, 'General Bruyère is killed.'

"'Ah!' exclaimed the emperor, and then he added, in a suppressed tone, 'this day will be fatal to us.' He immediately spurred his horse, and set off at a rapid gallop to a height which commanded Makersdorf, where the fighting was still going on. Marshal Mortier, Duroc, Kirgener, and I, followed him closely, but the wind blew the dust and smoke in our faces with such violence that we could not see each other. A tree near which the emperor passed was struck and knocked down by a ball. I arrived on the plateau at the same moment with the emperor. 'My lunette I bring me my lunette!' he called. I turned round, and found to my surprise that we were alone. Charles de Plaisance was galloping towards us. He looked pale and bewildered, and approaching me, he said, 'General Kirgener is killed; the Duke Frioul is——'

"'What!' exclaimed the emperor; 'what has happened, sir?'

"'Sire, General Kirgener and—the grand marshal are killed.'

"'Duroc killed! Go—go—it is a mistake—it is impossible—quite impossible. Caulincourt, you know he was this moment at my side.'

"Several *aides-de-camp* now joined us, and confirmed the fatal intelligence. Duroc was mortally wounded. The ball which had broken down the tree had in its rebound struck General Kirgener, and then the Duke de Frioul, whose bowels were literally ripped open. The emperor listened to these details with an air of torpid sorrow; and then in faltering accents he exclaimed, 'Duroc! Duroc!—Gracious Heaven!—My presentiments never deceive me. This is indeed a sad day—a fatal day!' He slowly paced from the plateau, and returned to the camp. On entering his tent, he walked about for some time in silent thoughtfulness. At intervals he stopped short, and addressed to me these broken sentences: 'Alas! when will fate relent?—When will there be an end of this?—Caulincourt, my eagles will yet triumph, but the happiness which accompanied them has fled.'

"I was myself too deeply oppressed by grief to attempt to offer him consolation. I loved Duroc as though be had been my brother. His unexpected death brought back with renewed force all the pangs I had suffered at the Battle of the Moskowa, where Duroc feelingly deplored with me the loss of my unfortunate brother Auguste.

"The Prince de Neufchatel entered, and announced that the Russians were once more repulsed.

"'It is high time,' said the emperor, bitterly. 'Two brave generals and Duroc lost in a miserable skirmish.'

"'Sire,' inquired Berthier, 'what orders has your Majesty to give?'

"'Wait till tomorrow.—Whither has he been conveyed?—How is he, Berthier?'

"'Sire, he is in a house at Makersdorf. Ivan and Larrey are in attendance on him. There is no hope.'

"'I must see him,' said Napoleon. 'Poor, poor Duroc!'

"In the evening Berthier and I accompanied the emperor on this sad visit Duroc, who was stretched on a camp-bed, was suffering the most excruciating agony. His features were so frightfully distorted, that he was scarcely recognisable. When we entered, he turned towards us, and fixed his eyes steadfastly on the emperor. It was the horrible, fixed gaze of death. There was in it an indefinable expression of reproach and affection. The emperor was overcome, and withdrew from the bedside. I took Duroc's hand in mine, but I was unable to speak; emotion choked my utterance. He articulated with difficulty; but he faintly said, 'I foresaw this at Dresden. The inward voice did not deceive me. Alas! the worst is not yet over!' His strength failed him, and he seemed to faint. The emperor again advanced to the bed, and embraced him several times. The doctors entered. 'Is there then no hope? inquired the emperor.—'None whatever,' was the answer. Poor Duroc for a moment recovered his consciousness, and turning his eyes towards the emperor, he said, 'For pity's sake, give me opium.' The emperor took his hand, pressed it to his bosom, embraced him once more, and then seizing my arm, hurried out of the room.

"'This is horrible,' he exclaimed. 'My excellent, my dear Duroc!—Oh, what a loss is this!'—I observed the tears dropping from his eyes as we returned in mournful silence to the camp.

"At five o'clock in the morning Ivan presented himself to the emperor, who immediately understood the purport of his visit. 'Ah, Ivan!' he exclaimed; 'all is over. He is released from misery. Well, he is happier than I.'

"The emperor gave directions for the purchase of a piece of ground at Makersdorf, for the erection of a monument over the grave of Duroc. Napoleon wrote with his own hand the following inscription:—

"'To the memory of General Duroc, Duke de Frioul, Grand Marechal du Palais to the Emperor Napoleon. He fell gloriously on the field of battle, being mortally wounded by a cannonball, and he expired in the arms of his friend, the emperor.'

"Napoleon placed the slip of paper in the hands of Berthier, without uttering a word.

"I have now," added the Duke de Vicenza, "told you all that passed in the last touching interview between Napoleon and Duroc' All the stories that have been propagated respecting the reproaches addressed by Duroc to the emperor are mere fabrications. Neither Duroc nor any one of us in his sad situation would have addressed reproaches to the emperor, weeping over the death-bed of a friend. If feelings of despair and regret really arose in the noble heart of Duroc, his tongue never gave utterance to them. They were buried with him in the grave.

"But wherefore," said the Duke de Vicenza, "should I conduct you through the sanguinary phases of the campaign of 1813? The gigantic efforts and the marvellous victories of the armies of Napoleon during that unequal conflict are not subjects adapted to fugitive conversation. To describe that period of heroism and treason, of glory and disgrace, is the task of the historian. For my part," added he, in a melancholy tone, and laying his hand on his heart, "I feel that my yet remaining span of life must be too brief to enable me to relate all I know of the base intrigue and treachery which hurled France from the pinnacle of glory to the lowest point of humiliation. Yet what I could disclose would present a useful lesson to the future! Illness and deeply-seated grief had paralysed the energies of the man who of all others was best qualified to write the history of the empire."

"Oh, Duke!" I exclaimed, "let me entreat you to continue your interesting narrations. Leave battles and victories if you will, but pray give us details of Napoleon. No one knows so much of him as you."

"That is true," replied the duke, smiling. "During the campaign of 1813, I conducted all the negotiations which were maintained with the view of bringing about peace. All who may write on this subject, even with the best intentions, must inevitably fall into error. Historical documents will, it is true, supply them with official facts; but the secret springs, the base intrigues, which rendered the conclusion of peace impossible, will baffle the investigation of the shrewdest observer.

"For example, it would be a serious mistake to imagine that the Emperor Napoleon was not fully aware of the position in which he stood. I, who have suffered so much from his irresolution, do not believe that he was under the influence of any illusion at the Congress of Châtillon. His resistance was the last effort of a powerfully organized mind—the last convulsion of mighty despair. Though I myself conjured him to come to an understanding with the allied powers at any price, yet I am not convinced that our concessions would have produced the wished for object. Nevertheless, it would have been politic to make the concessions, and thereby to have warranted a new appeal to the patriotism of the nation. The *levée en masse* might have been carried into effect, and France might have been saved a second time. Such was my opinion; but I could not bring the emperor to take the same view of things.

"I will relate a few facts, which will afford you an idea of the real position of the emperor in 1813.

"I had negotiated and concluded the armistice of Pleswitz with Prussia and Russia. Austria still affected to play the part of conciliatress; but her compact with France was broken, and we knew it. The armistice of Pleswitz was a misfortune, for the time had arrived when even the most rational measures proved disastrous to us. A suspension of arms was necessary to afford time for re-organising and newly equipping the army, and also to give the emperor a little respite, during which he could consider in the retirement of his closet the important questions involved in our political position. One evening, or rather one night, the emperor and I were discussing together some of the points then in dispute.

"We had been writing at a table, on which an immense number of papers and documents were lying; suddenly the emperor thrust the papers on one side, and rising from his chair, said—'We are a set of fools, Caulincourt. We are like children at play. These people will never come to any understanding—we have all changed ground. They have forgotten my conduct to them at Tilsit—I might then have crushed them, but I was magnanimous. Posterity will avenge me. These kings, by the grace of God and Napoleon, will appear petty indeed compared with me, who reign by the grace of my sword. But after all, my clemency was weakness—a school-boy would have acted more wisely than I did. He would have profited by the lessons of history, and would have known that these degenerate kings respect neither faith nor law.'

"The hurried and agitated manner in which the emperor uttered these broken sentences—the base deceptions which had provoked his recriminations—all imparted a terrific character to this burst of indignation. After a pause of some minutes, he thus resumed, in a more calm tone:—'How maladroitly these people conduct their own affairs. The pertinacity of their endeavours to force me to abandon the continental system sufficiently reveals their ulterior projects. I am of your opinion, Caulincourt England is the soul of this deadly war against France. England gorges them with gold to sustain the conflict. She will soon convince them that even the treaty of Luneville is too favourable to France. The Machiavelism of the British cabinet will overreach the short-sighted politicians of the alliance. They do not perceive that I am the only barrier that can check the interminable encroachments of English domination.

"Their greatest enemy is, not Napoleon, but England. Even were I to consent to the restitution of the Illyrian provinces, I should make a fruitless sacrifice. It would only be an acknowledgment of our weakness, and the signal for further exactions on the part of our enemies. Their hypocritical moderation covers a despicable afterthought. They now demand the abolition of the continental system, and the surrender of the Illyrian provinces. Tomorrow they will demand the division of Saxony, assigning the Elbe as my limit. Thus they will at the same time punish the King of Saxony for his fidelity to me. I will never consent to this indignity, and still less will I consent to parcelling out the dominions of the King of Saxony, my most devoted and faithful ally.'

"'Your Majesty,' observed I, 'regards the question in its worst point of view; this is pushing matters to the extremity. But admitting that your anticipations should be justified by the extravagant ultimatum of the Allied Powers, might it not be consistent with a bold line of policy to provoke the development. We are placed in critical circumstances; and candour is a duty which I owe to your Majesty. You are accused, Sire, of not wishing for peace, of wantonly sacrificing the blood of your subjects to your unbridled ambition. (Here he made a gesture of impatience.) Sire.' continued I, 'these perfidious insinuations have a most mischievous tendency. They mislead the public mind, and excite disaffection. in the army. There is but a step between discontent and that inertness which paralyzes the wisest operations. Grant what may be reasonably granted, and should new exactions force you to prolong the war, your position will be better, inasmuch as public opinion will be enabled to judge of the bad faith of the Allied Powers and the necessity of our resistance.'

"'Public opinion,' exclaimed the emperor, 'is ever ready to prostitute itself to its own interest. Do you not perceive, Caulincourt, what is passing around us. The men whom I have raised to eminence are now bent solely on enjoying the benefits I have heaped upon them. They do not see that they must still fight to win the repose they are thirsting for. And I!—do they imagine that I rest on a bed of roses? Do not I take my share of the fatigues and perils of war? Do I not every day offer my life as a sacrifice to my country? How base is their ingratitude!'

"I entirely concurred in his opinion respecting the demoralization of many of the commanders of the army," pursued the duke. "After their many exertions and perils, they naturally desired repose. But was that the time to seek it? Did not the safety of France, and the well-understood interest of all, command them, on the contrary, to rally round their able and still formidable chief? Complaints and murmurs could only tend to aggravate the difficulties of our position. You cannot conceive how greatly this selfish feeling annoyed and distressed the emperor, who was ever ready to sacrifice himself for the general welfare. I endeavoured by every means in my power to divert him from this train of painful reflection, but all in vain; he incessantly recurred to the subject.

"'The fact is, Caulincourt,' said he, 'that because you are not ungrateful yourself, you cannot comprehend ingratitude. But open your eyes, and look around. You will see that none but my poor soldiers and officers, who have not yet obtained the rank of princes, dukes, and counts, are worth anything. It is melancholy to say this; but it is the truth. I will tell you,' continued he, with increased warmth of manner, 'I will tell you what I ought to do. I ought to send all these newly-created nobles to repose on their down beds, or to strut about in their *chateaux*. I ought to rid myself of these growlers, and recommence the war with an army formed of the young and uncorrupted; of men who would look neither before nor behind them, but who would inscribe on their banners, as in 1793, the words—*Conquer or Die!* With that device in my heart I overran Egypt, subjugated Italy, and raised the

French eagles to a height to which none will raise them after me.'

"Here he threw himself on his chair. Large drops of perspiration stood on his forehead, and he was in a state of highly excited feeling. I gazed on him with admiration mingled with melancholy. I thought he never before appeared so great. Alas! it was fortune and not his genius that had forsaken him. What profound intuition that man possessed! What a ready power of judging men and things! He scanned at a glance the abyss which lay between his omnipotence and the first step of his adverse fortune. The men who once bowed so humbly to hint, now no longer trembled beneath his angry glance. Napoleon felt that he had outlived himself; that his will, to which all had crouched in ready obedience, was now evaded or questioned. Opposition was feebly and meanly attempted; there was now no longer peril in the attempt!

"The emperor informed me," pursued the duke, "that Louis de Narbonne, our ambassador at Vienna, had written from Prague, stating that the declaration of war by Austria against France would be immediately published. Thus our feeble hopes in that quarter were annihilated. Napoleon, who could not persuade himself that the case was without appeal, sent me on a private family mission to the Emperor Francis. 'Go, Caulincourt,' said he, 'you are a new man to the Austrian Cabinet; go and try what you can do with Metternich. If anything can be done, you will have some advantage, through your former friendly relations with the Emperor of Russia. My dear Caulincourt,' added he, cordially pressing my hand, 'you, I know, will not forsake me. At least, I am assured of that. See the Emperor of Austria as often as possible; tell him that I still cannot believe he means to injure his daughter and grandson, setting aside every other consideration which the Emperor Napoleon might urge.' He uttered these words with the air of pride naturally inspired by past recollections. He might, indeed, justly have appealed to the magnanimity of his conduct towards Austria. 'Tell the Emperor Francis,' said Napoleon at my farewell interview, 'that I do not send an ambassador to the Austrian Cabinet, but that I send to my father-in-law a friend who knows my heart, who is acquainted with my inmost thoughts.'

"I set out on my expedition in very depressed spirits. I plainly foresaw the utter uselessness of any efforts I could make. How different were my feelings when I departed on my brilliant mission to the court of Russia, whither a few years previously I had conveyed the commands of the most powerful monarch in the world.

"Whilst I was at Prague, I had the honour of seeing the Emperor Francis almost every day, He treated me with the utmost amiability. He was not so unintellectual a man as he had been represented. In ordinary times the Emperor Francis would have been one of those sovereigns whose subjects would have invoked blessings on their memory. In the critical circumstances in which he was placed, surrounded as it were by a general conflagration, he had not sufficient courage to make himself responsible for the consequences which might result to his country by the maintenance of his family compact with Napoleon. Francis was amiable, kind-hearted and benevolent; but there was not in his nature one spark of courage, energy, or heroism. The great Maria Theresa is to the House of Austria what Henry IV. is to the House of France, a splendid tradition. The blood of these great monarchs does not flow in the veins of their descendants. There is a remarkable degeneration in royal families. I am aware that this opinion will be pronounced by certain persons to be a democratic *bontade*; but that will not disprove the fact.

"The Emperor of Austria clearly saw the embarrassments of his peculiar position; but he had not strength to rise above them. On the one hand there was evident danger in remaining faithful to France; and on the other there was disgrace and even crime in forsaking her. Francis vacillated between his sovereign duties and his paternal affections; and the result was that he did violence to his heart and his conscience. He relieved himself from the responsibility, and threw the burthen on the shoulders of Metternich. It was not, therefore, the emperor whom I had to reason with and persuade. 'See Metternich explain this to Metternich,' were the only answers I could obtain to my indefatigable solicitations.

"In my conferences with the Austrian Prime Minister I had to dispute inch by inch the most absurd pretensions—to refute the most ridiculous prejudices—to reply with politeness to a man who, under an outward guise of cold civility, but ill concealed his firm determination to degrade and annihilate France. How often did that excellent man Louis de Narbonne calm my resentment and check my indignation. What parts are we playing here? said I—'Alas!' replied he, 'we are playing the part of the conquered, and we must pay the penalty!'

"Louis de Narbonne was a singular combination of talent and levity. The emperor used to say—'Narbonne is the type of the brilliant butterflies of the reign of Louis XV.' This was perfectly true. His *recherché* style of dress, his highly-polished manners, his gracefully ironical language, and above all, his incomparable levity, rendered him a living tradition of the old French court. He was a perfect model of the *grand seigneur* of past times. The indignation I expressed at the conduct of Metternich used to amuse him exceedingly:—'My dear duke,' he would say, 'you take these things too seriously. Metternich's conduct is base in the extreme;—but what then! Would you act the part of Don Quixote, and wage war against all the windmills you meet? The glorious days are past when we could dictate our own terms. We must now in our turn submit to be dictated to. What else can we do?' Poor Narbonne! He did not live to witness our disasters. Not even his gay spirit would have borne him up amidst the misfortunes of his country. He died in good time!

"With the exception of a few pleasant intervals, I was very miserable during my mission to Prague. The personal assurances of esteem and consideration which were lavished upon me, did not atone for the many annoyances incidental to my false position. Every link was not yet broken, and I was obliged sometimes to extend my hand to an irreconcilable enemy. This, I do assure you, is one of the greatest miseries attached to the hard lot of a statesman. Often, after taking my leave of the Austrian minister, I used to debate within myself, in the silence of night, whether the following day should not close the mortal career of one or the other of us. Why, thought I, do I refrain from sending an honourable challenge to the man who could coolly indite the terms of the message he intends sending to France?

"Oh! what torture of mind I then suffered! 'My dear friend,' said the incorrigible Narbonne, 'my grey hairs cover a head more cool than yours. Rely on my old experience. I am convinced that diplomacy and negotiation are now out of the question. The Allied Powers have formed their determination on the subject of France. They place no faith in our professions of moderation. They have traced out a line of policy for themselves, and they will pursue it. Your death, or that of Metternich, could work no change in the state of affairs. We are lost.' It was impossible to be angry with Narbonne, though our views were utterly at variance. I deeply felt the loss of his society when he left Prague to proceed to the emperor's headquarters at Dresden, where he arrived a few days before me.

CHAPTER 8

A Romantic Adventure

"During my sojourn at Prague," said the Duke de Vicenza, "there occurred to me a very strange adventure, which afforded a little diversion from my graver occupations. I will relate it to you," added he, with a smile, "but I forewarn you that I must make some reservations—I cannot tell all. Will you hear my story on this condition?"

"On any condition you choose to make, duke," replied I, eagerly. "Pray begin, I am all attention."

"One evening," said the duke, "in strict *incognito*, and attired in a brown *surtout*, with a pistol concealed in my bosom, I rode, followed by my groom, through one of the suburbs of Prague. I directed my course towards a house situated about half a league from the city. On arriving within sight of the walls of a park which surrounded a very pretty habitation, I alighted from my horse. Wait for me, Frank, said I to my groom; but if I am not here by midnight, you may take the horses back to the stable. I walked on at a rapid pace (directing my steps according to certain instructions I had received) until I reached a door, which, on my knocking, was immediately opened.

"A little female hand, was stretched out to me, and a soft voice murmured in my ear: 'Say not a word; but let me conduct you.' I am a fool, thought I; but no matter, I must go on. After several turnings and windings we reached a *kiosque*, the door of which was closed. My conductress stopped, listened, looked cautiously round her, and then opened the door. We entered, she again closed the door, and then, trembling with alarm, she threw herself on a sofa. In a few moments, having somewhat recovered herself, she gracefully motioned me to sit down, and resting her elbow on the cushions of the sofa, she languishingly leaned her head on her hand, and remained silent.

"This is a tolerably romantic commencement, is it not? But indeed the whole affair was nothing short of a romance, as you shall hear.

"After my first feeling of astonishment was somewhat dispelled, I began to survey the objects around me. A single light, burning in a globe of alabaster, illumined an apartment tastefully fitted up in the form of a tent, and decorated with various elegant and costly trifles, indicative of taste and wealth. On the table were an album, a box of colours, and several sketches. One of these designs was a view of the Palace of St. Petersburg, on the side occupied by the empress' apartments; the empress herself was represented standing in the balcony, and the likeness was striking. Here and there, in various parts of the room, were scattered books, journals, and music. I gazed on the lady, who now seemed to be quite overwhelmed by the consciousness of the strange step she had taken.

"She was young, and *coquettishly* dressed in a robe of clear white muslin, whose vapoury folds displayed to advantage her slender and graceful form. Her hair, which was of a bright chestnut brown, was negligently gathered up behind, and confined by a gold comb, whilst a profusion of long ringlets encircled, and indeed almost entirely shaded, her countenance. She raised towards me her large dark eyes, in whose expression pride and resolution were forcibly depicted; and rearing her head with an air of dignity, which I thought rather amusing, considering the position in which she had imprudently placed herself, she darted at me an interrogating glance, which informed me that I was expected to speak first. I said—'Madame, I have obeyed your summons.'

"'And you have taken your time to reflect on it, duke.'

"'Your "first message, *madame*—'

"'Did not presage a *bonne fortune*. You Frenchmen are so vain!'

"'Oh, *madame*,' I exclaimed, laughing, 'the mystification is perfect. It would indeed be unpardonable vanity to aspire to the honour of being distinguished by you. I would not for the world incur a second reproach, that of indiscreetly prolonging this agreeable visit. I am here, *madame*, in obedience to your commands, pray vouchsafe to inform me why I am summoned hither?'

"She turned upon me a look in which I could plainly read a mingled expression of hatred and curiosity.

"'I am a poor diplomatist, duke,' said she, 'I have not learned the art of dissembling and deceiving—of setting at nought solemn oaths and pledges of good faith. I am a true Muscovite, and I hate the French.' She uttered these latter words in a most emphatic tone, and evidently under the influence of uncontrollable excitement. 'Poor Elise!' she resumed, 'thou shouldst not have charged me with this commission. If thou hadst possessed a true Russian heart, no Frenchman could ever have wrung tears from thy eyes.'

"Elise!—on hearing that name a sudden thrill pervaded my whole frame. Surely, thought I, some demon is at the ground of all this; some treacherous snare is laid to entrap me! As these reflections crossed my mind, I involuntarily placed my hand on my pistol.

"'Duke,' exclaimed the lady, energetically, 'I know not what idea you have formed of me; but of all the conjectures which the seeming levity of my conduct may warrant, there probably is none which is not an insult' I made a sign of negation.

"'Do not interrupt, but hear me,' she continued. 'I am a native of Moscow—of Moscow, which is now devastated, and profaned by the French! I was twelve years of age when I lost my mother. My father, who occupied a distinguished rank at the court of Russia, placed me under the guardianship of—of—(Here the Duke de Vicenza paused, and begged I would excuse him mentioning the name of the person alluded to.) I was entered at the establishment for the education of noble young ladies at St. Petersburg. There I learned to love and revere my amiable protectress; and, indeed, I soon became as much attached to her as though she had been my mother. My affection for her was filial, enthusiastic, devoted, and submissive, and her name was daily mingled with my prayers.

"'This, duke, will suffice to explain to you why you are here— why I have consented to see and to converse with an enemy of my country!

"'On the day on which I completed my fifteenth year, my father came to visit me: "Feodora," said he, "this evening you are to sign in the emperor's cabinet your contract of marriage with Count ——, and in a week hence he will become your husband. Go and pay your respects to your mistress, and take leave of your companions; you must leave this establishment immediately." I was overjoyed; for I was now to be freed from school restraint, whilst at the same time I could see my beloved protectress as often as I wished. Eight days after this I was married. I was now no longer a child, no longer even a young girl, though only fifteen years of age. I became the friend and confidant of my adopted mother, my dear Elise. I was speedily introduced into the brilliant sphere of fashionable life, composed as it is of pleasure and grief, honours and humiliations, burning recollections and bitter regrets.

"Elise, the noble-minded Elise, had been the victim of love. The man on whom she conferred her whole heart and affection forsook her sacrificed her to some necessity. You are moved, duke. You are possibly at a loss to comprehend how a man can break a heart that has been surrendered to him—a heart that has been faithful to its vows and to the religion of love! Poor, confiding Elise! The man she adored once said to her,—"Ask for my life, my blood, but do not ask me for what I cannot give you; for I would rather die than refuse you anything." Yet scarcely had two years elapsed, when Elise, kneeling at the feet of this man, said to him—"Do not depart, Armand. Behold me at your feet! You know I cannot live without you. I cannot exist where you are not. Grant me this sacrifice, the only one I will ever seek in return for the many I have made to you. Your country, then, is dearer to you than I—than my love! Rank, wealth, honours, are offered to you here.

"Accept them, Armand, accept them, I conjure you! We count many illustrious French names among the inhabitants of Russia. Remain with us, then, dear Armand. Your duty, you say, calls you 800 leagues from me. Alas! I fear you never truly loved me. When you offered me your life you were insincere; for in this fatal hour there is something which you prefer to me. You tell me now that honour is more powerful than love, that you can die for me, but not live dishonoured with me. Alas! why did you not tell me when I first, laid my head on your bosom, that the love you vowed to me was merely conditional. Had you told me so I would have plunged into the Neva." She said all this, duke, and many more touching things. Yet this man forsook her!'

"I was almost petrified," said the Duke de Vicenza. "The scene which this mysterious female had described was still fresh in my recollection, it carried me back to a happy period of my life. I cannot tell how I armed myself with courage to resist the seductions of the passion which then possessed me, for I adored Elise. My love for her was of that ardent and engrossing kind which will not permit us either to calculate or to measure danger; and this *liaison* was attended with great peril both to her and to me. Circumstances must have been very imperious—honour must have appealed with a very loud voice, before I could have resolved to break those sweet bands—to renounce that happiness for which I daily placed my life in jeopardy. But a woman of ardent feeling, who gives more than her life in exchange for love, cannot comprehend that there must arrive a fatal hour when she must be sacrificed to inexorable destiny! I was lost in my reveries, when the voice of Feodora roused me.

"'Well, duke,' said she, 'have you nothing to communicate to me?'

"'*Madame*,' replied I, 'you have pronounced a name with which is connected a secret that must for ever remain buried in my heart. That name which I used fondly to repeat in the days of my happiness shall never again be uttered by my lips. Have you been entrusted with any message for me? The sacrifice of my honour excepted, she knows well that I am devoted to her in life and death.'

"'Ah!' said my interlocutor, contemptuously, 'again there is a restriction to your devotedness!' She approached the table, and touching a spring, opened a drawer, which was ingeniously concealed by the markings of the wood. From the drawer she took a richly-embossed portfolio, and presenting it to me, she said,—'This contains a letter. I will take charge of your answer, Duke.'

"I eagerly seized the portfolio, and took leave of the countess. She conducted me from the *kiosque* with the same precautions as those observed on my entrance. This is not precisely a *bonne fortune*, thought I, as I mounted my horse, which speedily carried me back to my hotel. During the whole night my imagination was busily employed in retracing the circumstances of this strange interview. This mysterious woman had evidently been made the depositary of an important secret. The letter presented to me left no doubt of the unbounded confidence reposed in Feodora. And what a strange being was she! So frank and bold in expressing her hatred of the French, and yet so beautiful and captivating in spite of her rebellious spirit.

"I carried to Feodora my answer to the letter she had given me in the portfolio. I don't know how it happened, but I took pleasure in trying to tame this fierce little Muscovite, and the consequence was that my visits to her became more and more frequent, and at length daily. In truth, Feodora was a very charming woman.

"One morning, a few days previously to my departure from Prague, my valet delivered to me a packet which a courier had left late on the preceding night. On tearing off the envelop I found three letters; two of them, which were in the same handwriting as that I had first received, showed by their date that they had not been punctually forwarded. Poor Feodora had not been over anxious to remind me of the love I owed to another. She was well aware that the transient impression she herself had produced could not efface the profound sentiment which was concealed in the inmost recesses of my heart.

But even as it was, this little infidelity oppressed me with the weight of remorse, and for the thousandth time in my life I felt how much women are superior to men.

"I mechanically opened Feodora's letter. It ran as follows:—

When you peruse these lines, Armand, there will be between you and Feodora the abyss which separates repentance and guilt. Yes, Armand, I say guilt, for can there be a greater crime than to betray a benefactress in her confidence and in her love? It is base to forget the duties of daughter and wife for the enemy of one's country—for a Frenchman! But I need not vent on you reproaches which you cannot comprehend.

The period of expiation commenced yesterday. You were to have come, and you failed to do so. Throughout the long night, during which I looked for you in vain, I uttered imprecations on you. On my knees I confessed the fault of which I have been guilty, and I felt all the horror of remorse. I now look upon you as a demon in the form of an angel, and the remembrance of you will henceforth haunt me like a frightful phantom. Noble Elise, you are avenged.'

"When I perused this extraordinary note I could with difficulty persuade myself that I was not dreaming; Indeed, the singular circumstances attending my introduction to this woman are enveloped in a veil of mystery, which time has not yet raised. Feodora's letter was accompanied by a little *billet*, containing the following lines:—

The cause of the Emperor Napoleon is lost—nothing can save France from ruin. Your efforts are vain. Abandon the Corsican tyrant. The magnanimous Alexander will receive you, and ,in serving him you may usefully serve your country. The illustrious General Moreau felt that he had a divine mission to fulfil. He has crossed the seas to overthrow the oppressor of his country. Moreau is now in the camp of the Allied Powers.'

"I was lost in a maze of conjectures. Who was this Feodora. I made inquiries respecting her. 'The Russian lady set off twenty-four hours ago,' replied the porter of the house in which she resided. I questioned some Russians of my acquaintance; but in the first place I did not know her family name, and next, I had strong reasons for being guarded in my investigations. In fine, the beautiful and haughty Muscovite is to this day known to me only as the mysterious Feodora."

Chapter 9

Austria Declares War against France

"I will now," said the Duke de Vicenza, "relate to you what occurred after I joined the Emperor at Gorlitz, together with some curious details of the terrific catastrophe of Leipsic. On hearing them you will probably concur with me in thinking that if contemporaries have the right to impute faults to Napoleon, those faults have been far exceeded by the magnitude of the expiation.

"On the 18th of August I reached the headquarters at Gorlitz, and if I did not bring from Bohemia the official declaration of war on the part of Austria, the information I had acquired left me no doubt on the subject When I entered the emperor's apartments at Gorlitz, the Prince de Neufchatel was in the act of dispatching orders to the different corps. 'Berthier,' said the emperor, 'send off orderlies this instant. Detain Gourgand; tell him to await my orders.' Then advancing to me, he added—'Well, Caulincourt, what news have you?'

"At that moment a cabinet usher announced the Duke of Otranto. My looks must have reflected the feelings that were passing in my mind, for the emperor said to me, 'Ah! you will see some others whom you little expect.' The sight of Fouché certainly surprised as well as annoyed me; I could not conceive why his presence was required at the headquarters of the army. I felt towards Fouché one of those instinctive aversions which almost always find their justification in after circumstances. Intercourse with the world never taught me to disguise my antipathies with any degree of success. Fouché, therefore, was well aware that I did not like him, and he on his part cordially returned my aversion.

"'Duke of Otranto,' said the emperor, addressing Fouché, 'in appointing you Governor of my Illyrian Provinces I give a signal proof of my confidence in your capacity. You must oppose the machinations of

Baron Stein with your utmost ability. Keep your eye upon intriguers. Banish all plotters without mercy. Send them to any town in France, with notes to the prefect and commissary-general of the department, and at the same time direct to them the attention of the general police of Paris. I have fire-brands enough in my capital without getting more from Germany. Your powers give you great latitude; and, except in cases of very grave importance, you may decide without referring to me. There must be firmness, and, above all, promptitude, in the operations of the police. No concessions—no compromise with agitators. Half measures are always injurious, and they never gain over an enemy. Politics and sentiment do not accord; you know that well. Go, then, Duke of Otranto; I count on your zeal and ability.'

"'Your Majesty knows that I am devoted to you in life and death; and the post to which you have appointed me will afford opportunities of giving renewed proofs of my devotedness.'

"'I know it—I know it; you will send me every day an accurate report of the feeling of the inhabitants for and against my government. The well-disposed you may stroke with a cat's-paw; but show claws to the disaffected. Imbue your mind thoroughly with the truth that public feeling is at the disposal of him who knows how to dispose of it Proclaim on the housetops my resolution never to abandon the Illyrian Provinces. You understand! This is the only means of checking defections and defeating guilty schemes and hopes. See that the supplies of the garrisons are properly kept up. Neglect nothing that is useful; and report to me every fact with which you think I ought to be made acquainted. In present circumstances, a governor-general of conquered provinces must be like a vigilant *vidette* at an advanced post.'

"The governor-general of the Illyrian Provinces took his leave, placing his hand on his heart, and bowing to the very ground; but in the sinister expression of Fouché's eyes hideous things could be read. Two years afterwards, this man insulted and persecuted his unfortunate sovereign and master.

"When Fouché had withdrawn, the emperor took up some papers, which he glanced over without saying a word. This was quite characteristic of Napoleon. The fact is, he had fully seized the ideas which were passing in my mind, and though we had never entered into any explanation of our mutual opinions of Fouché, yet I feel assured that on this occasion Napoleon shared all my apprehensions. But his self-love (and Napoleon had a large share of that quality) would not permit him to condescend to a sort of defence of the Duke of Otranto, who had been justly disgraced; nevertheless, my silent disapprobation annoyed him. He wished that I should provoke an explanation, and I was determined not to do so. This was not often the sort of footing on which we stood, in reference to one another, and he frequently called me *barre de fer*.

"According to his custom, he explained to roe a few days afterwards the motives which had determined him to give the government of the Illyrian Provinces to the Duke of Otranto. This appointment was in reality an act of policy. Mallet's affair was present in the emperor's mind. This bold enterprise showed what a man of daring spirit might attempt with success, and the emperor deemed it unsafe to have behind him in Paris a man so dissatisfied and dangerous as Fouché. He adroitly concealed his distrust under the plausible reason of opposing the artful police of Fouché to the occult but all-powerful police of Baron Stein, the leader of the sects of *illuminati* which were then rising up on all sides. Stein constituted himself a director of public opinion, and by the aid of quasi democratic professions he had stirred up an insurrectionary spirit in numerous public schools and universities. There was at that time a rage for secret associations in Germany, and the indefatigable Stein was found at the head of them all.

"The emperor, whose eagle eye could penetrate revolutions, said to me—'It answers my policy to have it understood that I am opposing Fouché to Baron Stein; but, after all, what can be done by Fouché and all our French police in Illyria against the formidable influence of the secret societies which infest Germany? At the present moment these associations are wonderfully serviceable to the Allied Powers, who employ them as active and devoted auxiliaries in opposing me. They will use them as machines for working their own ends, until the time arrive when they will find it convenient to consign all these young fanatical heads to the axe of the executioner.'

"As to Fouché, he was perfectly aware of the real motives which influenced his appointment to the government of Illyria. He therefore left Paris with anything but satisfied feelings, though he affected gratification. He bowed beneath the rod which had hitherto spared him, and which now indicted so paternal a chastisement. The time had not yet arrived when he could with impunity defy and insult his benefactor. On this subject I can relate to you many horrible traits to which I was witness at Fontainbleau and Paris, after Waterloo.

"Having received the emperor's instruction respecting the duties, of his new appointment, Fouché took his leave. After he had withdrawn, I was left alone with the emperor; I remained silent, expecting he would address me. After a short pause, he said, with an air of impatience—'Well, duke, I presume you bring bad news from Prague, since you seem so unwilling to tell it.'

"I was waiting till your Majesty should question me.

"'Speak out, speak out. Has Austria officially declared herself against me?'

"I believe, Sire, that Austria will make common cause with Prussia and Russia.

"'That may be your opinion,' said he, sharply, 'but it is not therefore a fact.'

"It is a fact, Sire; and your Majesty may be assured that, on a subject of such importance, my opinion is not founded on mere conjecture.

"'On what, then, is it founded?

"Two days preceding that fixed for the rupture of the armistice, Blücher, at the head of a hundred thousand men, inarched into Silesia, and took possession of Breslau.

"'This is indeed a serious affair! Are you sure of it, Caulincourt?'

"I had, Sire, a warm altercation with Metternich on the subject, the day before my departure front Prague.

"On the very day on which Breslau was taken, General Jomini deserted the staff of Marshal Ney, and he is at this moment with the Emperor Alexander.

"'Jomini! a man overwhelmed with my favours!—the traitor! To abandon his post on the eve of a battle! To go over to the enemy with a report of our forces and means! Incredible!' As he uttered these words, there was, mingled with the feeling of deep indignation portrayed in his countenance, an expression of increasing uneasiness, which he evidently could not subdue. I was unable to proceed.

"'Is this all,' resumed he, holding out his hand to me. 'Speak, Caulincourt! Let me know all! I must know all!'

"Sire, the coalition has taken a wide range. Sweden, too, is in arms against us.

"'What do you say? interrupted he, with impetuosity. 'Bernadotte! Bernadotte in arms against France. This is the ass's kick, indeed!'

"Bernadotte, resumed I, not satisfied with turning his arms against his country, has recruited for deserters among our Allies, as if unable singly to endure the maledictions of his countrymen.

"'What mean you?'

"General Moreau is in the camp of the Allies!

"'Moreau with the Allies! This is not possible! Caulincourt, I cannot believe this. Bernadotte, the King of Sweden, may colour his odious treason by some specious pretext; but Moreau—Moreau take revenge on his countrymen—on his country! No, no, it cannot be. Moreau is weak, devoid of energy and exalted ambition. Yet there is a wide difference between him and Jomini—a renegade—a traitor. No, this report is not to be credited. How did you hear it?'

"I did not, as you will readily suppose," said the Duke de Vicenza, addressing himself to me, "reply categorically to this question. The distressing nature of the intelligence I had brought from Prague prevented me from amusing the emperor with the episode of the romantic Feodora.

"'The occupation of Breslau,' resumed the emperor, 'is important in many points of view. It is an event big with incalculable consequences. We must now fight again, and we must conquer under pain of being driven beyond the Rhine. But after all, what does the Emperor of Austria mean? Did he not freely consent to the treaties? And have I violated them? Under what pretence does the Cabinet of Vienna mask its conduct towards me?'

"I remained silent. The emperor knew from my correspondence that I had exhausted on this question every possible argument without obtaining satisfaction.

"'Well!' exclaimed he, 'the die is cast. I have three hundred thousand infantry, forty thousand cavalry, and a formidable artillery force. Saxony is, and will continue, faithful to me. That country shall be the scene of my operations. I will force them to make peace. All is not lost, Caulincourt! I have here,' continued he, pointing to his forehead, 'abundance of resources and resolution. I will not despair. I have conceived a bold project—one of those ideas which come as it were by inspiration, and which command fortune. But to put this scheme into execution, great sacrifices will be necessary. Look here, Caulincourt!' He passed his finger over a map of Prussia which was lying open on the table.

"'From Duben I may march direct on Berlin, and take possession of the Prussian capital without firing a cannon-ball. I shall dismay Bernadotte and Blücher, whose improvidence has left Berlin uncovered. Blücher is a good swordsman, but a bad general. On making myself master of the heart of Prussia, I shall relieve my fortresses.' He observed the surprise that was depicted on my countenance. 'Oh! I am aware that you will think this a bold idea; but it is only by going out of beaten tracks that we can disconcert a plan of campaign long meditated by the enemy. Taking advantage of the first moment of stupor, I may, by a desperate blow, change the aspect of things. Look at the map, Caulincourt; follow me attentively. Duben is a point of junction which will serve to mask my projects. The enemy will imagine that I am preparing to make Leipsic my *point d'appui*, whilst, with all my forces combined, I shall be marching straight on Berlin. This is a stupendous project; but if I am understood and seconded, I am convinced that it will succeed, and that it will decide the fate of the campaign.'

"The emperor's plan was indeed admirable," said the Duke de Vicenza ," it was one of those lofty conceptions which raise Napoleon in the rank of military commanders higher than Alexander the Great

"His plan for carrying Berlin was one of the grandest combinations of his genius. We considered it under every point of view, and I fully shared the emperor's opinion that its success was at the least very probable. In the desperate circumstances in which we were placed, temerity might serve us better than prudence. The result proved that in all possible hypotheses the plan of marching upon Berlin could not be more disastrous than our retrograde movement on Leipsic. But to carry this plan into effect it was necessary, as the emperor observed, to find men resolutely determined to make the greatest sacrifices. I will, at a future opportunity, describe to you the scene I witnessed when at Duben. The emperor's plans became known just at the moment when they were on the point of execution. Napoleon must not be made the scapegoat to bear the responsibility of all the disasters of France. Let every one answer for his own sins!

"The night was far advanced, but neither the emperor nor I thought of retiring to rest. Napoleon, whose mind was disturbed by a thousand anxious thoughts, paced with hurried steps up and down his chamber. Suddenly stopping short, and without introducing the subject by any preliminary remark, he said: 'Murat has arrived.' Then, after some hesitation, he added,—'I have given him the command of my guard.'

"I could not repress a gesture of astonishment.

"'*Ah, parbleu!* I thought you would be surprised! At first I gave him a bad reception, but finally I yielded to his importunities. He at least will not betray me. He is a brave man and a good soldier. Caulincourt, there are certain forebodings which it is our duty to endeavour to overcome. As long as I am fortunate, Murat will follow my fortune. But the business of the present is sufficient: to occupy me, I need not be looking into the future.'

"The emperor must have put a great restraint upon his feelings before he could have consented to receive Murat. The King of Naples had abandoned, at Smorghoni, the mutilated remains of our unfortunate army, of which he had been made commander-in-chief. Since then his conduct towards Napoleon had been, to say the least of it, equivocal. Latterly, he had offered his services to Austria, to act as mediator between France and the coalition. This will scarcely seem credible, but it is nevertheless true. Not only was the proposition absurd, (for he was perfectly aware that he had no influence over the emperor,) but there was a guilty afterthought in the absurdity. This subsequently became evident. We also knew his intrigues with Lord Bentinck, with whom he had had an interview in the Isle of Pouza.

"On being made acquainted with these proceedings, the emperor became greatly irritated, and said,—'Murat is a traitor and a madman; he ought either to be shot or sent to Charenton.' Events hurried on with astounding rapidity. The emperor had arrived at that extremity when he was forced every day to put in practice the old adage 'necessity knows no law.' It was indeed a hard necessity which forced him to refrain from expressing his contempt for such ingratitude. But let me say no more! The grave has closed over Murat and his errors!

"Whilst I was in Bohemia the emperor had seen the empress at Mentz. He told me, with all the ardour of a young man, the happiness he had experienced in meeting *his Louise*. This subject brought about a short truce to care, and Napoleon's radiant countenance presented no trace of the painful emotion he had suffered at (he commencement of our conversation. He drew from his waistcoat pocket a little miniature portrait of the King of Rome, painted by Isabey. It was the faithful representation of a most beautiful child. Napoleon was affectionately attached to the empress and his son. The occasional impoliteness of his manners to females in public was quite at variance with the kindness and suavity which distinguished him in his domestic relations.

"Only those who knew Napoleon in the intercourse of private life can render justice to his character. For my own part, I know him, as it were, by heart; and in proportion as time separates us, he appears to me like a beautiful dream. And would you believe that, in my recollections of Napoleon, that which seems to me to approach most nearly to ideal excellence is not the hero, filling the world with his gigantic fame, but

100

the man, viewed in the relations of private life. This is a contrast which often affords me a theme for carious and interesting reflection.

"In his intervals of gaiety, Napoleon's now of spirits sometimes betrayed him into almost boyish playfulness. He was an excellent mimic, when he chose to exercise his talent in that way, and woe to those who fell under the lash of his pleasantry. I have seen him give admirable imitations of Cambaceres and Kourakin; and as he *knew everything* (to use his own expression), he often amused us by very droll details."

"Oh, duke!" said I, "how much I should like to bear a few of those droll details. Pray oblige me by relating some."

"It is not very easy to comply with that request, I assure you," replied the duke, smiling; "if I were to begin you might soon find it necessary to call me to order."

"Nay! surely you can remember some which are not likely to incur any such interruption."

"Well," resumed the duke, "I will relate to you an incident which afforded the emperor no little merriment at the expense of his Excellency Prince Kourakin, the Russian Ambassador.

"In the year 1812 some dramatic performances were given at court. You know the arrangements which used to be observed on these occasions. The empress, with her ladies, occupied a large box in the centre of the *salle*. The boxes on either side were filled by the ladies of the high functionaries of the empire, all specially invited by their Majesties. At the extremity of the tier, on the right hand side, was the emperor's box, and the corresponding one on the opposite side was assigned to the *corps diplomatique*.

"Poor Prince Kourakin, who was certainly the most ugly of men, was afflicted with the infatuation of adorning himself with diamonds. The emperor used to say, that the chandeliers were eclipsed by the splendour of Kourakin, and that when the Russian Ambassador attended the play the expense of a hundred wax-lights might very well be spared. One evening the performance consisted of an act of the opera of *Jerusalem Delivered*. The charming Grassini (who then sang only at the court theatre), Crivelli, and Porto, sustained the principal characters. Tacchinardi conducted the chorusses, and the performance was altogether so exquisite that it absorbed the interest and riveted the attention of all present. Kourakin, radiant as the sun, was seated in frost of the ambassadors' box, with an amusing air of self-complacency. He paid no attention to the music, to the charms of which he was utterly insensible.

"His eyes, however, appeared to be under the influence of a fascination from which his ears' were exempt. Etiquette, of course, prohibited him from turning his back to the emperor, and, at the risk of getting a stiff neck, he sat with his head turned towards the Countess L——, whose box was in the second tier, and to whom he directed languishing glances with the most amusing air imaginable. Sometimes he beat time on the front of his box, with his great clumsy fingers covered with brilliant rings; and sometimes he twirled his aiguillettes, which were studded with costly diamonds. Duroc and I, who were stationed behind the emperor, had several times remarked the grotesque glances directed by Kourakin to the young and pretty Countess L——, who was not without a little of *coquetry* in her disposition. Yet the more censorious observer could never have suspected her to be guilty of any levity in reference to Kourakin.

"At the conclusion of the performance the emperor conducted the empress to her apartments. Her Majesty wore that evening on her bosom a bouquet formed of jewels, of various colours, set in imitation of flowers. It was a magnificent ornament, and the emperor, who was a connoisseur in jewels, expressed his admiration of it. Then turning to Kourakin, he entered into a dissertation on the beauty and value of the diamonds with which the ambassador was profusely decorated: 'Really, Prince,' said he, 'you carry about with you the mines of Golconda.'

"Kourakin bowed.

"'You are quite dazzling.'

"Another bow, still lower than the former.

"'You are irresistible.'

"'Ah, Sire!'

"Kourakin reared his head like a peacock, at the same time directing an amorous glance at the elegant Countess L——, who seemed to experience no little difficulty in preserving her gravity.

"About an hour afterwards the emperor entered his cabinet in high spirits, and entertained Duroc and me with the description of a little farce that had formed a sequel to the *Jerusalem Delivered*.

"'Kourakin,' said he, 'has actually persuaded himself that he is in love with Madame L——; and after sighing and languishing for some time without success, be at length ventured on a declaration. The malicious woman wrote at the bottom of the *billet-doux*, which she returned to him—"Your Excellency has made a little mistake; this declaration is intended for Mademoiselle Bigotini." Kourakin, instead of being disheartened, sent another message, to which no answer was returned. His Excellency then determined to change his plan of attack. He looked in the mirror, and began to suspect the possibility of recommending his suit by something more agreeable to the lady than his personal appearance. Accordingly, every morning there arrived at the residence of Madame L—— a colossal bouquet, accompanied by a basket filled with a variety of elegant And costly trifles, selected from the Magasin of Sike, the expense of which speedily exceeded 20,000 *francs*. But the best of the joke is, that Madame L—— alleged, in the most innocent manner possible, "that she was indebted for all these pretty presents to the gallantry of the general her husband, who had recourse to these agreeable surprises to keep alive her recollection of him during his long absence.'"

"At this we could not help laughing heartily, for we well knew that throughout the whole course of his life General L—— had never had reason to reproach himself with any act of extravagance.

"'Yesterday evening,' pursued the emperor, 'Madame L—— went to the opera, and afterwards to the Princess Pauline's ball, at Neuilly. On her return home, at about three o'clock in the morning, the servant handed out of the carriage, along with his mistress's cloak, a Russian leather box. "What is that, Jean?" inquired the lady. "This box was on the seat of the carriage, along with the cloak, *Madame*."—"Oh, yes, very true. I had forgotten it—it is quite right, Jean,"

"'The box was carried up to Madame L——'s apartment, and when the countess found herself alone, curiosity naturally prompted her to open it. Its contents, almost dazzled her. "*Mon Dieu!*" she exclaimed, "what magnificent diamonds!" And then, with a deep sigh, she added, "How unfortunate that he is so very ugly!" As the emperor uttered these words he mimicked so admirably the whining voice and mincing manners of Madame L——, that we were ready to expire with laughter.

"And what has been the upshot of all this, Sire? inquired I.

"'*Par Dieu!* that is the best of the joke! You shall hear. This morning I caused an intimation to be given to Madame L——, that it would be advisable for her to send back the Russia leather box to its owner, unless she felt inclined to retire to her old castle in Auvergne, to reflect on the dangers of *coquetry*. I cannot permit ladies who enjoy the honour of being admitted to pay their court to the empress, to amuse themselves with these little *espiegleries*, which are worthy of the noble dames of the Regent's Court. Kourakin may be let off with the payment of his bills to Madame Bernard, Sike, and others. It is right that he should have a lesson, but he must keep his diamonds.'

"We renewed our laughter, and the eperor, rubbing his hands with an air of triumph, said—'You see gentlemen, I know everything that is going on. You cannot keep any secrets from me.'

"But," said the Duke de Vicenza, "this anecdote has led me very far from the thread of my narrative. From the Tuileries, in January 1803, to Gorlitz, in August 1613, there is an immeasurable distance. In 1812, all was prosperity and happiness, and the future was full of brilliant promise. In 1813, death had thinned our ranks—all was gloomy and menacing, and the clouds which overhang the present obscured the future. Alas! what disasters had that future in store for us!

"A few days after my arrival at Gorlitz the declaration of war by Austria against France was officially notified. The most disheartening intelligence poured in from all sides. Treason was everywhere at work. We could now no longer count on Bavaria. Every succeeding hour was marked by some base defection, some new misfortune. And yet the future historian will coolly record this terrible phasis, which dealt so many death-blows among the spectators of the last convulsions of the empire!

"Prince Schwartzenberg commanded the Austrian Army, amounting to 130,000 men, and 80,000 Russians were marching on Dresden. The emperor sent Murat with a part of the imperial guard to protect Dresden, and to give confidence to the excellent King of Saxony, who had declared his resolution to make common cause with Napoleon. Two days after the departure of the King of Naples, a courier arrived with intelligence that the enemy was at the gates of Dresden. 'Am I doomed not to have a day's respite?' said the emperor, in a tone of deep despondency. He sent for Gourgand, a brave and intelligent officer, to whom he was much attached.

"'Gourgand,' said the emperor, 'depart this instant for Dresden, and travel with the utmost possible speed, for you must be there tonight. As soon as you arrive, at whatever hour it may be, you must request an interview with the King of Saxony. Tell him from me that tomorrow I shall set out in person for Pyrna. Tell the King of Naples, Marshal St Cyr, the Duke de Bassano, and Durosnel, that they must not suffer themselves to be intimidated by a *coup de main* which the enemy may attempt upon Dresden; tell them they must hold out for four-and-twenty hours longer. I shall bring with me forty-thousand men, and I shall be able to assemble the whole army in thirty-six hours before the walk of Dresden. See the commander of the engineers, and with him inspect the redoubts and fortifications round the city. When you have examined everything, make notes of your observations, and return without loss of time to meet me at Stolpen. I shall be there tonight. Go, Gourgand, and use the utmost speed.'

"Next night, at eleven o'clock, the indefatigable Gourgand returned to the headquarters, at Stolpen. This mission, which Gourgand executed with all his characteristic intelligence, was of the highest importance. He brought back a most alarming account. Dresden was exposed to imminent danger. The Russian Army was advancing by forced marches. Platoff, with his hordes, a truly satanic advanced guard, spread fire and destruction wherever they appeared. The Cossacks had already entered and set fire to a village situated about half-a-league from the great gardens; and St. Cyr betrayed a disposition to evacuate his position, not having forces sufficient to defend it.

"'Well!' said the emperor, when Gourgand had closed his narrative of disasters, 'what is the opinion of the Duke de Bassano?'

"'Sire, he does not think it will be practicable to hold oat twenty-four hours longer.'

"'Impossible! And you, Gourgand I what do you think?'

"'I firmly believe, Sire, that Dresden will be taken tomorrow, unless your Majesty be there in person,'

"'Gourgand, be cautious how you advance this opinion if you do not feel assured it is well founded.'

"'Sire, I have seen all, and carefully examined all; and I am ready to answer for it with my life that your Majesty's presence alone can save Dresden.'

"This reply decided the Emperor. He reflected tor a few moments and then sent for General Haxo. Drawing his finger over the map, he described, with amazing rapidity and clearness, the movements of the different scattered corps which he was assembling, as if by the touch of a fairy's wand, to fly, as be expressed it, to the defence of Dresden. He analyzed clearly the enemy's plan, and ranged in opposition to it his own combinations. A moment sufficed to enable him to scan at a glance the whole circle of operations.

"'Set off immediately, Haxo,' said he, 'and see that my orders are obeyed. I make you responsible for their immediate execution. Tell Vandamme that, entrenched as he is in the inaccessible denies of Peteswalde, he may await the result of the operations at Dresden. For him I have reserved the honour of picking up the sword of the vanquished. Cool collectedness is necessary, and Vandamme is of an ardent temperament. Explain to him clearly what I expect him to do. Depart without delay, General Haxo.'

"Then, turning to Gourgand, he thus addressed him:—

"'Order a fresh horse, my dear Gourgand, end return to Dresden with your utmost speed. Make known my intention of commanding in person. My old guard will precede me. Tell the King of Naples that he must sustain the honour of our arms until my arrival. Let everyone centuple his activity, and be at his post. I cannot be present everywhere. Proclaim to the troops that tomorrow evening I shall be with them. Go, Gourgand. Use dispatch. Lame a dozen horses, if it must be so, but reach your journey's end speedily. Remember, the fate of Dresden depends on your punctuality.'

"Orderlies were dispatched in every direction. The old guard, which had been hastily assembled, defiled before our windows, raising shouts of '*Vive l'Empereur!* Forward on Dresden!' The whole town was in commotion. Every one was at his post. The will of one man acted, as it were, with the power of electricity on the will of all. The events which I am here describing are of such recent date that we do not regard them with the degree of wonder they are naturally calculated to excite. The time will come when they will appear nothing short of miraculous. It is but just also to consider the share of merit due to every individual who took part in the glories of Napoleon.

"It must be acknowledged that never did a chief meet with more ready and devoted obedience on the part of those who were subordinate to his authority. With the rapidity of lightning orders were transmitted from one place to another, without any calculation of difficulties or distances, or any concern about fatigue or privation. All vied with each other for the honour of occupying the most dangerous posts, and executing the most difficult missions. Life was lightly prized when balanced in the scale with duty. It would be necessary to name every officer in the army to render justice to each individually.

"I will not," said the Duke de Vicenza, "enter into the details of the terrible Battle of Dresden, which lasted three days. You have, of course, read many accounts of it. Besides," added he, with a smile, "I know you would rather hear particulars relating to the emperor personally; or, to borrow your own. expression, *les choses de Napoleon.*"

"Thank you, Duke," said I, shaking hands with him; "and though you consider me incapable of adequately comprehending the details of a battle, I am nevertheless an attentive auditor of whatsoever you may please to narrate. Be assured I shall never forget either your inexhaustible kindness or *les choses de Napoleon*. Both will remain indelibly engraven in my memory and in my heart."

CHAPTER 10

Napoleon's Entrance into Dresden

We entered Dresden," said the Duke de Vicenza, "on the morning of the 20th of August. It would be impossible to describe the demonstrations of joy evinced by the troops when they beheld the emperor at the further end of the bridge. Both the young and old guard marched forward to meet him. At one moment the bridge was so crowded that our horses pressed closely against each other, and could not move a step.

"The joyous enthusiasm of the troops was raised to the highest possible degree. 'There he is! there he is!—that is he!' they exclaimed; and shouts resounded along the whole bank of the river. The authority of the officers was insufficient to restrain the troops. 'Let them alone! let them alone!' said the emperor; 'they will presently make room for me to lead them on to face the enemy.' These words were repeated from mouth to mouth, and in a few moments the troops were almost stifling each other in their efforts to make room for us.

"Napoleon's entry into Dresden was truly triumphal; and it will never be forgotten by those who witnessed it. As we approached the city nothing was heard but clapping of hands and cries of enthusiasm. Men, women, and children, mingled with the troops, and escorted us to the palace. The King of Saxony came out to receive Napoleon, and embraced him in the presence of his assembled subjects. The consternation and alarm which had hitherto prevailed were now succeeded by boundless joy and confidence. The enemy's lines already crowned the heights which surrounded the city. It was at once a grand and consolatory sight to witness the defiling of the Imperial Guard and the proud *cuirassiers*, commanded by Latour Maubourg, inarching with upraised heads, and casting looks of defiance on the heights, where vast numbers of the enemy's forces were collected.

"The troops continued to defile until evening, when they all occupied the positions allotted to them. The Emperor went to inspect every point, with the view of preparing for a general attack. The Russians and Austrians likewise made their arrangements. The Prussian columns were posted in the Gross-Garten. A general movement pervaded the two camps; and there was something indescribably solemn and gloomy in this expectation of a great event. Friends pressed each other's hands in silence. We were no longer marching to those brilliant conquests which, in every campaign, extended the domination of France. Each man seemed now to be intent only on defending his own home and family. This was a bitterly mortifying reflection.

"The battle commenced at three o'clock, and was maintained with unexampled obstinacy till nine at night. We returned to the palace about midnight. The emperor had had no rest for six-and-thirty hours, and yet he sat up the whole night dictating orders. It required a constitution of iron to bear up under the fatigues to which we had been exposed for the space of five months. I several times fell soundly asleep as I sat on my horse, whilst the report of cannon was thundering in my ears.

"But how could we think of ourselves when we saw the emperor exposing his life and health to continual danger? At four o'clock he threw himself on his camp bed, and in about twenty minutes after he suddenly awoke, exclaiming, 'Caulincourt, are you there? Proceed to the camp, and take with you the plan which I have drawn up with Dalbe. The corps of Marmont and Victor have arrived tonight. Examine the amount of their forces, and see whether they are strong enough to maintain the positions which I have assigned to them on the field. This is essential, Caulincourt. See with your own eyes; and trust only to your own observation.'

"The rain poured in torrents, and the camp was the image of desolation. Our men, who had arrived by forced marches, and were exhausted by fatigue, were bivouacking on the muddy ground. The fires were extinguished by the torrent of rain. I took out my notes and gave some orders relating to the Imperial escort for the day. I returned to the emperor, whom I found standing near a window, looking anxiously at the state of the weather. Day was beginning to dawn. 'What terrible weather,' said he, in a tone of dissatisfaction; 'this is an evil presage.'

"Napoleon was superstitious, and he did not like people who regarded superstition as a weakness. He used to say that none but fools affected to despise it.

"At six in the morning the emperor mounted his horse, and we left Dresden by the gate of Fribourg to proceed to the camp. The firing recommenced with terrific fury. It was on this second day of the battle that Moreau received his mortal wound. The King of Naples performed prodigies of valour; he had two horses killed under him. Murat was truly sublime on the field of battle. His tall figure, his noble countenance, brilliant eyes, and elegant costume, altogether imparted to him a picturesque appearance. When it was his task to conduct a charge his courage prompted him to the most glorious feats: he commanded universal admiration.

"In the direction of Gorlitz we had a terrible engagement with the Austrians; and we lost a vast number of troops without succeeding in forcing the enemy's centre. The emperor sent for Murat. 'Go thither,' said he, pointing to wards Gorlitz with his lunette. 'Take with you Latour Maubourg's *cuirassiers*, and decide the victory.' The King of Naples immediately placed himself at the head of the cavalry and galloped forward to the scene of the engagement. He made some admirable charges, and decided the partial advantage. Three brigades, commanded by Metzko, were repulsed, and ten thousand men surrendered themselves prisoners. It was a most gallant affair.

"'They have had a rough lesson to begin with,' said the emperor, as he saw the column of Austrian prisoners file off towards Pyrna. I saw him smile at some remarks made by a wounded dragoon who was following in the rear of the column, on his way to the *ambulance*. The pain of his wound seemed to be momentarily eased by the pleasure he enjoyed in jeering the Austrians, towards whom our soldiers cherished the bitterest animosity. The lower class of people seem to be endowed with an exquisite instinct for distinguishing right from wrong, justice from injustice. 'Are you not ashamed of yourselves, you *Parpaillots* of Austrians? What unnatural dogs you must be to fight in this manner against your own flesh and blood.' It seemed as though every soldier regarded as his own personal affair the family quarrel which was about to be decided on the field of battle between Napoleon and Austria.

"During the action the emperor commanded in person a terrific cannonade which was directed on the heights of Rocknitz, where the allied forces were planted in such masses as to preclude the practicability of any other form of attack. It was easy to perceive, from a certain degree of nervous agitation in his manner, that his feelings were painfully ruffled at finding himself thus face to face opposed to the

Austrian troops. He turned round to me and said, 'The wicked advisers of the Emperor Francis deserve to be hanged. This is an iniquitous, impious war . . . How will it all end?'

"I could relate many traits of those brave old guards, who were treated with so much indignity after the fall of Napoleon. I, who had the opportunity of being a close observer of the gallant conduct of this corps, must ever be its panegyrist. The humble uniform of every private soldier enveloped a hero, who, though rude in aspect, was endowed with chivalrous loyalty and courage. The glory of the Roman *phalanxes* is eclipsed by that of the Imperial guard. History will inscribe that glory in letters of gold when she records the events of Fontainebleau and Waterloo. It is one of the most extraordinary traditions of the empire.

"It was curious to observe the attachment, confidence, and familiarity, which existed between the humblest of the soldiers and the most absolute sovereign that ever existed. There was not one of Napoleon's intimate friends, however high in rank, who would have ventured to indulge in the sort of *camaraderie* which was kept up between the emperor and his old *moustaches*. And these same men would not have ventured to speak to me of their lieutenants in the familiar tone in which they addressed the redoubted chief of the army. They regarded Napoleon as a being differing from all others, and combining within himself the attributes of sovereign, country, and family. He inspired them with a language which they addressed only to him, and words which they uttered only in his presence.' Nothing used to amuse Napoleon so much as this familiarity of the soldiery, and he always replied to them with truly paternal kindness.

"About the middle of the day the rain began to descend with redoubled violence. The emperor, who had been on horseback since daybreak, was literally soaked to the skin, and an appearance of extreme lassitude was observable in all his movements.

"On the left, in the direction of the Gross-Garten, a battalion of grenadiers of the old guard grouped round a battery, had sustained, since the commencement of the action, the violent assaults of the cavalry of Beningsen. The conservation of that battery was exceedingly important. At one moment the enemy's firing appeared to relax, and the emperor observing this circumstance, spurred his horse, and galloped, amidst the heat of the engagement, between the enemy's cavalry and our artillery. The ground was thickly strewed with the bodies of the slain. 'This position costs us dear,' said he, petulantly; then a moment afterwards, he added, with a look of satisfaction, 'I knew that my guard would not surrender it to the Russians.'

"'Let them come back again at their peril,' exclaimed, with a menacing gesture, an old artilleryman, whose head had just received a sabre wound, and was bandaged up with a handkerchief saturated with blood. Then turning to the emperor, he said, 'This is not a fit place for you. Go away. You are more ill than any of us; go and take some rest.'

"'I will, when we have won the battle,' said the emperor.

"'My comrade is right, Sire,' said a veteran grenadier. 'Your Majesty is wet to the skin. Pray go and get your clothes changed.' The brave fellow uttered these words in the tone of supplication, which a son might be expected to employ towards a beloved father.

"'I will rest when you can all rest, my lads; that is to say, when the battle is ended.'

"'I know that your Majesty has that battery at heart,' said the grenadier, 'but we will take care that the Russians don't get it. Will we not, comrades?' He was answered by a shout of acquiescence. 'Now, Sire, since we answer for the safety of the battery, surely you may go and take a little rest.'

"'Very well, my good fellows, very well. I trust to you;' and he galloped off, smiling.

"Never did the emperor execute finer manoeuvres or display more surprising presence of mind and activity. He was present at all the points exposed to the greatest danger, frequently facing a shower of grape-shot, like any private soldier. In short, be seemed to become more and more heroic in proportion as difficulties accumulated.

"At the approach of evening we were victorious on all points. Thirty thousand of the enemy's troops *hors de combat*, two hundred pieces of artillery, and a vast quantity of baggage, were the trophies of these two days. Dresden was literally filled with our captures. Our troops performed prodigies during the action. The officers could scarcely restrain the ardour of the men, who, without waiting the word of command, rushed headlong to the attack. Whilst he was looking on, the emperor several times exclaimed enthusiastically, 'What troops! These are mere raw recruits! It is incredible!'

"We had not more than a hundred thousand men engaged; the force opposed to us was more than three times as numerous. The enemies' troops were fresh on entering the field; ours, on the contrary, had not had a single day's rest for the space of three months; had frequently been in want of absolute necessaries, and were harassed by the fatigue of forced marches during the few days preceding the battle. Yet they gained the victory by dint of courage and self-sacrifice. Oh, whatever have been our disasters, and the humiliating situation of France, since 1814, yet how many glorious recollections remain to console us!"

Here the Duke de Vicenza paused. Whenever his memory carried him back to the triumphant days of the empire, his countenance seemed to beam with the light of inspiration; and his brow, though furrowed with care, once more bore the expression of pride and confidence. But these bursts of animation were always succeeded by such profound melancholy, that it was painful to see him. What a sad contrast was presented by the brilliant existence of Napoleon's grand equerry and that of the poor invalid seated in a humble apartment at Plombières, and whilst relating the marvels of the emperor's reign, striving to conceal the active part he himself had played in the great history.

"We did not return to the Palace of Dresden till eleven o'clock," resumed the duke. "The emperor was so wet that the water dripped from his clothes. He was taken ill in the night with a sort of ague fit; yet when I entered his apartment at four in the morning, I found him up and ready to mount his horse. 'The work is not ended yet,' said he, 'we must follow the enemy in his retreat, and drive him completely from the environs of Dresden. The King of Naples and Victor will pursue him on the Sayda road; Marmont, on Altemberg; Saint Cyr, on Dohna; and Mortier, with the young guard, on the high road of Pyrna. It is always the same thing over again,' he added, with a sigh. 'Gentlemen, let us to the camp.'

"We went down to the courtyard of the palace. Day was just beginning to dawn. When the emperor saw the squadron on duty, drawn up in the courtyard, he could not repress an exclamation of surprise. The squadron was composed of the same grenadiers of the old guard, who, on the preceding day, had served as the emperor's escort, and who had returned with us to Dresden, soaked through with rain. To see them again at five in the morning in smart uniforms, presenting arms, and looking as trim as if they had been on parade at the Tuileries, seemed like the work of magic.

"'Why, my lads, you must have spent the night in equipping yourselves, instead of taking your rest,' said the emperor, in a tone of kind reproach.

"'Rest!—we have not had much of that,' replied one of the men. 'But no matter! We have had as much as your Majesty!'

"'I am accustomed to go without rest.' He cast his eye on a gruff-looking quarter-master, and recognising his countenance, he said—

"'You served in Egypt, I think?'

"'I am proud to say I did. I was at Aboukir; and I remember it was hot enough there.'

"'You have no decoration, I perceive.'

"'It will come sometime or other,' said the quartermaster, somewhat sullenly.

"'It has come,' said the emperor. 'I give you the cross.'

"The poor fellow was quite overcome by joy and gratitude. He fixed on the emperor a look which it is impossible to describe, and the tears overflowed his eyes. 'I shall lay down my life for your Majesty today, that is certain,' said he. In his transport he seized the skirt of the emperor's famous grey great-coat, and putting it into his mouth bit off a fragment, which he placed in his button-hole.

"'This will do till I get the red riband, please your Majesty.'

"The emperor was deeply moved by this incident. He spurred his horse and galloped off, his escort following and raising shouts of joy. The King of Saxony, who was a witness of this scene, sent that same evening twenty gold Napoleons to the quarter-master, with a message, informing him that the money was 'to purchase a red riband.'

"You will, I doubt not," said the Duke de Vicenza, "readily believe me, when I say that even now, after the lapse of thirteen years, my heart glows at the remembrance of these incidents. They were, indeed, of such common occurrence, that we ceased to wonder at the fervent adulation paid by the soldiery to Napoleon. I retain a pious recollection of it, and it serves to counteract in my mind the pain excited by the vile apostasies I have witnessed.

"Even since the fall of the emperor, I have occasionally met with curious examples of the veneration in which he was held. Last year, for instance, when I was proceeding to my country seat, I stopped to change horses at a little village beyond Alençon. Whilst the new postilion was assisting to harness the horses, I observed him gazing at me with marked attention. I could not account for the man's curiosity. At length he bestrode his horse, and with several tremendous smacks of his whip, drove off at a furious gallop. I expected every moment to be overturned; and, moreover, being an invalid, I felt incommoded by the excessive speed. I called to him to slacken his pace, and pulling up his horses, he turned round and made me a military salute, saying— 'General, you see I know, you!'

"You know me! Well! and is that the reason why you with to break my neck?

"'On the contrary, general, I wish to do you honour, in memory of ——. You know who I mean! Were you not his most intimate friend, and always with him?'

"What do you mean? I do not understand you?

"'Well then, general, I mean the emperor! That name will not offend your ears! I served in the guides. *Mille Tounerres!* Those were glorious days, general! Glorious days!'

"On arriving at the next relay, I offered the poor fellow some money, but he declined to accept it.

"'General,' said he, I have a little favour to request of you, and if you will grant it, it will make me richer than the present you offer. Can you spare a quarter of an hour to honour me with a visit in my humble abode, which is hard by. There is a report that *he* is dead; but I cannot believe it. I drink his health every day.'

"I was so amused with the man's blunt simplicity of manner, that I accepted this strange invitation; and, having alighted from the *calache*, I followed the old Imperial guide to his dwelling-place. There I drank half a glass of very sour wine, which, however, did not do me any harm. I admired some wretchedly daubed coloured drawings, representing Napoleon on foot and on horseback; and a sort of caricature of the King of Rome, dressed in the uniform of a grenadier of the guard. At the bottom of this picture were written, in pencil, the words *il grandira*. I was next shown several eagles, and a silver cross, with an image of Napoleon. These things were taken out of a press, where they had been deposited along with some old uniform coats, carefully folded up. The soldier, as he showed me these relics, said, with emotion, 'I would not part with them for worlds. I worship them as though they were sacred. And I have preferred turning to the vile business of *trottemenu* (postilion), rather than I would serve any other sovereign. Such is my way of thinking; I know it differs from that of many others.'

"You perceive," said the duke, "that I cannot cure myself of the habit of relating without order, or connexion, all that comes into my head. We were, I think, at Dresden, and on the bloodstained field of battle.

"We were once more victorious, and this victory was destined to be the last ray of the star which lighted the fortune of Napoleon. The rest of the campaign was a succession of misfortunes, aggravated by the basest treason. Every feeling held sacred by mankind was then turned to scoff and derision. Military capitulations and treaties of alliance were openly violated, and physical force superseded the law of nations. All was set at defiance; even the judgment which history will pronounce on such deeds. Sovereigns did not then appear to understand that, by demoralizing their subjects, they were creating to themselves incessant sources of torment. Not even kings can set bad examples with impunity.

"But it was not enough to forsake, the emperor, or to maintain a base and dishonourable neutrality; our allies waited till they were on the field of battle to desert from our ranks. Thus we saw the Saxons, at Leipsic, turn their arms against those Frenchmen with whom, but a few minutes previously, they had had the honour to share glory and danger. But the time will come when party spirit shall give place to justice, and then the historian will scarcely find words sufficiently severe to qualify such turpitude. The anathemas uttered by the victims on the field of Leipsic will be re-echoed by the voice of posterity."

CHAPTER 11

Arrival at Leipsic

"We left Dresden on the 7th of October. We had already heard of the defection of a Westphalian regiment, which went over to the enemy with arms and baggage. General Vandamme, too, led away by his natural impetuosity, had transgressed the orders transmitted to him by the emperor through General Haxo. Vandamme had been surrounded on all sides, and overpowered by numbers; his ten thousand men had been cut to pieces, and himself made prisoner, at the very moment when we so dearly earned the victory of Dresden.

"On hearing this sad news, the emperor said—'Surely some fatality hangs over us. This unfortunate event takes from us a valuable resource. There is no excuse for the disobedience of Vandamme. My orders were precise. He ought to have known, that against a retreating enemy one must raise a bridge of gold or a barrier of steel.'

"Marshal Saint Cyr remained in Dresden with thirty thousand men. The King of Saxony insisted on accompanying the emperor. He entered the carriage together with the queen and the Princess Augusta, The party was escorted by the Imperial staff. At Eilenburgh, on the banks of the Mulda, the Saxon troops rejoined the French army, and were reviewed by the Emperor and the King of Saxony. I read and translated to the Saxon troops the proclamation addressed to them by the emperor. In this proclamation Napoleon exhorted the Saxons to second the efforts he was making to maintain the independence of their country.

"He called their attention to the example of fidelity set by their sovereign, his dear and honoured ally; and reminded them that Prussia was threatening Saxony, and seeking to invade her finest provinces. Then, appealing to them in the name of military honour, he conjured them to emulate the valiant soldiers of the grand army, with whom the Saxons had made common cause, and in whose ranks they were about to fight.

"Shouts of enthusiasm followed this address. All swore to remain faithful until death. Some officers stepped forward, sword in hand, and, surrounding the two sovereigns, exclaimed—'*Vive notre Roi! Vive l'Empereur* Napoleon, the friend of the Saxons!'

"Our troops, who had been dispirited by so many successive defections, now felt their confidence revive. On that foreign land they had found friends and companions in arms. They shook hands, embraced, and shared their wine and provisions together. French cordiality soon thawed the ice of German reserve. Within an hour after the review, the troops seemed to be united by the bonds of fraternity. A month later, all these feelings were obliterated.

""We left at Eilenburgh the King of Saxony, his family, and the Duke de Bassano. The latter was invested with the most extended powers, and the emperor's confidence was never more worthily bestowed. With high talent the Duke de Bassano combines every honourable quality. He is one of those men whose characters shed lustre on the empire. After the fall of Napoleon, the honour of General Maret was unsullied by any act of meanness or ingratitude.

"Eilenburgh became the depot of the great park of artillery and all the baggage wagons. We took the direction of Duben. The plans on which the emperor had been deliberating were then made known. At length it was understood that he intended to march on Berlin, and not on Leipsic.

"When the emperor's purpose became known, there was an almost general explosion of dissatisfaction. Blind obedience was suddenly superseded by rebellion. 'Must we, then,' it was said, 'expose ourselves to another failure in Prussia? Is the wreck of our army to be buried in Berlin? Has there not been blood enough spilt? Is this never to end? Is it too late to enter upon this hazardous campaign. Having gained our position on the Rhine, we will keep possession of our winter-quarters; and in the spring of the year (if it must needs be so) we will enter the field again.'

"These complaints were uttered aloud and without any sort of reserve. When the emperor spoke of his plans, and explained the chances of success offered to us by the improvidence of Blücher, he found himself surrounded by cold looks, and not an approving word seconded the generous enterprise. Whilst these feelings of doubt and dissatisfaction prevailed amongst the principal commanders of the army, intelligence arrived of the defection of Bavaria. Then the spirit of discontent knew no bounds, and for the first time the emperor heard remonstrances.

"There was something very odious in an insurrection thus excited solely by unmerited misfortune. Was not Napoleon still Emperor of France? Was he not still the able chief who had so often led us to victory? Scarcely a day had elapsed since his will was law! Yet now, the sublime conceptions of his genius were met by a frantic cry of disapproval. 'We have had enough of fighting. We want to go back to France!' were words echoed from mouth to mouth. Alas! how severely have subsequent events chastised this baseness!

"I was in the emperor's saloon when the officers of his staff came to implore him to abandon his design on Berlin and to march to Leipsic. It was a most distressing scene. None but those who knew the emperor as I knew him can form any notion of what he must have suffered at that moment. The subject was opened by a marshal of France. I will not name him. His existence has since been poisoned by bitter regret! After he had spoken, several others delivered their opinions; and, as it often happens in similar cases, the person who spoke loudest and with most vehemence, whether right or wrong, converted to his way of thinking all who had differed from him. It is possible that, before the interview with the emperor, strong arguments and effective remonstrances might have been prepared; but in the presence of him, whose look of displeasure was not easily braved, no one had courage to deliver the speeches previously prepared, and such feeble arguments were advanced as ill justified the bold step that had been taken.

"Whilst the emperor's blood boiled, and his eyes flashed, with indignation, his insulted pride armed him with strength to restrain the expression of his resentment. He maintained a dignified coolness; but a slight tremor was observable in his voice, when he made the following reply:—'I have maturely reflected on my plan; and have weighed the defection of Bavaria in the balance of circumstances adverse to our interests. I am convinced of the advantage of marching on Berlin. A retrograde movement, in the circumstances in which we are placed, would be attended by disastrous consequences; and those who oppose my plan are taking upon themselves a fearful responsibility. I will consider of what you have said, gentlemen.' He then retired into his cabinet.

"In the course of the day I several times went to the emperor's door. He was alone in the cabinet, with nothing to occupy him but

119

his own thoughts. This solitude and the absence of occupation, which was so much at variance with his usual active habits, rendered me uneasy, and in the evening I directed a servant to tap at the door and to request that the emperor would admit me. He made no reply. I was awaiting his answer in the saloon adjoining his cabinet. It was a cold and dark night; the wind howled through the corridors of the gloomy castle of Duben, and shook the windows, which were fixed in curious old leaden frames. An air of portentous melancholy prevailed around. Everyone had tacitly absolved himself from the oath of allegiance. The sovereign had said—'I will reflect,' and his rebellious subjects, having given their ultimatum, took no pains to conceal their indifference as to the *veto* which might be affixed to it.

"The incidents of this eventful drama were now hurrying on with a degree of rapidity which exceeded even my worst forebodings. The denouement, which at first appeared doubtful and obscure, now developed itself with frightful certainty.

"Alas! thought I, we shall mark by a long track of blood the path we have yet to traverse; and the abyss which is to. swallow us up will be our last halting-place!

"Night advanced, and the same silence prevailed in the emperor's cabinet. I tore a leaf from my memorandum book, and with my pencil wrote these words—'I am here; will your Majesty be pleased to see me?' I summoned an usher, and gave him positive orders to enter the emperor's apartment, and to give him the slip of paper. I approached the door of the cabinet, which now stood ajar. The emperor read what I had written. A faint smile lighted up his dejected countenance, and he said—'Come in, Caulincourt,'

"I found him lying on a sofa, beside which stood a little table covered with maps and papers. But it was evident he had not been perusing them. His eyes were dim and fixed, and the sardonic expression of his mouth betrayed the bitter reflections which had occupied his mind. His hands were convulsively agitated, and he took up and threw down, unconsciously, any object that happened to lie within his reach. His aspect altogether denoted that he was suffering under deep and absorbing affliction.

"I approached him and said—'Sire, this state of mind will kill you.'

"He made no reply; but an impatient gesture revealed this thought, and seemed to say—'It matters not.'

"'Sire,' returned I, 'the representations which have been made to you are submitted to your Majesty's approbation.'

"He fixed his eyes on me and said—'You are not under the delusion, Caulincourt; no, it cannot be. You must be aware of the fatal results of this spirit of insubordination which is every day showing itself. It must be followed by fearful and incalculable consequences. When bayonets deliberate, power escapes from the sceptre of the sovereign. I see growing up around me a power of inertness, more dangerous than positive revolt. A hundred generals in open insurrection could not embarrass me. My troops would put down the fiercest rebellion. They do not argue, they obey, and are willing to follow me to the furthest extremity of the world. But in the critical circumstances in which we are at present placed, it is a question of life or death to the country that a good understanding should exist between the leaders of the army and myself. Distrust and hesitation will bring about our destruction more speedily than the swords of the allies.'

"He rose from the sofa, and paced two or three times up and down his cabinet. Then he said, as if speaking to himself—'All is lost! I am vainly contending against Fate! The French people know not how to bear reverses!' He again threw himself on the sofa, and fell into his reverie. All my efforts to rouse him were unavailing. His faculties seemed to be suspended, and his genius disarmed, by the listlessness of those in whose co-operation he confided. This miserable apathy was demoralizing the army and extinguishing that sacred flame of patriotism which had wrought so many miracles. And what but a miracle could now defend France from the invasion of the five powers combined against her?

"Throughout the following day the emperor's mind was racked by anguish and indecision. In making the sacrifice of his personal conviction he seemed to feel that he was annihilating, by a single blow, all his fortune. His presentiments were but too fully realised. At length, towards evening, he came to a decision. He then became apparently calm, as he always did when he had made up his mind to anything. I shall never forget his prophetic words:—'Fate marks the fall of nations.'

"'But, Sire,' observed I, 'the will of a people may counterbalance the decree of Fate.'

"'Yes,' replied he, laying his hand on my arm; 'but that will has not been shown. Bear this in mind, Caulincourt! Let not the French invoke maledictions on my memory.'

"The emperor announced his determination to march on Leipsic.

'May they who have urged this movement not have reason to repent it,' added he. Orders for departure were immediately given; and, as if the triumph over the emperor's wish had satisfied all the exigencies of our ill-fortune, the bulk of the army manifested the most boundless joy. It was a melancholy spectacle to those who did not share this almost general feeling of gratification. The emperor, in yielding, had been overcome by one of those necessities against which the most energetic resistance cannot hold out.

"Augereau arrived at headquarters, bringing with him the twenty thousand men of his division. Augereau, with his excellent good sense and discernment, foresaw the fatal consequences of our retrograde movement. 'This,' said he to me, 'appears like madness. All eyes are now directed to one point, which is France. Do they not perceive that defection has echeloned along our route enemies the more formidable, inasmuch as they know the strong and the weak side of our resources. The emperor was wrong to yield to this clamour, and I told him so not an hour ago. He should have turned adrift all these fellows who are so anxious to get home, and should have marched forward with the well-disposed part of the army. We had none of this in '93. There was no clamouring then. Every man carried his fortune at the end of his musket, and never turned to look behind him. Had I been in the emperor's place I would have sent one half of them back to France to plant their cabbages.'

"The marshal, in his soldier-like honesty, could not conceive the idea of men betraying their duty; but he saw only one side of our disasters. Misfortune had come accompanied by every base feeling. At the close of 1813 France was not a place to which the discontented could be sent with safety. Whilst her heroic sons had been shedding their blood on the field of battle, vile conspirators had been secretly forging chains to bind their mutilated limbs. Woe to those who rewarded such heroism by such ingratitude!

"On the morning of the 15th of October the emperor left Duben, and he reached Leipsic early in the day. He immediately began to trace his plans. The abrupt and impatient manner in which he issued his commands denoted his disturbed state of mind. Our numerical force was frightfully disproportionate to that of the enemy, and it was evident that this battle must be decisive! Whilst pointing out to me on the map the plan he had traced out, the emperor said; 'There are no scientific combinations which can compensate on this point for the thinness of our squares. We shall be overpowered by mere numbers.

One hundred and twenty-five thousand men against three hundred and fifty thousand, and this in a pitched battle! Well! they would have it thus!' This phrase, which he repeated for the second time in a tone of despair, rang in my ears like a sentence of death.

"The flower of the French Army was buried on the field of Leipsic. There, as everywhere, our officers and troops earned imperishable laurels. I was with the emperor when the Austrian general, Meerfeld, was conducted to his presence. The general had been defeated and repulsed, with all his division, at Daelitz, by the Poles and the old guard. Meerfeld, now our prisoner, had formerly been one of the negotiators of Campo Formio. At Austerlitz, too, he had been the bearer of the first proposition for an armistice. Napoleon, who, contrary to all evidence, still cherished hope of the success of new overtures to Austria, sent Meerfeld on a mission to the Emperor Francis.

"The general was instructed to urge on the attention of his Majesty such considerations as were calculated to convince him that the policy he was pursuing threatened the destruction of his daughter and grandson. He demanded an armistice on reasonable conditions. 'Depart,' said Napoleon to General Meerfeld, 'on your honourable mission of peace-maker. Should your efforts be crowned with success, you will secure the affection and gratitude of a great nation. The French people, as well as myself, earnestly wish for peace; if it be refused, we will defend the. inviolability of our territory to the last drop of our blood. The French have already shown that they know how to defend their country against foreign invaders.' Meerfeld left the French camp, and never returned.

"I was at a loss to comprehend how this fixed idea could have got possession of the superior mind of Napoleon. To the very last moment he laboured under a delusion with respect to Austria.

"On the night of the 17th the emperor was in a painful state of agitation, and anxiously looking for General Meerfeld, who, however, was destined not to return. Every movement in the camp annoyed him; his anxiety increased every moment; his features were contracted, and his countenance lividly pale. He threw himself into an easy chair which stood at the further end of the tent. 'I feel very ill,' said he, laying his hand on his stomach; 'my mind bears up, but my body sinks.'

"I will send for Ivan, exclaimed I, hurrying towards the door.

"'No, Caulincourt, I desire that you do not. The tent of a sovereign is as transparent as glass. I must be up, to see that every one is at his post.'

"Sire, said I, taking his burning hands in mine, I implore you to lie down and take some rest. Lie down, I entreat you.

"'I cannot—it is impossible—I must be up.'

"Permit me, Sire, to send for Ivan..

"'No, no—a sick soldier would, receive an hospital order; but I—I cannot share the indulgence that would be granted to the poor soldier.' As he uttered these words he heaved a deep sigh, and his head sunk languidly on his bosom.

"This scene," pursued the duke, "will never be effaced from my memory. The recollection of it inspired me with courage at the time when all was irreparably lost! At that terrible moment, when energy was nearly exhausted, when resolution was on the point of yielding in the struggle with despondency, then I thought of Napoleon on the night of the 17th of October. How trivial my own sufferings appeared in comparison with those of the noble victim.

"I approached the emperor. He took my hand, and pressing it feebly, he said, 'It is nothing—I shall soon be better. Take care that no one enters.'

"I was in an agony of alarm and apprehension at seeing the emperor in this sad condition. The enemy was pressing us on all sides. The fate of the thousands who were on the field of battle hung on the fate of Napoleon. I offered up to Heaven one of those tacit prayers to which no language can give adequate expression.

"After a little interval, the emperor, though still breathing with difficulty, said, 'I feel somewhat better, my dear Caulincourt.' He took my arm and walked two or three times slowly up and down the tent His countenance gradually resumed its wonted animation. Half an hour after this serious fit of illness, the emperor was surrounded by his staff, and was giving orders and dispatching messages to the different commanders of corps. He sent the Prince de Neufchatel to Randnitz, where the reserve of his guard was subsequently to support Ney. Day was beginning to dawn and the carnage was about to recommence.

"'This day,' said the emperor, as he mounted his horse, 'this day will resolve a great question. The destiny of France is about to be decided on the field of Leipsic Should we be victorious, all our misfortunes may yet be repaired; should we be conquered, it is impossible to foresee what may be the consequences of our defeat.' All the officers of the escort might have heard these words.

"About noon we were attacked on all points by the whole combined forces of the allies. Our army, reduced to less than a hundred thousand men, had now to oppose a force of three hundred and fifty thousand, concentrated *en masse* in a semi-circle of from three to four leagues in extent, and with twelve hundred pieces of cannon. Thus the enemy had constantly fresh troops in reserve to fill up the gaps caused by our artillery.

"Throughout that fatal day every hour was marked by a new misfortune—a new loss. The deaths of Generals Vial and Rochambeau were successively announced. The fog, the smoke, and the tumult of the *mêlée*, scarcely permitted us to recognise each other. We found it very difficult to follow the emperor. We repeatedly lost sight of him. He was continually moving from place to place, braving the greatest dangers, and disdaining life without victory.

"Hitherto the conflict had been maintained with various chances on both sides. An *aide-de-camp* of General Regnier arrived. He brought intelligence that the Saxon Army and the Wurtemberg cavalry, under General Normann,—that is to say, twelve thousand men and forty pieces of artillery, had gone over to Bernadotte. The latter had ordered the commander of the Saxon artillery to turn his guns and fire on the French. For some moments the emperor sat on his horse as motionless as a statue. He raised his eyes as if appealing to the justice of Heaven. 'Infamous!' he exclaimed. The word was repeated by a thousand voices.

"Imprecations and expressions of rage resounded on all sides. Several Saxon officers, who remained faithful to us, broke their swords, and overcome by shame for the baseness of their countrymen, retired to the rear of the army. 'No matter,' said a dragoon of the escort; 'we can do without the cowardly dogs. Your Majesty has still your French army to count upon!' He darted with the rapidity of lightning into the midst of the mêlée. Shouts of *Vive l'Empereur! Mort aux Saxons!* were echoed from mouth to mouth. All the escort followed the dragoon. The officers alone remained at their post near the emperor.

"A few minutes afterwards a young officer of hussars, whose name I forget, rushed headlong into the enemy's ranks. In a charge some of the miserable renegades had carried off one of our eagles. The gallant young officer rescued it, but it was at the cost of his life. He threw it at the emperor's feet, and then he himself fell, mortally wounded, and bathed in his blood. The emperor was deeply moved by this incident: 'With such men,' said he, 'what resources does France possess!'

"But valour and courage could not overcome destiny. Our ammunition was exhausted before our blood. For the first time we re-

125

tired from the field of battle without having conquered; and we commenced that fatal retreat, in which the unfortunate men who had escaped death in the conflict found their graves in the waters of the Elster, Thus perished Poniatowski, the idol of the brave and devoted Poles.

"On the morning of the 19th, the emperor proceeded to the palace of the King of Saxony. The sovereigns took an affectionate leave of each other. The king was inconsolable for the conduct of the Saxon Army; the blush of shame overspread his venerable forehead. The queen and the Princess Augusta offered the emperor every assurance of their friendly feeling: they were alarmed at the dangers to which he was exposed, and with uplifted hands, and eyes streaming with tears, they supplicated him to depart. The King of Saxony threw himself into Napoleon's arms, calling him his son and his friend, and the emperor tore himself from the embraces of this excellent family, whose conduct presented a consolatory picture amidst the many examples of royal turpitude!

"Murat separated from the emperor at Erfurt, under the pretext that his presence at Naples was indispensable for the defence of his kingdom. At the advanced posts, on the 22nd of October, he had stipulated conventions with Austria and England. I will not add a word to this fact. Murat expiated his crime by a terrible death: I respect his misfortune.

"Every day of our retreat was marked by a new engagement. We were doomed to reach France only by marching over the bleeding corses of our countrymen. At Hanau, the Imperial guard, the precious wreck of our valiant grand army, gained a victory over the combined Bavarian forces, commanded by General Wrede. This man, too, had earned all the distinction he was possessed of by serving for the space of ten years under the French flag. The emperor had conferred many favours on Wrede.

"On the 2nd of November we entered Mentz, and all our troops crossed the Rhine. The emperor then determined to proceed to Saint Cloud. Only six months had elapsed since we quitted that residence, and in that short space of time we had lost all—even hope!"

CHAPTER 12

Illness of the Duke de Vicenza

Several days elapsed before we had an opportunity of renewing our conversation with the Duke de Vicenza, who was so ill as to be compelled to keep his room. We visited him regularly; but the restorative which I had formerly employed with success was now no longer at my command. The pleasing recollections of Russia were exhausted, and I was, of course, anxious to divert the mind of the invalid from painful reminiscences.

But that knowledge of the heart, that exquisite tact with which the Duke de Vicenza was so eminently gifted, enabled him to discern the motives of my reserve.

Holding out his hand to me, he said, in a tone of kindness, "I observe that your questions have ceased, yet I feel assured that your curiosity is not gratified. But I see how it is: you check your curiosity from feelings of consideration towards me. You are reluctant to call back my memory to a period to which I cannot revert without pain; yet that period is almost constantly present in my thoughts. Profit, therefore, I entreat you, by the faint spark of life which yet animates me, and which will ere long be extinct."

"Oh! duke!" I exclaimed, "I entertain no such gloomy anticipations. On our return to Paris I trust we shall frequently have the happiness of enjoying your society; then your health will be improved, and I shall not hesitate to put your goodness under contribution."

"Now or never," said he, sorrowfully. "I feel that my life is fast ebbing away. To me the future has no promise. Grant me but a few days, and then we will resume our favourite subject."

"Well!" replied I, with difficulty restraining my tears, "we shall remain at Plombières until you depart If you continue ill, our services are at your command, and if you get better, we will take advantage of every fine day to renew our walks and conversations."

In mountainous districts the autumn is short Plombières, which had been so gay and so full of company on my arrival, was now almost asserted. The birds of passage, who had gone thither in quest of health or pleasure, were rapidly taking flight. The season for the waters was past, and we were almost the only visitors remaining in Plombières; yet how gladly would I have continued there the whole winter through, to hear the Duke de Vicenza describe the stirring events of the Empire. There were yet many incidents in the career of Napoleon which I wished to hear authentically related. The last acts of the great drama were of recent occurrence, and yet I knew them but superficially.

I was, above all, curious to be made acquainted with that striking period in the emperor's reign, the close of the year. 1813, when intrigue and treason were hatched under the very eyes of the sovereign, and in the bosom of the capital. Who so well qualified as the Minister for Foreign Affairs to furnish me with a key to the odious machinations which so powerfully contributed to overthrow the Imperial government?

I wished to accompany the faithful equerry of Napoleon to that, sacred apartment at Fontainbleau, to which the duke was one among the few admitted. I wished to follow him to the Palace of the Tuileries, where, during the Hundred Days, the brilliant hopes with which national enthusiasm had inspired the intrepid deserter from Elba vanished like a dream—I wished to hear the duke describe the dramatic scenes of Malmaison—that fairy palace, whose gilded saloons and perfumed gardens, once the abode of taste and happiness, became in 1813 the temporary jail of the condemned sovereign.

The duke's health gradually improved, and, after a little time, we resumed our morning excursions and our evening conversations.

"Do you recollect at what point I stopped?" said he.

"Perfectly," replied I. "You had brought the emperor from Mentz to St. Cloud."

"Well," pursued the duke, "I left him there and returned to Paris. I cannot describe the sort of boyish pleasure I felt at once more finding myself at home. To have an apartment to myself, and to lie on a bed, appeared to me the highest of all possible luxuries. Even now I cannot refrain from smiling when I think of the perfect contentment I enjoyed on the first night of my arrival. When I stretched myself on my bed, instead of falling asleep I contemplated by the light of the fire the interior of my chamber, which appeared to me a most magnificent place in comparison with the huts and hovels in which I had slept during the preceding six months.

"What had wrought this change in my ideas? Why did I feel thus joyful at my return? Had I not been present at every battle that had been fought for the space of fifteen years? Had I not slept at the bivouac, and endured every physical privation? But then, we were all light at heart and gay in spirit, and we readily forgot our sufferings and fatigues in the glory of the conquest, the pride of the victory.

"This last campaign, on the contrary, had been throughout gloomy and discouraging; there had been nothing to mitigate the misery which inevitably follows in the train of war. For the first time I enjoyed happiness unalloyed by that sort of mental torture which the Emperor so well defined when he exclaimed—*Phis un jour de repos!* What would I not have given to have been free to go and pass the winter fifty leagues from Paris, to escape the torments of every kind which I saw crowding upon me, and which were the unavoidable consequences of my political position.

"My first visit on my arrival in Paris was to an old female relative of mine, Madame de ——. She was an excellent woman, but an obstinate and uncompromising adherent of the Bourbons. In spite of her numerous absurdities, Madame de —— was animated by that pure and disinterested spirit of loyalty which never bends to circumstances. The emperor in the zenith of his glory was never, in her eyes, anything more than a fortunate adventurer, to whom, to her great regret, she saw me devoted, heart and soul. How often, in our disputes on this subject, have I smiled at her eternal remark—'Well, well, we shall see what will be the end of all this!' The commencement of the long predicted *end* had now arrived.

"I usually paid my visits to Madame de —— in the morning. She made an exception in my favour, but received me at what she termed her *petit lever*. Her circle of friends, consisting exclusively of *frondeurs* hostile to the empire, were of course not very agreeable to me, and I avoided coming into contact with them.

"Madame de —— uttered an exclamation of joy when she beheld me. 'Ah! My dear Armand,' she said, 'how happy I am to see you at home again! How have you managed to escape the many dangers yon have been exposed to? But few have returned to tell the tale of horror. What news do you bring?'

"None! you would not weep to hear it; and therefore I will not tell you my news.

"'Ah! my dear Armand, I can guess the riddle. Your enchanter has lost his wand, and the ludicrous metamorphoses he wrought are at an end. Of all the sovereigns he created nothing now remains but the shadow of an emperor; and I know one who has vowed to rid us of even that shadow.'

"My dear *madame!* do not speak thus, I entreat you. You have no idea how much you grieve me.

"'What! are you still under the influence of the sorcerer's spell? Have you not had enough of this imperial foolery? But, to be serious, my dear duke, do you not know what is going on.'

"No, said I, eagerly. I arrived only yesterday evening from the army.

"'Then you do not know that the empire, as you are pleased to call it, is rapidly tottering down—that all the powers of Europe have entered into a compact—

"What! interrupted I.

"'Have entered into a compact not to lay down arms until they hare razed from the list of sovereigns this great Usurper, who, for the space of fourteen years, has been playing a game with all the crowns in Europe. A distinguished individual (whose name I need not mention), who is too sharp-witted ever to be taken by surprise, has already made overtures to the Allied Powers, and taken precautions for every possible event that may ensue. If I were not afraid you would accuse me of slander, I should say that he has already sold the lion's skin for a good price. Others, too, have followed his example, and have taken active measures for making their peace with the rightful power. The revolution is imminent, yet a little while, and there will be but one man less in France, whilst tranquillity will be restored in Europe. Now do you understand?'

"Do you imagine, said I, that because a few miserable traitors are plotting the emperor's ruin, that that ruin is certain. The army is devoted to its chief, and its fidelity is incorruptible. There exists in the mass of the people an ardent sympathy with Napoleon; and among the higher ranks so many persons are compromised in his cause, whilst so many others have their existence attached to his fortune, that their interests are blended with his. Some will be actuated by honour, and others by affection, to support the man who has raised them from nothing; and their efforts will neutralise the base intrigues of those who would deliver France up to the power of foreigners.'

"'My dear duke, where have you come from? Your romantic notions will make you the laughing-stock of all Paris. Sympathy, fidelity, honour, and all those fine things, merely belong to the traditions of by-gone days: the revolution of '92 exploded all those notions. Formerly, honour consisted in the religious observance of an oath, in the fulfilment of the most sacred of duties, in fidelity to one's sovereign. If that sovereign were unfortunate, the greater were his claims to sacrifices and respect. But the good old times of Henri IV. are past, never to return. Who cares now for an unfortunate king? Now-a-days, my dear Armand, honour consists in preserving one's rank, one's fortune, no matter by what means, even though it should be by walking over the body of him to whom we owe that rank and fortune. Alas! we live in a very wicked world.'

"These words conveyed a horrible truth:—they were a revelation of the misfortunes of the future. I remained silent, overwhelmed by gloomy reflections.

"'In a word, my dear duke,' pursued Madame de ——, your hero has descended from his pedestal. He has been conquered, and that is a crime which the world never pardons. Were you to visit, this very night, twenty of the best drawing-rooms in Paris, you would find the condemnation of Napoleon written in every face and uttered by every mouth. Those who have solicited Imperial favours may be distinguished by the fury of their attacks and the bitterness of their language. Truly! one would suppose the poor emperor to be responsible for all the meanness to which they resorted, to gain admittance to his service. Then there are the newly-made nobles, the senators, with their endowments of a hundred thousand *francs*, the *parvenu* duchesses, countesses, baronesses, &c.

"'All these people imagined that their greatness was to last for ever, and they cannot endure the thought of descending again to their proper level. The possibility of this metamorphosis drives them mad. There is a host of people here in Paris who owe everything to your Napoleon, and who are the loudest in abusing him for his ambition, and for staking their places and dignities on the result of a battle. Really, this ingratitude is disgusting! Even the very valets in the ante-chambers look with contempt on their masters! However, happen what may, my dear Armand, I would rather see you in the class of dupes than in that of traitors!'

"I took leave of Madame de ——, racked by the most painful feelings. I beheld with horror the abyss which was yawning before us. We were manoeuvring over a volcano. Public opinion was rising against the emperor. Opposed to that formidable power, the wisest combinations must fail. The ruin of France was evident from this simple fact.

"In the evening I made some visits to persons attached to the court. Though no one ventured, in my presence, to express feelings of hostility to the emperor, yet I could discern, through the air of reserve and the polite restraint which pervaded the conversation in reference to political events, that discontent and opposition were the uppermost feelings in every mind. Madame de —— had given me a true picture of the state of affairs. Of this I was fully convinced, when I observed the moral physiognomy of the saloons of Paris, at the end of the year 1813.

"I returned home, weary and disgusted at the utter want of principle manifested in what are called the higher ranks; and I almost looked back with regret on my camp life. There every hardship and privation was counterbalanced by the consolation of witnessing acts of heroism and noble disinterestedness, by being surrounded by generous spirits, who would willingly have made any sacrifice to serve a sovereign from whom, possibly, they had received no personal favours.

"The melancholy picture of human nature which I now beheld around me, produced a depression of spirits which speedily affected my health.

"Circumstances did not permit me to live entirely in seclusion, but I restricted my circle of association as much as possible, and with the exception of a few friends with whom I could, as it were, think aloud, I maintained no intercourse with society.

"The intelligence of the death of Count Louis de Narbonne," pursued the Duke de Vicenza, "came upon me like a thunder-bolt. The event took place at Torgan, on the 17th of November. After the count's embassy to Vienna, the emperor had appointed him governor of the fortress of Torgan. His death was caused by a fall from his horse. I never understood the reasons which prompted the strange nomination of Narbonne to the command of a fortress. The emperor never gave me any explanation on this point, but it is certain that the emperor's mind fostered an unjust prejudice, to which he yielded without being willing to avow it. During the latter period of his embassy to Vienna, Narbonne found himself placed quite in a false position.

"The emperor observed that Narbonne was born to be an ambassador. So he was; but what availed all his skill and finesse when opposed to the determined resolution not to accede to any proposition made by France? Ill fortune sometimes renders men unjust; and this was the emperor's case in reference to Narbonne. Napoleon was dissatisfied with his ambassador because he had not succeeded in enforcing his propositions. I am the more inclined to believe that this was the ground of the emperor's unfavourable feeling towards Narbonne, judging from the lukewarm reception he gave me on my return from Prague, where I had also failed in the object of my mission.

"Poor Narbonne! he was severely mortified at the sort of disgrace into which he had fallen, though unconscious of the real cause. He begged of me to sound the emperor on the subject. I did so. But Napoleon gave no explanation, and Narbonne departed from Torgan.

"I called to mind the last conversations I had had with Narbonne at Vienna and at Prague. He was gifted with that sort of happy temperament which enables its possessor to see only the bright side of things. He always knew how to find a pleasant point even in the most untoward events.

"Count de Narbonne's perfect elegance of manner and language, joined to his good-humoured cheerfulness, and a certain *savoir faire*, rendered him a peculiar favourite in the highest circles in Vienna, and likewise had their effect in charming the emperor. You will perhaps smile when I tell you that, in spite of his advanced age (he was then sixty), I could name more than one young and pretty woman who was not insensible to the gallantry of our *vieux jeune homme*. One day at Prague, when I was complimenting him on his *bonnes fortunes*, he said,—'My dear duke, at twenty, a man adores women for their own sakes, and he would load his back with the towers of Notre Dame to lay them at their feet; because men at twenty years of age are fools. At forty, we love women for our sakes; because, at forty, we grow selfish. At sixty, we do not love at all; in fact, we care nothing at all about women, except in so far as they may be useful to us; because, at sixty, men are calculators, and nothing more.'

"What an *infidel* you are, count, said I, laughing.

"'Not at all,' replied he, 'I am merely confessing that I am sixty years of age, and not in love. The truth is, that, in paying my court to the fair ladies of Vienna, I find opportunities of forwarding my ambassadorial interests. I do not see why I should entertain any scruples on this head; we have a right to gain an advantage over the enemy by any means in our power. I am absolutely incensed against these Austrians; their conduct is like that of savages. After the Emperor Francis has given us his daughter, they affect to treat us as parvenus. They are lamentably deficient in good-breeding.'

133

"With this sort of levity the gay Count de Narbonne treated the most serious affairs in the world. He was a diplomatist after his own fashion; and a very able one, too, I assure you.

"I shall remember as long as I live the time when he was with the army, in 1812. The emperor wrote to Narbonne, desiring him to come and receive his instructions. We had then no quarters but such as the field of battle afforded; and it was irresistibly droll to hear Narbonne, in his tent, lamenting the absence of all those comforts and elegancies which he had never before experienced the want of. 'Seriously,' said he, 'I cannot comprehend the possibility of sleeping and living in these canvass apartments, open to the wind and to every intruder, and in which a man cannot even dress or undress without being observed.' To Narbonne, the business of the *toilette* was a most important affair; and he invariably devoted to it at least two hours every day. Whilst he was employed in adorning his person, the interior of his tent would have furnished an admirable subject for a caricaturist.

"For want of a carpet, a luxury which he regarded as indispensable, even on a field of battle, his *valet de chambre* had spread over the floor of his tent all the spare bed-covers and curtains he could collect. His table was like the counter of a perfumer's shop, covered with gallipots, scent-bottles, brushes, combs, &c, and the count, in his elegant *robe de chambre* and slippers, paced up and down with an air of ludicrous misery, venting imprecations on the inconveniences to which he was subjected. 'Tents may be all very well for military men,' said he, 'but ambassadors are quite out of their element in them. It was a strange whim of his Majesty to command my presence here.' At length, when he was dressed, powdered, and perfumed, *vaille que vaille*, to use his own expression, he would cast a last glance at his little mirror, and taking his hat and gloves from the hands of his *valet de chambre*, would sally forth from his tent to wait on his Majesty. Then the poor count was beset by new troubles, and it was the most ridiculous thing imaginable to see him in full court costume striding over *caissons*, knapsacks, and all the numberless impediments that intercepted his passage.

"The soldiers stared at him as though he had been some wonderful curiosity. Narbonne happened to be at that time the only man in the camp who attached any vast importance to dress and appearance. This circumstance in itself would have sufficed to render him remarkable, independently of the eccentricity of his costume, which was in every particular that of the last century. On finding himself thus the object of general observation, he would shrug his shoulders and say, 'I wish to heaven his Majesty would grant me my farewell audience. How happy should I be to make my bow.'

"I heard of the death of Count de Narbonne at the Tuileries, from the mouth of the emperor himself. He sent for me one evening, and on my arrival I found him just concluding the perusal of a dispatch. He looked dejected, and laying the dispatch on his desk, he said to me, abruptly, 'Narbonne is dead!'

"Narbonne dead! exclaimed I, with astonishment, and scarcely able to believe what I heard.

"'I am sorry, very sorry for it,' continued the emperor. 'Narbonne was an excellent man—his honour and patriotism were of the true antique mould. He was one of those noblemen of Old France, of whom so few specimens are extant. This is a severe loss.'

"Possibly Napoleon's recollection of the injustice with which he had treated the count caused him to feel the event more keenly than he might otherwise have done. He paced up and down the room with his hands crossed behind his back, and said,—'During the last two years ill-fortune has pursued me with remarkable tenacity. Death has mercilessly thinned the number of my friends. Duroc, Bessières, and others, are now no more. All my most faithful and valued servants are gradually disappearing. When will fate relent?'

"The mind of Napoleon," pursued the Duke de Vicenza, "was of too elastic a temperament to remain long depressed by any event of ordinary occurrence. He could pass from one subject to another with inconceivable celerity. Thus, by a sudden transition, breaking the train of gloomy reflections which had been conjured up by the death of the Count de Narbonne, he said to me:—

"'Caulincourt, I am going to give you the portfolio of foreign affairs.'

"How, Sire?

"'A new congress is to be opened at Manheim. I mean to send you thither as my plenipotentiary. You are the man to negotiate with the sovereigns.'

"I made a gesture indicative of dissent

"'*Parbleu!* I say you are the negotiator who will succeed best You are to go to Manheim—therefore prepare for your departure as speedily as possible.'

"But, Sire, is there any connexion between the mission which I am about to fulfil at Manheim, and my appointment to the department of foreign affairs ?"

"'I will explain this matter to you. A set of dissatisfied meddling people have started a question which I wish to resolve by giving you the portfolio of foreign affairs. Maret is accused of having dissuaded me from concluding the peace for which you were negotiating at Prague. This is an egregious absurdity. But to deprive the credulous and ill-disposed of every pretext for believing this nonsense, and to drive the allies to the wall, you are made both minister and plenipotentiary. This, I think, will satisfy them.'

"Your Majesty knows that I am entirely at your command.

"'What else can we do, Caulincourt,' interrupted he. 'If the burden be heavy to you it certainly is not light to me. We must no longer count on our strength—we must spare no efforts.'

"My appointment," continued the duke, "was ordered to be announced in the *Moniteur* before I was made acquainted with it. It appeared in that journal in the morning, and I did not quit the Tuileries until two hours after midnight. This is the way things were managed at that time. It never occurred to the emperor that anyone would hesitate to serve him at the sacrifice of any personal convenience.

"I made my preparations in the course of the day, and about ten at night I proceeded to the Tuileries, where I had a long conference with the emperor. I begged of him to tell me whether it was his fixed intention to adhere to the last-basis laid down by the Allied Powers, and which had been communicated by Prince Metternich. I urged him to give me his sincere ultimatum, that I might be enabled to close decidedly with the Allied Plenipotentiaries, who were doubtless furnished with positive instructions. The emperor did not answer my questions categorically. He managed, with wonderful address, to veil the secret of his real designs.

"This was one of the striking peculiarities of Napoleon. In conversation on general topics, his interlocutor would find himself perfectly at his ease, and Napoleon maintained his share in the discussion with a grace and *bonhommie* which never failed to exercise a captivating influence. But in a conversation on any important subject the emperor was cautious and reserved; he was always master of himself, and he imposed a certain degree of restraint on the person with whom he was discoursing. He seemed, as it were, to take advantage of his exalted position, and willingly, or reluctantly, his interlocutor was almost always brought over to his way of thinking.

"But at the period to which I here refer, Napoleon was struggling against a host of adverse circumstances. In pointing out this unamiable trait in his manner, I feel bound to bear evidence to the many amiable points which counterbalanced it. At Schoenbrunn and at Tilsit, where, being victorious, he might have unrestrainedly exercised his power, he was magnanimous and merciful, and he proved himself, in the strict sense of the term, a great sovereign. When at the pinnacle of his glory, he yielded to every noble and glorious inspiration—he was al-powerful, and yet he never abused his power over the conquered. Then he disdained art and dissimulation, those resources of the weak. He felt the consciousness of his greatness, and he was sincere and generous. The benefits conferred by Napoleon have been vilely forgotten. France ought to enregister them among her proudest titles of glory.

"But I am wandering from the thread of my narrative," said the duke, smiling. "I will return to it.

"The emperor closed his last instructions to me with these remarkable words:—'I wish for peace—I wish for it without any reservation or afterthought. But, Caulincourt, I will never accede to dishonourable conditions. It is wished that peace should be based on the independence of all nations;—be it so. This is one of the Utopian dreams of which experience will prove the fallacy. My policy is more enlightened than that of these men who are *born kings*, (This expression, so highly significant in the mouth of the *soldier of fortune*, was frequently employed by Napoleon in his moments of irritation.) Those men have never quitted their gilded cages, and have never read history, except with their tutors!'

"After remaining for some moments silent, he thus resumed:—'Tell them—I impress upon them, with all the authority we are entitled to exercise, that peace can be durable only inasmuch as it shall be reasonable and just towards all parties. To demand absurd concessions,—to impose conditions which cannot be acceded to consistently with the dignity and importance of France, is to declare a deadly war against me. I will never consent to leave France less than I found her. Were I to do so, the whole nation *en masse* would be entitled to call me to account. Go, Caulincourt; you comprehend all the difficulties of my position—you have a perfect knowledge of men and things. Depart, and Heaven grant that you may succeed!'

"Whilst I was taking leave of him, he added—'Do not spare couriers. Send me intelligence every hour. You know how anxious I shall be.'

"The negotiations of Manheim were a source of mortification and disappointment. I must, however, affirm,—for I will not compromise

137

my opinion, in deference to unjust prejudice or senseless clamour—I must affirm that I obtained countenance and assistance from the Emperor of Russia. That sovereign possessed a just and elevated mind. He wished to put it out of the power of France to injure him; but he was far from wishing her destruction. This fact is evident from his conduct in 1814. I cannot say as much for the friendly disposition of the diplomatic agents at the Congress. But Alexander was his own master, and in satisfying public feeling in Russia, which was violently roused against France, he found that he could consent to a peace honourable to Napoleon.

"Our real enemies, they who had vowed our destruction, were England, Austria, and Sweden. There was a determined resolution to exterminate Napoleon, and consequently all negotiations proved fruitless. Every succeeding day gave birth to a new conflict. In proportion as we accepted what was offered, new pretensions rose up; and no sooner was one difficulty smoothed down than we had to encounter another. I know not how I mustered sufficient firmness and forbearance to remain calm amidst so many outrages.

"The bases proposed in the correspondence with Austria were nearly acceptable, though the emperor, as I have already observed, still hesitated. I left the Tuileries with powers to treat, with the exception of some restrictions. On my arrival at the Congress, Metternich, under pretext that the emperor had not given his sanction with sufficient promptitude, withdrew his propositions, and the new conditions presented to me were ridiculous. I demanded that the points in dispute should be restored to the footing on which they stood at the time the first plan of the treaty was drawn up. As far as Russia was concerned, my demand would have been complied with; but in relation to the other coalesced powers my negotiations fell to the ground.

"The opinions of the committee organised in Paris for the subversion of the Imperial government, reacted like a directing power in the deliberations of the allies. The destinies of France were in the hands of an able coterie, who were stimulated and encouraged by our recent defeats. France, with the wreck of her incomparable army, held out against all Europe; but treason, organised in the heart of the capital, furnished to the enemy the secret of our last means of defence, gave him the exact cipher of our squares, and indicated with atrocious precision the final term of our resistance."

"Oh! I exclaimed, indignantly, surely there is not, either in this world or the next, a punishment sufficiently severe to expiate the crimes of men who would betray their country."

"The punishment is yet to come," murmured the duke.

"I was convinced of the uselessness of my efforts, and plainly perceived the Machiavelic after-thought which protracted these lingering discussions without any intention of bringing them to a result. I accordingly wrote to the emperor, assuring him that these conferences, pompously invested with the title of a congress, served merely to mask the irrevocably fixed determination not to treat with France; that the time we were thus losing was employed by the Allied Powers in assembling their forces for the purpose of invading us on all points at once—that by further temporizing we should unavoidably augment the disadvantages of our position.

"The extraordinary levy of three hundred thousand men was then definitively determined on, and the famous declaration of Frankfort immediately made its appearance. The motive of the *Senatus Consultum* was represented by the Allies, in their incendiary proclamation, as a new provocation of the Emperor Napoleon to the coalesced powers, with the view of enforcing peace.

"The negotiations were once more broken off, and though I had personally received at the Congress every mark of esteem and consideration, yet my mission was attended by so many unpleasant circumstances, that I could not regret its termination.

"I verily believe that no diplomatist ever found himself placed in so unpleasant a position as I was during my missions to Prague, Frankfort, and Châtillon. Two years had scarcely elapsed since the time when France laid down the law to Europe, and now it was her turn to be ruled insolently and arrogantly by those whom she had spared.

"I arrived in Paris at two in the morning, and I drove straight to the Tuileries. The emperor had given orders that I should be conducted to him at whatever hour I might arrive. When I entered his cabinet he was dictating to his secretaries. He immediately dismissed them. As soon as they were gone he darted a scrutinizing glance on me, and said, in a voice faltering with emotion:—

"'Well! you have not succeeded in bringing them to reasonable terms. They regard me as a lost man, with whom they may trifle with impunity.' As he uttered these words his contracted lips gave a fearful expression to his countenance.

"Sire, said I, the declaration of Frankfort is so explicit that there is no possibility of misunderstanding the intentions which dictated it. The deceitful assurances given to France emanate from an atrocious conspiracy. The object of the Allied Powers is to separate the cause of France from that of your Majesty.

"'But,' interrupted he, eagerly, 'the French people have too much good sense to be caught by such a bait as that to abandon me would be to overwhelm themselves with disgrace. The interests of the country would perish in the abyss into which my subjects would hurl me.'

"Sire, in the circumstances in which we are placed I see but one resource.

"'What is it?' and then, without awaiting my reply, he added, 'Who would presume to seat himself on the throne of France after me? Who would pretend to govern a people whom twenty years of conquest have impressed with the consciousness of their own power and importance? Where is the bold adventurer, who, regardless of the future, could conceive the idea of enslaving a nation which is to be ruled only by glory? Since the 21st of January, of sanguinary memory, what can a king of France be, unless be govern by the authority of his own acts. He must be a slave, or, what is worse, *a man too much*. The impulse is given—sons are inspired by the recollections of their fathers. The heroic phasis of the Empire will be to the French people the palladium before which must fall all common-place mediocrity imposed by foreign domination. There is no other national spirit in France but the love of glory and the hatred of foreigners.'

"Whilst the emperor spoke thus he stood with his elbow resting on the mantelpiece, and one leg crossed over the other. The candelabra lighted his whole figure from head to foot, and enabled me to observe all the play of his expressive countenance. The fire of inspiration which beamed in his eyes, his animated gestures, his prophetic language altogether, presented a somewhat supernatural effect He looked as though he had been born to rule the world. I gazed on him with a mingled feeling of admiration and sorrow. In the zenith of his glory, the hero saw tottering on every side the edifice which his own genius had raised. His courage seemed to increase with his misfortunes, and he beheld them undismayed.

"These recollections are indelible," added the Duke de Vicenza, in a tone of deep emotion. "In calling to mind the scene which I have just described, I can almost fancy I behold Napoleon before me; the inflexions of his voice seem even now to vibrate in my ear.

"The emperor remained for some moments silent, and then, as if awakening from a dream, he said:—'What is your opinion, Caulincourt? What course would you suggest?

"Sire, replied I, it appears to me that, at the point at which affairs have arrived, your Majesty owes to the French nation a full and candid publication of the documents which were the first bases of the conferences of Manheim. It will be unsafe to conceal the bad faith of the Allied Powers, or any of the causes which render, on your Majesty's part, the conclusion of peace impossible.

"'That will not do,' said he. 'Why excite alarm and discouragement in the public mind? Besides, there is already a tendency to exaggerate the difficulties of my position.'

"Unfortunately, Sire, the reality is so bad that it scarcely admits of exaggeration. As I uttered these words he made a gesture of dissatisfaction and impatience. Our position, proceeded I, is desperate, unless by a great effort of national power the whole people voluntarily concur in the defence of their territory. It ought to be made known to the French people that the Allies refuse to treat with France. A candid declaration on the part of your Majesty would acquaint the nation with its danger, and at the same time show the resources we yet possess, and the chances of success insured to us, if we rise *en masse* in defence of our frontiers.

"'*Ah baste!*' said the emperor, 'You take a chivalrous view of everything, Caulincourt. An appeal to the patriotism of the nation! Only reflect on the consequences! Doubtless such an appeal would have an electric effect; but consider the power it would throw into the bands of the plebeian class, who always play so conspicuous a part in these revolutionary movements, and who render them so dangerous. On the day after a popular victory, the throne would be the spoil of the first bold adventurer who—'

"And yet, interrupted I, it is by means of levies *en masse* that the Allied Powers have, in the space of a few months, driven us from their fortresses and their territories; it is with their unprepared militias that they now hem in our frontiers.

"'If you wish to form an accurate judgment of things, you must not compare the French people to any other. What has succeeded in other countries, would ruin me in France. But, at all events, in any hypothesis, I have always your scheme as a resource in the last extremity. It would be premature now.'

"Now, Sire, I exclaimed, irritated at the inconceivable blindness of the emperor,—we are now arrived at the last extremity.

"'I am not of your opinion,' said he, petulantly.'

"Has your Majesty any orders for me? said I, taking up my hat.

"He looked at me steadfastly, and then advancing to me, said, 'Caulincourt, you allow your imagination to mislead you. It is necessary to meet misfortunes coolly, or they will overcome us. I see you are fatigued; go and take some rest, and come to me again in the forenoon. We will have a little conversation before the meeting of the Council.'"

CHAPTER 13

The Continental Blockade

"The clock of the Tuileries struck six," said the Duke de Vicenza, "as I closed that conversation with the emperor which I related to you yesterday. I was much fatigued, for I had travelled from Frankfort to Paris without stopping. I never alighted from my carriage till I arrived at the Tuileries. On reaching home, I immediately threw myself on my bed to take a few hours' rest, and in the morning I again waited on the emperor, whom I found quite restored to good humour.

"Napoleon was subject to fits of irritability. When he could not find good arguments to convince those who differed from him, he would manifest his dissent by a dry answer. If after this he was still contradicted, he would become irritated, and his anger would sometimes be carried to violent lengths. I was not of a temper to tolerate these paroxysms patiently; and therefore, whenever I found the conversation taking an unpleasant turn, I always contrived to cut it short, and to take my leave. This used to vex him exceedingly; and yet he would seldom suffer me to depart without soothing by a kind word any unpleasant feeling to which his warmth might have given rise. Then, without any further explanation, harmony was restored between us. Sometimes he would jokingly call me *Monsieur de Tufier*, but he had too much tact and dignity of mind to wish me to play the courtier to his faults.

"During the campaign of Moscow, a very sharp discussion ensued between the emperor and me. I consequently quitted the headquarters and removed to a garret which an officer had the goodness to give up to me, together with his straw mattress. This, considering the privations of the time, was a tolerably comfortable abode. Berthier was sent by the emperor to request me to return; but I refused, for I was resolved to relinquish those functions which brought me into personal contact with Napoleon. I even wrote to beg that he would give me a command in Spain. He sent back my letter, at the bottom of which were written, in his own hand, the following words:—

'I have no wish to send you to Spain to be shot. Come and see me; I expect you.'

The emperor, as soon as he saw me, laughed, and holding out his hand, said:—'You know, Caulincourt, we are like two lovers. We cannot live apart.'

"Our misunderstanding had lasted three days. This was very long; but after that time our quarrels became much less frequent.

"About the end of 1813 the emperor, contrary to his custom, often appeared in public, accompanied by the empress. One evening he attended the opera; the performance was *Cleopatra*, and it was for the benefit of Madame Grassini. The theatre was crowded, and their Majesties were vehemently applauded on their entrance. At the close of one of the acts the Emperor retired to the ante-room adjoining his box, and, without any observation to lead to the subject, he said to me:—'So, the Faubourg Saint-Germain is stirring again!—These people are quite incorrigible.' I was on my guard; and I made no reply.

"'They speak violently against me. Have you heard anything, Caulincourt?'

"No one, said I, would dare to attack your Majesty in my hearing.

"'They are intriguing with their usual stupidity; these petty *maniganceurs* are not dangerous; but, nevertheless, I cannot help feeling indignant at the ingratitude of a set of people, most of whom I have extricated from misery. I restored to them their sequestrated estates; and, in compliance with their obsequious and mean supplications, I have given them appointments about my court And here they are, like ungrateful valets, speaking all the ill they can of the master who has fed them. Really, this is odious! The fact is, I have done too much for the Fabourg Saint-Germain. I will put an end to all this intriguing by and by.'

"It is very certain," pursued the Duke de Vicenza, "that if the emperor had followed the advice then given him, which was, to send a certain personage to Vincennes, he would have done right That traitor was the soul of all the intrigues and plots then brewing; and his long-established intimacy with almost all the members of the foreign *corps diplomatiques* gave him very great influence. The rest of the intriguers were sufficiently ill-disposed, but they were persons without weight or importance. The emperor thought them too insignificant to do much mischief; but he was wrong.

"A few days afterwards, on the breaking up of the council, Savary, the minister of the police, presented to the emperor a packet of papers and a portfolio.

"'What is this!' inquired Napoleon.

"'Sire, these are proofs corroborative of the facts to which I have often, but in vain, called the attention of your Majesty.'

"The emperor drew one of the letters from the packet, and whilst he perused it I observed a frown gather on his brow. When he had finished reading the letter, Savary related the following circumstances:—

"Madame La ―― (I will not mention her name, from feelings of respect to the honourable family of which she is a member,) had been pointed out to the police as one of the most active agents of the *coterie* of the Faubourg Saint-Germain. Being a spirited and enterprising woman, she was selected by the directing committee to convey to Germany information useful to the cause for which the royalists were intriguing. It must be confessed that admirable discernment was manifested in the choice of the messenger. Madame La ―― was still young and pretty, and possessed a vast share of talent and intelligence. In addition to these powers of fascination she was distinguished for a degree of enthusiasm and courage which it was expected would enable her to subdue any difficulties she might encounter in the fulfilment of her mission.

"I know not what pretext she set forth as the motive of her departure from France; but, having obtained a regular passport for Mentz, the female ambassador quitted Paris about the 3rd or 4th of December. She set off in an elegant *calèche*, laden with trunks, filled with a choice assortment of superb dresses. This was the lady's diplomatic baggage. But who could possibly have suspected any mischief? Nothing ever appeared more innocent than the lady and her journey.

"Accompanied by a confidential domestic, Madame La ―― proceeded with confident security on her journey to Mentz, dreaming of parties, balls, conquests, &c. Alas! these delightful dreams were of short duration; and on waking from them, the lady found herself surrounded by a party of *gendarmes*. The door of the carriage was rudely opened; and, without ceremony, Madame La ―― was informed that she most alight. Tears and supplications were unavailing; the lady was compelled to obey, and the agents of the police commenced a minute

145

search in the interior of the *calèche*. They were well convinced that something was to be found, and yet they could find nothing. Meanwhile, the lady, who was kept standing in the road shivering with cold, finding that the search was likely to prove fruitless, began to regain her courage, and ventured to utter threats. She declared her determination to complain of the shameful violation of personal liberty;—her passport was perfectly *en regle*. Had the age of terror returned, that such acts of violence could be committed with impunity on a poor inoffensive female? These, and a thousand similar lamentations were uttered by Madame La ——, until she was suddenly silenced by the discovery of a place of concealment which had been most ingeniously contrived at the back of the carriage. In it were found the correspondence, a portfolio containing bills of exchange on Frankfort and other places, and fifteen thousand *francs* in gold.

"Threats were now succeeded by tears and supplications, accompanied by offers of large rewards to the *gendarmes*. The lady's distress might have melted hearts of stone; but the *gendarmes* were insensible, and above all, incorruptible. Madame La —— found that there was no alternative but to return to Paris in company with three *sbirri*, who very cavalierly seated themselves in the carriage with the fair traveller. At daybreak the equipage entered the court yard of the minister of the police. The papers, &c., were taken from their hiding place, and verified in the presence of the lady, who, after a long examination, was, together with her servant, consigned to a place of security.

"The contents of the papers were exceedingly curious. They proved that, however active might be the vigilance of the police, there was still a possibility of eluding it. We read several proclamations, printed at Sceaux, by a press which had been clandestinely fitted up in the cellars of a *château* belonging to a M. Lamy. The information was very carefully drawn up, and presented a perfectly correct picture of the state of France. The impression produced on the public mind by the levy of the three hundred thousand men was described;—mention was made of the misery of the working classes, the distressed state of agriculture, and the stagnation of trade, which excited general discontent. A great deal was said respecting the diminished popularity of the emperor since his reverses, and the disaffection openly manifested towards him. The conclusion was, that the French people looked to the Allies as their liberators, and earnestly prayed for their arrival.

"There were numerous little perfumed *billets*, sealed with crests, and addressed to the Count de Saint Priest. Their contents were appeals to old relationship or friendship, and entreaties that the count would use his influence with his Majesty the Emperor of Russia. Every arrangement was said to have been made for seconding the Allies in their generous enterprise. Agents were established in all the principal towns of France to facilitate the entrance of the invaders.

"Many other letters, written in the same spirit, were addressed to foreign diplomatists; and among the papers there were documents obtained, I know not how, from the ministers of the war department and the interior. This seizure was very important, and it gave rise to serious alarm. We were lost in conjecture as to the means by which the legitimists had procured certain information;—there now seemed every reason to apprehend that they might renew, with better success, the attempt which had recently failed.

"The emperor inquired whether every precaution had been taken for keeping the arrest of Madame La —— a secret. Savary replied, that the servant and the postilion, the only individuals who had witnessed the arrest, were lodged in a place of security, so that there was no possibility of the affair becoming known.

"Savary urged the emperor to adopt measures for putting a stop to these plots against his government. The removal of some of the ringleaders of these dangerous conspiracies would have sufficed to awe the rest. None of the criminals cherished a grateful remembrance of Napoleon's magnanimity. The emperor might on this occasion have made a terrible example; but he disdained revenge.

"After Savary's departure he read over most of the documents, and truly their contents were of a nature to irritate him. He uttered a few indignant exclamations, but did not evince any violent anger. He threw some of the papers into the fire, and placed the rest in a drawer of his desk. He appeared much grieved; and, after a few moments silence, he said to me:—'Caulincourt, could you have conceived such atrocity?'

"Napoleon was always averse to punish; he never, without deep regret, inflicted punishment on persons whom he had known. During the space of a few months so many illusions had vanished, and he had witnessed so much deception, that he became almost indifferent to the injuries of which he was the object. He felt the necessity of summoning all his energies to meet the great events that were impending, and he could not bend his mind to little things. I likewise remarked that his habitual petulance had given place, on many occasions, to a calmness which was not natural to him. It might be that his physical organization was beginning to sink beneath the exhausting efforts of every kind to which he had been exposed.

"Every successive day brought some disastrous intelligence to add to the embarrassment of our situation. The fortresses which we still defended in Germany were escaping from us one by one; and thus we were losing men, ammunition, provisions, and valuable resources of every description, which went to enrich the enemy. The levy of three hundred thousand men was easily effected; but we were pressed for time. It was now December, and the Allies were advancing by forced marches. On the 1st of January, 1814, they crossed the French frontiers.

"The emperor said no more to me respecting my proposition of appealing to the French people, nevertheless, I am still of opinion that this was the only measure that could hare averted our ruin. National intelligence must have perceived that the simultaneous concurrence of all in the common defence would ensure to every man the inviolability of his home, and the preservation of his property. The foreign powers could not have effected their invasion in defiance of armed France. How often, during this terrible period of the campaign of 1814, did the words used by Napoleon at Duben recur to my memory—'*Fate decrees the fall of nations!*' We now saw this axiom fearfully verified.

"In obedience to the emperor's orders I departed, at the beginning of January, for the headquarters of the Allies, where new and useless negotiations were opened. I have already spoken to you of the Congress of Châtillon, and I really have not courage to turn back to that gloomy page of my recollections. It was, I think, on the 25th, that the emperor quitted the capital to place himself at the head of the army, which had already fallen back to Saint-Dizier.

"Then commenced that miraculous campaign in which the genius of Napoleon shone with immortal lustre. Never did troops execute more scientific manoeuvres, or display greater prodigies of valour. In the campaign of France were renewed the wonders which marked Napoleon's heroic career in Italy. The close of the emperor's military life exhibits the most extraordinary defence recorded in the annals of war.

"I rejoined the emperor at Saint-Dizier, after the rupture of the conferences, and I was very glad to find myself again at headquarters. I cannot attempt to describe the misery I suffered during the negotiations at Châtillon. I could obtain only evasive answers, at a time when it was incumbent on me to treat at any sacrifice. The veil of illusion

148

was raised, and the reality was visible in all its horror. But even then we might look forward to the future—now, the grave is all that remains."

"The letters, duke," said I, "which you wrote at the time you are now alluding to, will remain. a lasting monument of your efforts and courage. Baron Fain's *Manuscrit de* 1814, devotes to you some fine pages in the history of our misfortunes."

"My letters presented but a faint outline of the sentiments I expressed in my private conversations with the emperor. On the eve of my departure from Châtillon I returned home, weary of those eternal conferences in which the bad faith and bad spirit of the Allies were but too manifest. The ground was no longer tenable. I found it necessary that I should communicate personally with the emperor, and I gave orders for my departure.

"With a mind harassed and unfitted for occupation, I threw myself on a sofa. I was unable to sleep, and I had fallen into a train of melancholy reveries, from which I was aroused by the sound of the rustling of paper. Turning my eyes in the direction whence the sound proceeded, I perceived a pamphlet, which someone was thrusting under the door. Who is there? said I; an emphatic *hush!* warned me to be silent. I rose eagerly, seized the pamphlet, and I heard the footsteps of the person recede from the door. The moon was shining brightly. I went to the window, and, drawing aside the curtain, I perceived a young man, wrapped in a cloak, and with his hat drawn down over his forehead. He crossed the court yard at a rapid pace; but before he passed through the gate leading to the street, he stopped, and turning his eyes towards the window of my cabinet, he placed his finger on his lip, and disappeared.

"By the tall figure of the stranger, and his fair curled hair, I immediately recognised one of the secretaries of the Russian Embassy. Alexander is no more, and I will not name the young secretary, for fear of compromising him,

"The pamphlet which was thus mysteriously conveyed to me had been brought to Châtillon on the preceding night by an extraordinary courier; and a copy had been presented to each ambassador. It was entitled—*De la nécessité de renverser Bonaparte, et de retablir les Bourbons, par le Lieutenant-Colonel du génie de Brichambault.*

"This libel, emanating from the pen of a French officer, was calculated to produce a great effect on the Allied Sovereigns, by directing their attention to the consequences so speciously pointed out. There was a diabolical Machiavelism in the idea of conjuring up before the eyes of the sovereigns the fearful phantom of a universal republic, and representing it as a necessity which Napoleon would not scruple to employ for the purpose of tempting the French people to pardon a dishonourable peace. To this libel were joined statements and calculations relating to the actual force of the army, its state of moral discouragement, &c.

"Safely entrenched in the midst of the enemy's camp, the author, a French officer, disgraced by the emperor, and exiled to Nancy, had basely kindled this torch of revenge on his country.

"The perfidious insinuation presented to the Holy Alliance was of a nature to exercise great influence on the final determination of the Sovereigns, and it in some degree justified their implacable resentment This pamphlet was an affair of the utmost importance, and I felt anxious and impatient to make the emperor acquainted with it; I therefore hurried my departure from Châtillon. I set out on the 20th of March, and after numberless circuits, I arrived on the 23rd at Saint-Dizier, where the Imperial headquarters were established.

"When I entered the emperor's cabinet, I found him dictating orders; three secretaries were employed in writing for him.

"'Ah!' he exclaimed, fixing his keen glance upon me. 'Leave us, gentlemen. Well, Caulincourt, what news have you?'

"He knew of the rupture of the conferences, but he did not expect to see me quite so soon. Without uttering a word, I presented the pamphlet to him. I attentively observed the expression of his countenance whilst he glanced over it. His features became contracted, and his lips were agitated by that sort of convulsive movement peculiar to him when his feelings were powerfully excited. He read the pamphlet to the very last line, and turned back to peruse again some passages which he had marked with his nail. When he had finished, he threw it down on the desk near which he had been sitting, and rising from his chair, he paced rapidly up and down the room.

"Then, stopping short, and his eyes flashing with rage, he said: 'This is an infernal production. The diabolical idea of reviving the name of the republic may have an incalculable effect. It will afford the Allies a powerful reason for concluding neither truce nor peace with France. The question becomes an affair of life and death to every sovereign. A lever is raised which will descend with terrific weight on France. The republic! the republic! As a last resource,' added he, in a more calm tone, 'it might, perhaps, be tried; but in present circumstances this suggestion is a serious misfortune—a crime. Caulincourt, the author of this libel deserves the severest punishment. Do you know what effect it has produced? Where did you get it?—how did it fall into your hands?'

"Sire, it came to me from the only quarter in which there exists sympathy or good faith to your Majesty; and I related the mysterious visit of the Secretary to the Russian Embassy.

"'Bah!—are you sure of this? Quite sure, Caulincourt?' and then, without awaiting my reply, he continued. 'But yes! I know him well! He has a noble, generous heart. He did not understand me. It was necessary to sacrifice everything—everything for the maintenance of the continental blockade. Caulincourt, the Emperor Alexander did not look to the future.'

"Nay, Sire, said I, impelled by a sense of justice to refute this allegation; the Emperor Alexander perfectly well understood the consequences of the continental blockade, had it been executed in good faith. That system, which would temporarily have ruined Russia, was endurable only so long as France, by fidelity to her engagements, concurred in abridging its duration. Instead of that, we violated our pledges by granting licences——

"'Ah I there you are again, at the old story of the licences. No more of that. Come hither, Caulincourt,' said he, beckoning me to approach a table on which were spread several maps of France. With the aid of his pins, he described to me, in a few words, an admirable plan of the respective position of the contending parties, the places occupied, the movements of the armies, and their relative force.

"'I was at work last night with Dalbe,' pursued he, 'I have got all my plans arranged here (tapping his forehead)—I still possess immense resources. My troops are admirable. What a brave nation are the French! I will accept no humiliating conditions. No, I will never bend my neck to them; we have not yet come to that extremity. But tell me, what effect do you think this vile pamphlet has produced?'

"The effect is sufficiently apparent from the circumstances which have brought about the rupture of the conferences.

"He again walked up and down the room. 'Sit down, Caulincourt,' said he; 'never mind me; you know I cannot rest in one place. So they flatter themselves that they can impose still harder conditions on me! But I can tell them' now that I will not condescend to treat with prisoners. Yes, I say, with prisoners! Do you understand me, Caulincourt?'

"Convinced as I was of the utter hopelessness of our position, and amazed at the incredible blindness of the emperor, I described to him in energetic terms the deplorable state of France—the exhaustion of the country, which was invaded on every side—and the evident discouragement of the commanders of the army.

"'Is it for the sake of calumniating the army that you have deserted your friends, Caulincourt?' said the emperor, and as he spoke he stood before me with his arms crossed, his head reared, and with an angry expression of countenance.

"I could not bear this. I took up my hat, and after a difficult struggle with my feelings, I summoned all my resolution, and rushed towards the door.

"He held me back by the skirt of my coat. 'Where are you going?—Nonsense! What a couple of fools we are. It is four o'clock. I am tired, and so are you, my dear Caulincourt.' Then stretching out his hand to me, with an air of languor, he added,—'I will try and sleep for two hours. Go you and take some rest, and come to breakfast with me tomorrow.'

"I cannot, Sire; I beg of your Majesty to grant me a *congé*.

"'No, Caulincourt, I will not—you must not—you ought not to leave me—I need your aid, my friend. This is not the time to forsake me!'"

CHAPTER 14

The Battle of Arcis-sur-Aube

"The emperor was surrounded by men distinguished for heroic courage and fidelity; and, notwithstanding the adverse aspect of affairs, every partial victory which we obtained revived hope and confidence. I arrived at headquarters just after the battle of Arcis-sur-Aube. A general feeling of joy and enthusiasm prevailed, and the details of the battle were repeated from mouth to mouth.

"The following anecdote was related to me by Colonel Mondreville, a brave and excellent officer, then at headquarters:—

"'During the heat of the battle, a division of Russian cavalry, about 6,000 strong, preceded by a body of Cossacks, broke our lines and drove back our cavalry, which was of inferior force. The emperor, whose glance rapidly surveyed every movement of the battle, perceived an impenetrable cloud of dust rising before him so densely, that nothing beyond it was visible. He immediately proceeded to the spot. Some horsemen rode up at full speed,—some wounded, others terrified. In a moment, a crowd of troopers in full retreat surrounded the emperor. "What means this?" said he. "What means this? Dragoons, whither are you flying? Halt, halt!"—"The Cossacks! the Cossacks!" was the only cry; and the tumult was becoming almost a complete rout.

"'At this moment an officer without a helmet, and covered with blood, rode up, and perceiving the emperor, rushed towards him. "Sire," said he, "the Cossacks, supported by an immense body of cavalry, have broken our ranks and driven us back." The emperor, instantly raising himself up in his stirrups, called out in a voice of thunder, "Dragoons, rally! Do you fly, and I here? Close your ranks, dragoons, and advance." At the same moment he darted forward, sword in hand, in front of a cloud of Cossacks. He was followed by his staff, by some of his body guards, and by those very men who an instant before were flying in

153

confusion and terror. In a moment they dashed on the enemy with cries of "*Vive l'Empereur*." The Russian column was driven back, and pursued with great slaughter. Immediately after this the emperor returned tranquilly to the midst of the battle, which he continued to direct till its close. During this partial engagement we had not more than a thousand horse to oppose to six thousand Russians, much better mounted, yet it was at the head of the wreck of a troop of dragoons that the emperor ventured to repel this superior force, and he succeeded.

"'The battle was not over till midnight, but we were not able to snatch a victory. The French on this occasion combated with six thousand exhausted men, against thirty thousand fresh troops, commanded by De Wrede.'

"I had no recollection of any instance in which I had seen Napoleon engaged sword in hand, and I afterwards mentioned to him the affair of Arcis-sur-Aube. He looked at me with astonishment,—'*Ma foi*,' said he, laughing, 'it is a long time since anything of that kind occurred to me. By the way, I now recollect that I had some difficulty in getting at my scabbard to get out my weapon,' and he laughed heartily at his own awkwardness; 'but,' he added, good humouredly, 'the fact is, that my redoubtable sword is one of the worst blades in the whole army.' We laughed at this; but it was true. One of the whims of the emperor was, that he would not have a new hilt substituted for the shabby mother-o'-pearl one. Not an officer in the army would have worn such a sword.

"This conversation put him into good humour; and taking my arm, he drew me aside, and said, 'You are not aware that I made an attempt to carry off my father-in-law! That would have been a glorious capture! I have manoeuvred incessantly to take the headquarters of the Allies; that would have greatly advanced our affairs at Châtillon. What do you say to it, Caulincourt?—(Here his countenance darkened.) But I was teased on all sides to cover Paris!—To cover Paris! I know that is essential; but I thus lost the opportunity of effecting all my other intended operations. By abandoning Paris to its own defence, I should be master of my own movements—nothing could hinder my march to the Rhine—uniting its garrisons with those of the Moselle—organising on that whole line *your* levy *en masse*,— shutting up the roads, and thus cutting off the communications of the enemy's forces engaged in the heart of France.' He paused for a few moments, pensively, then added, 'Since the opening of this campaign, this scheme has been constantly in my thoughts—I have matured it—developed it—my plan is fixed. What is your opinion, Caulincourt?'

"Sire, the plan certainly appears well-digested,—

"'But to carry it into effect,' interrupted the emperor, eagerly, 'Paris must be abandoned—what will Joseph do? Will he resist with energy? That is the whole question. My head is filled with a thousand plans, but I am checked by uncertainty; and in this war, which resembles no other, I go on thus from day to day. The accounts which I receive from Paris are most alarming. I know not what may be the result.'

"In the evening Berthier came to my quarters: I had a thousand things to ask him as to what had occurred during my absence; and he, whose heart was sad and heavy, sought a friend to whom he could unbosom himself. We were, therefore, glad to find ourselves together. Berthier was then getting old; the fatigues of the campaign seemed to have overcome him.

"Berthier confirmed the opinion I had formed as to the real cause of the emperor's indecision during the negotiations at Châtillon. 'There is no doubt,' said he, 'that those alternate victories and reverses produced in the emperor that fluctuation of ideas which rendered your position at Châtillon so difficult during the conferences. The emperor still reposed faith in the good feeling of Austria, if not towards him, at least towards his wife and son. This error will be our ruin. Letters after letters were, by his desire, written by the empress to her father. You know Maria Louisa is a complete nullity; she is not another Maria Theresa, who would energetically declare her determination to defend the capital, and that rather than deliver it up she would bury herself and its faithful inhabitants under the ruins, as long as the emperor should maintain the war at the head of his army. That Austrian marriage has brought misfortune to us,' added Berthier, with a sigh.

"Berthier described to me a scene which took place between the emperor and the Duke de Belluno, after the Battle of Montereau, where we gained a victory at the expense of so much blood. 'If you had executed my orders on the preceding day,' said the emperor to the Duke de Belluno, 'you would have arrived in time to surprise the bridge, and possibly this sanguinary affair at Montereau might have been obviated.' 'I was so exhausted by fatigue that I found it impossible to proceed as you directed,' replied the marshal, who unfortunately had no better excuse to offer. On hearing this reply, the emperor stood for some moments mute with astonishment, and he then vented a most angry reprimand on the Duke de Belluno.

"'After all,' pursued Berthier, 'there are moments when a man's strength may betray his courage. We all know that Victor is brave and devoted; but the emperor is indefatigable, and he cannot understand that every one is not constituted like himself. However, harmony was restored, but poor Victor is greatly afflicted.'

"'On the morning of the 19th or 20th of February,' Berthier continued, 'the emperor breakfasted at Bray, near Nogent, at the same house which the Emperor of Russia had quitted on the preceding evening. We there found a curious letter, which had been left by mistake on the chimney-piece. The letter was from Wintzingerode, who informed the Emperor Alexander that the country people could not safely be relied on—that the French peasantry had commenced an active guerilla warfare against the Allied troops, "This very night," added Wintzingerode, "an officer and twenty Russian soldiers were massacred within two leagues from the camp," Wintzingerode called Alexander's attention to the fact, that for some days past, many similar cases had occurred.'

"'*Parbleu!*' said the emperor, putting the letter into his pocket, 'this information is beyond suspicion. If we are thus seconded by these brave peasantry, it may come to pass that not a man of the Allied forces shall quit France. The French are born soldiers. By arming the country people, and organizing the peasantry in free corps, we should have immense resources.'

"Berthier went on to state 'that the Duke de Ragusa had acted admirably in this campaign, and obtained brilliant success in several actions; but at Corbeny he had allowed himself to be surprised in his bivouac. His division was cut to pieces; two thousand men were killed; his artillery and baggage were almost wholly lost,. and he was, with the remnant, obliged to repass the Aisne with the enemy at his heels.'

"'Well,' added Berthier, 'you know the emperor would consider himself justified in running his sword through the body of any commander who could allow himself to be surprised in that manner. The emperor reproached him in the severest terms, but such is his partiality for Marmont, that he was soon appeased, and continued him in his command. Belluno was much more severely treated for a less serious fault.'

"We again adverted to the Battle of Arcis-sur-Aube.

"'I have reason to believe,' said Berthier, 'that the emperor sought death in that battle.'

"How? cried I.

"'I am convinced,' replied he, 'that it was his earnest wish to be killed that day. Alarmed by the dangers which the emperor encountered, his staff and body-guard advanced and kept quite close round him; but every now and then he separated from them, and advanced toward the enemy. Alarmed at his intention, which I at once understood, I ventured to observe that in the position in which he then stood he was terribly exposed, and served as a mark to the enemy. "I am very well here," said he, drily. It was only when, as I just now described to you, he rushed forward sword in hand in front of the Cossacks that he quitted that dangerous position. At this period of the engagement he became several times involved in the whirlwind of the charges. His escort could not keep up with him.

"'A howitzer-shell fell at his feet, and he was instantly lost sight of in a cloud of dust and smoke. A cry of terror arose from all parts. He was given over as lost. He soon reappeared, and, throwing himself on a fresh horse, he placed himself under the fire of a battery, which several battalions of the old and young guard were striving in vain to carry. The presence of the emperor in the midst of them, and the dangers to which he exposed himself, electrified those brave fellows. They redoubled their efforts, and at last forced the position, and drove back the enemy, but not until they lost more than 400 of their comrades. It is impossible to describe this scene of carnage. The appearance of the dead was most hideous. My dear Caulincourt,' added Berthier, much affected, 'the emperor wished to get killed at Arcis-sur-Aube.'

"This was a painful subject, but nevertheless I closely questioned Berthier upon it. We did not separate till daylight.

"On the day after my return," continued the Duke de Vicenza, "I resumed, under the dictation of the emperor, my correspondence with Metternich. We had a serious affair on the 26th at St. Dizier. Wintzingerode was beaten, and driven across the Marne. We took 2,000 prisoners, a park of artillery, and a considerable quantity of bridge equipage likewise fell into our hands. The prisoners, however, only embarrassed us, for we did not know what to do with, or where to send them. This was another useless victory; but these partial advantages continued to feed in Napoleon's mind the hope of obtaining peace on less rigorous conditions. Fatal confidence!

"After the Battle of St. Dizier, the emperor lost sight for a moment of the march of the Allies, and his uneasiness about the condition of the capital returned. We arrived on the evening of the 27th at Vitry.

There we obtained some intelligence from the statements of prisoners, and the accounts of our troops who had escaped from the hands of the enemy. Some of the peasants of Vitry brought us proclamations and bulletins. These left us no longer in doubt as to the movements of the Allies. They were marching on Paris. An officer arrived at our headquarters; he was wounded, and had escaped by a miracle from the enemy, by whom he had been made prisoner. He understood the Russian language perfectly, and he informed us that a doubt had arisen amongst the Allies, in a council held recently, whether they should continue to harass the army under Napoleon, or at all hazards advance on Paris. The emperor Alexander feared an 'Imperial Vendean rising.' The Allies spoke of retiring on the Rhine, and the junction of all their forces was necessary either for an advance or a retreat.

"Oh!" said the duke, "if at this moment the emperor had made reasonable offers, there would have been some chance of their being accepted, and we might have been saved. But how was this to be foreseen?

"The officer added, 'that the council separated without coming to any decision; but, during the night, a secret emissary, sent from Paris, had an interview with the Emperor of Russia. At daybreak the council was again re-assembled. The intelligence that Alexander had received put an end to all irresolution. It was announced that a powerful party awaited the arrival of the Allies in the capital; that Paris was without the means of defence, without order, and stripped of her troops, and that the Allied Powers might enter without striking a blow.'

"The emperor listened to these details with a mournful air: and when the officer ceased speaking, he exclaimed, 'I shall be in Paris before them.' We returned to St. Dizier. The emperor passed the whole night shut up in his cabinet perusing his maps. This was another cruel night. Not a word was uttered. Deep sighs sometimes escaped from his oppressed bosom. He seemed as if he had lost the power of breathing. Good Heaven! how much he suffered!

"Orders for our departure were given," continued the duke, "and we moved on by the way of Doulevent to Troyes. Just as the emperor was mounting his horse, some peasants arrived, bringing with them carts filled with prisoners, whose carriages had been seized by the inhabitants of St Thibaut Amongst the prisoners was M. de Weissemberg, the ambassador from Austria to England, who had been summoned to the headquarters of the Allies; also a Swedish general, named Brandt, a *conseiller de guerre*, whose name I forget, and two Russian officers, MM.

Tolstoi and Marcoff.

"I had known Tolstoi and his family at St, Petersburg. In the midst of my troubles it was some relief to recall the happy days passed with him during my embassy to Russia. Tolstoi, who was gay, young, and frank, said to me, 'My dear duke, I am in raptures with France. I am all anxiety to see Paris.' Hold, my dear friend, said I, you sting me to the very heart—remember, you are speaking to a Frenchman. But nothing could prevent him from expressing the joy he felt in visiting France. His companion, Marcoff, was much more reserved, and also much less agreeable.

"The prisoners must have considered themselves very fortunate that their lucky stars had brought them to the emperor, who treated them very well. He took no other advantage of their arrival, than that of attempting a direct communication to his father-in-law. M. de Weissemberg, after a long interview, departed with a message to the Emperor of Austria. Napoleon ordered the portfolios and despatches belonging to the prisoners to be delivered up to them, and charged me to procure them horses, and to see that they were provided with safe-conducts. Tolstoi embraced me, and throwing himself on his horse, went off in his usual light and joyous manner. How different had been our fortune since we met at St. Petersburg! I saw him again in Paris, where he did everything in his power to oblige me. Alexander learnt from Tolstoi all the details of the interview of the prisoners with Napoleon.

"By some fatality, the Emperor Francis was separated from the headquarters, and he narrowly escaped being taken. He got on the road to Dijon, where he eventually arrived. M. de Weissemberg consequently did not know where to rejoin him. In the meantime, the fatal *denouement* approached. Napoleon, attacked on all sides, definitively abandoned his project of marching with his forces on the Rhine, and manoeuvred to cover Paris. The enemy continued to advance by forced marches on the capital. In order to prevent the junction of the several corps of the Allies, to disseminate their forces, and to continue our advance to Paris, we had to sustain a combat every day. The fighting might be said to be continuous. The ardour and devotedness of the troops seemed to increase with the danger, and they seemed indefatigable. The heart beats at the remembrance of the heroism displayed in the last days of the crisis.

"On the 30th of March we were at Troyes. The emperor traced out the route of the army, so that on the 2nd of April the whole

159

should unite before Paris. At ten o'clock he set out, accompanied by Berthier and myself. We made the journey from Troyes to Montereau, a distance of ten leagues, in two hours. A crazy vehicle; drawn by two horses, which were kept at full gallop, brought us across some fields on the road to Paris, between Essonne and Villejuif. Whilst waiting for our relays we saw some disbanded troops, who had, they said, evacuated Paris in the evening after the capitulation. It was then ten at night. These people are mad,' said the emperor. He descended from his carriage, and ordered that an officer should come to him. At that moment Belliard arrived, who announced the taking of Paris, and gave him all the details which led to that event.

"Large drops of perspiration rolled down the forehead of the emperor. His mouth became contracted, and the livid paleness of his face was frightful. 'You hear this, Caulincourt,' said he, turning towards me, his eyes fixed on mine with horrible intensity. He wished to march on Paris with the armies of the two marshals, who had received his orders at Troyes. 'The guard,' he said, 'will arrive on the night of the 31st.' He wished to make an attack on the Boulevards at the moment of the entrance of the Allied. Sovereigns. 'The national guard and the people will support me,' added he, 'and when I shall enter within the walls of Paris, I will not quit them except as a conqueror or a corpse.'

"Soon after there successively arrived, the guards of honour, the commanders of corps, and the general officers who had concurred in the defence of Paris, under the orders of Marmont. It sickens me to pronounce this name," added the duke, in a sorrowing accent. "The emperor, continually standing, constantly repeated to himself those dreadful details which preyed upon him. He then loudly announced his intention of marching on Paris. It was suggested to him that that would be a violation of the capitulation, in virtue of which the troops had evacuated the capital; that these troops were few in number, and greatly harassed; that four thousand men had fallen under the walls of Paris; and that if that bold enterprise failed, the city would be given up to pillage, to fire, and sword.

"All these reasons were plausible, no doubt; but it is a melancholy truth, that none of the advice given was disinterested. Each person gave his advice from selfish calculations. The human heart contains many foul recesses.

"The emperor was not deceived as to the motives which influenced his counsellors. 'Enough,' said he, drily. He then ordered that the corps of Mortier and Marmont should take up a position behind the

River Essonne: then, turning towards me, he said, 'Do you set off at full speed to Paris, Caulincourt, and see if it be yet possible to do anything by treaty. I am delivered up and sold; but no matter. Depart this instant; I give you full powers, and I await you here—go. The distance is not great,' added he, with a deep sigh; 'go.'

"The emperor was separated only by the Seine from the advanced posts of the enemy, whose forces were spread over the plains of Villeneuve Saint-Georges. The fires of their bivouacs illumined the right bank, while Napoleon remained in darkness on the opposite side, with two post carriages and some servants.

"I rode with excessive speed, and I felt an extraordinary sensation within me. My horse had the swiftness of the wind, and it almost seemed to me that I carried him. I arrived too soon at the advanced posts to learn that all was lost—that the ruin of France was consummated, and that the fate of the emperor was at the mercy of wretches, who, as he had just said, had delivered him up and sold him.

"From a miserable roadside inn, already occupied by Russians and Prussians, I forwarded him an express. A feverish anxiety seized me, when I thought of the despair into which my letter would plunge him. I immediately mounted the first horse I could get, and rejoined the emperor at the moment he had finished reading my dispatch. We conversed for some moments. 'I only asked them,' said Napoleon, 'to defend Paris for twenty-four hours longer—the traitors!—Marmont—Marmont, who had sworn that he would allow himself to be cut to pieces under the walls of Paris rather than surrender!—and Joseph flying!—my brother to deliver up my capital to the enemy! They had my orders; they knew that on the 2nd of April I should be at the head of seventy thousand men; my brave military schools and my National-guards, who had promised to defend my son. Every man of courage would have been at my side. The traitors have capitulated—they have betrayed their brethren in arms, their country, and their sovereign—they have degraded France in the eyes of all Europe. To enter a capital with a population of eight hundred thousand souls, and without striking a blow!'

"The emperor seemed plunged in the most profound grief. I was deeply affected, and burning tears overflowed my eyes.

"'My dear Caulincourt, return—return to headquarters, and try to see the Emperor Alexander. You have full powers from me. Go, Caulincourt, go.'

"Sire, answered I, I have not been able even to come near Alexander. They distrust me. The sovereigns will enter Paris tomorrow, and they are now busied with preparations for that event. These are the reasons assigned for refusing me permission to approach the Emperor Alexander.

"'Return—I have now no hope but in you, Caulincourt,' continued he, holding out his hand.

"I go, Sire,—dead or alive I will gain entrance into Paris, and will speak to the Emperor Alexander.

"The emperor then took the road to Fontainebleau, and I repaired to Paris. I will tell you how he fulfilled that mission; it is very curious. My head is burning," said the duke, raising his hand to his forehead. "I am quite feverish. I should live a hundred years before I could forget these scenes. They are the fixed ideas of my sleepless nights. My reminiscences are frightful—they kill me. Tomorrow, if I can, I will describe to you those twenty days of torture passed at Paris or at Fontainebleau. The repose of the tomb is sweet after such sufferings."

CHAPTER 15

Arrival of the Grand Duke Constantine

"I have now arrived," observed the Duke de Vicenza, "at the most disastrous epoch of the reign of Napoleon. If I felt any very great anxiety for the ease of the short span of life which still remains to me, I should, instead of reviving the memory of the period to which I am now about to allude, banish all recollection of those moments of torment which no words have power to describe. But I have by sad experience learned how much a man can bear, when he is resolved rather to die, struggling against obstacles, than to desert the cause he has embraced.

"Whilst the emperor was proceeding to Fontainebleau, I pursued my route to Paris, in fulfilment of the mission with which I was entrusted to the Emperor Alexander.

"My wearied horse proceeded slowly, and I retrained from urging him on. The high spirit which had sustained me during my recent toilsome journeys, was now succeeded by a frightful depression. The vivid emotions which I had experienced for the last twenty-four hours, seemed to have exhausted all my moral strength. My head was all vagueness and confusion. I had only one distinct idea, and that had reference to the emperor's last words, 'I have no longer hope, except in you, Caulincourt.' Still it required a very powerful mental effort to enable me to discover the meaning of this expression, and to perceive all its consequences.

"To return to the headquarters of the Allies was to me a mission of humiliation and disgust. All my feelings of dignity and pride rebelled against the duty which was imposed on me. But there are certain necessities before which every sensation of repugnance fades away; and we feel bound to attain the end which we have in view, let our personal sacrifices be what they may. To the word *honour*, a man's destiny is inseparably attached.

"'The road which I took was crowded with the remains of different regiments, which marched as chance directed them. A *chef-d'escadron* of the guards of honour, who had received a wound in his head, and who with difficulty kept his seat on his horse, came up to me and asked me to direct him to the head quarters. In an instant I was surrounded by a multitude of these fugitives. 'Where is the emperor?' they cried, 'we wish to rejoin him.' 'We have no commanders.' 'Where shall we go ?' 'The emperor does not know what is going on at Paris. We fought well; we are ready to fight again; and yet we have been made to yield to the enemy!' In the countenances of these men was expressed a sort of wild grief; while their mouths uttered imprecations and furious menaces against the traitors; for they looked upon themselves as betrayed, and not conquered.

"In masses of men there is an instinctive sagacity which enables them to take just views of great events. I was much struck with the words uttered by a *cuirassier* of the old guard with a feeling of fierce indignation. 'We defeated them in every point,' said he, raising his head with a look of pride, 'and we might still have gained the battle. Neither we nor the emperor quitted the field; we did not capitulate. There is treason, but no capitulation. Lead us back to Paris, and the foreigners will never enter it without first passing over the body of the last French soldier.' ... 'Where is our emperor? If he is dead, all is over! still let us know the sad truth.' He spoke these last words in a tone of the most poignant sorrow, while the tears dropped from his eyes.

"I endeavoured to soothe the exasperation of these brave men, and directed their officers to proceed in good order on Fontainebleau, where they would find the emperor. At this magic name, loud shouts and '*vivas*' burst from the multitude. As much enthusiasm—as much affection for Napoleon, as ever had been felt during his most prosperous days, was then manifested. At that moment, when a few miserable individuals in their gilded saloons were, by their agreement to disgraceful treaties, sealing the ruin of France, a handful of poor soldiers, worn out by fatigue and famine, wounded and abandoned on the high roads, still found strength to march forward, for the purpose of shedding all their remaining blood in their country's defence. Their confidence in the emperor—their devotion to his person, existed in all its force; now, when be was so shamefully deserted by those whom he had raised up. Good Heaven! what has become of that fine army, so national, so devoted. At every step I met parties of troops. They asked the same questions, and expressed the same indignation. I directed them to proceed to Fontainebleau.

"The Russian Army, divided into several corps, covered the roads to Chartres, Orleans, Melon, and Essonne, by the latter of which I travelled. The day was breaking when I perceived the bivouacs of our enemies. With them there was nothing but triumph and rejoicing. This contrast with the scenes of the preceding night was horrible. The Russian troops destined for the military occupation of Paris were parading about in their best uniforms, and indulging in al! the boisterous joy of victory. The officers collected at the head of their regiments seemed, by their exulting looks, to defy both heaven and earth. Every countenance was radiant with satisfaction. Acclamations and hurras were raised as each corps filed off for the march.

"The aspect of the scene,—the movement of the camp,—the exultation,—the sound of trumpets, almost drove me mad. Impelled by an emotion which every man of feeling will easily understand, I convulsively grasped the hilt of my sword. The blush of shame covered my forehead—the blood boiled in my veins. The idea that these men were about to enter Paris in triumph, under my very eyes, maddened me. In my delusion I inwardly debated the possibility of engaging them one by one, and of not allowing them to enter our capital unless they passed over my body. I thought that true honour consisted in offering such a resistance much more than in discharging the duty consigned me of imploring the conqueror, ... This over-excitement—this fever of the soul—passed away; reason returned, and I perceived that it was more magnanimous to meet misfortune than to seek a useless death.

"But how is it possible for cold reasoning to prevail against those emotions which excite in us the most ardent passions. I saw that it was necessary for me to turn from this scene, and burying my spurs in my horse's flanks, I galloped off in another direction.

"After riding a league, I alighted at the door of a farmhouse, where I passed a portion of the day. About six o'clock I returned to the advanced posts, and signified that I was the bearer of a message for the Emperor of Russia. I was informed by the commanding officer that the most positive orders had been issued not to allow any individual belonging to the French Army to enter Paris. At this moment a Russian general officer made his appearance. I mentioned my name, and said, that being entrusted by the Emperor Napoleon, my master, with an important despatch, I desired to be conducted to the Emperor Alexander, to whom the despatch was addressed. The officer replied, that he could not take upon him the responsibility of complying with my request; because he had received orders of the most positive description to allow no one coming from the Emperor Napoleon to enter Paris; and that a special direction had been given not to admit me, the Duke de Vicenza, under any pretext whatsoever.

"But, general, replied I, somewhat sharply, you take upon yourself an immense responsibility in refusing admission into the city to an envoy (whatever other rank he may possess) entrusted with official communications for your sovereign.. . . .Do these orders emanate directly from the Emperor of Russia? 'Sir,' returned the general, 'I have received my instructions. I am not in any way bound to satisfy your curiosity; but I have no objections to inform your Excellency that these orders were agreed on at a council of the Allied Monarchs, assembled at the house of Prince de Talleyrand Perigord, where the Emperor Alexander alighted. This very night they were forwarded to me by an *estafette*, sent from the prince's mansion.'

"You are certain, General, I observed, with some indignation, that the Emperor Alexander alighted at M. de Talleyrand's. . . . . 'Quite certain.' Oh, I exclaimed, this surpasses any anticipation that could have been formed of human turpitude! This man—this Talleyrand— received the emperor's orders to escort the empress to the bank of the Loire; and it is he, this very Talleyrand, who is doing the honours of Paris to the Allies! Infamous!

"I inquired for several Russian generals—Woronsoff, Csemichoff, Onwarrow, and others with whom I was personally acquainted. They had, however, accompanied the Emperor Alexander to Paris.

"I will not attempt to describe to you," continued the duke, "all that I suffered at the sight of these foreign soldiers, who guarded our *barrières*, and forbade me admission into Paris. I drank the cup of bitterness even to the very dregs! Indignation and anger excited me, and I felt a sort of mad desire to challenge one of these victorious chiefs, and demand satisfaction for the humiliation of my country. During these few short moments I experienced all the misery reserved for the conquered partisans of a great and noble cause. Suddenly I heard a general movement around me—all eyes were turned towards a carriage which had just driven up. The drums were beat, and I mechanically went in front of the carriage, and found myself near the coach door, at the moment when the individual whom it contained stepped out of it. This was the Grand Duke Constantine!

"'What do you want. Sir? Who are you?' he asked, in a tone of severity. Prince, I am the Duke de Vicenza, replied I, trembling with rage. The duke regarded me with a look of profound astonishment. 'Excuse me. Sir,' he observed, 'I did not at first recognise your Excellency;' and taking my arm, he led me away in the direction of Essonne. 'In what way can I personally be of service to you?' he inquired. Prince, admission into Paris is refused me, and yet I must enter the capital,—I must! I repeated, with an air of exasperation, which, spite of all my efforts, I was unable to dissemble.

"'Becalm, duke,' said Constantine. 'Do you look upon me only as an enemy? Is, then, the recollection of St. Petersburg so utterly effaced?'

"Prince, I rejoined, overcome by the kind tone of Constantine, deign to excuse me. I am so unfortunate that I distrust all . . . .

"'Distrust not me, my dear duke, you know well enough that in our family you will find none but friends.'

"Well, then, prince! I exclaimed, in the name of that precious friendship with which you honour me, I claim a favour of you—allow me to enter Paris.

"'What do you mean to do there?'

"To plead the cause of my sovereign—the cause of my country.

"'My dear duke, nothing can be done for Napoleon—the powers will listen to no proposition coming from him.'

"Prince, the emperor, my master, has entrusted me with a secret message for the Emperor Alexander, and I am bound to discharge this sacred duty, and at the peril of my existence I will enter Paris.

"'It grieves me greatly to add to your disappointment by refusing your request; but I cannot take upon myself to break orders which have been formally given; that would be a terrible responsibility.'

"I withdrew my arm from Constantine's. 'My dear duke,' said he, grasping my hand, 'hear what I have to say,' you oblige me to tell you that a promise not to receive you has been exacted from the Emperor Alexander.'

"What baseness! I exclaimed; but I am determined to make my way into Paris, dead or alive. I should be vile indeed, if I deserted the cause which has been entrusted to my honour. Prince, no power shall withhold me from advancing. Every man has his destiny.

"I turned to go away, but the grand duke detained me. 'Duke de Vicenza,' he said, 'I should never forgive myself were I to leave you in this distressed state of feeling. Be the consequences what they may, you shall go with me. That is the only possible way in which you can gain access to the capital. Attend to my instructions, my dear duke. Leave me; remount your horse, pass our last posts, and be at hand on the road. The rest is my business. Leave me coolly and immediately.'

"I took leave of the prince, and passed through the camp at a gallop. When out of sight, I ordered my servant to wait for me at the first village; and on foot, like a malefactor, avoiding public roads, I turned and went back, threading my way behind the trees. At a short distance I saw the grand duke's carriage, which had stopped on one side of the road.

"Harassed by fatigue, but still more by the violent emotions which I had suffered during twenty-four hours, I sat myself down beside a bush, and kept looking in the direction in which I expected the prince would come, I spent a sad, tedious hour, in a horrible fever of expectation, anxiety, and bitter reflections. The most painful recollections arose in my mind. My imagination carried me through the immeasurable distance which separated my Russian Embassy from the day in which the ruin of the empire was consummated.

"I thought of the time I had passed in the palace of St. Petersburg, when the glory of the great Napoleon reflected lustre on his ambassador, and assured to him the most brilliant position that the ambition of man could desire. During those four years all had been happiness and splendour. Ages had not passed away since that period of poetic existence. Three short years, and all was gone! Three years had undone twenty years of conquests, of miracles, of every sort. Death and destruction marked the distance which separated St. Petersburg from Paris, and nothing remained of the most powerful, of the most colossal, empire of modern times, except its immortal founder, a prisoner at Fontainebleau.

"My memory recalled, with fatal tenacity, places, dates, and melancholy coincidences.—Thus I recollected that precisely six years previously, on the night of March 31, I gave a magnificent *fête* at St. Petersburg. This date I could not forget; a memorial of the heart rendered it ineffaceable. Ah! had any one in the palace of the embassy then sketched out the frightful course through which I have since travelled, I should have thought him fit for the *Hopital des Fous*.

"Night having set in, I quitted my resting place, where the painful recollection of the pleasures of the past had only rendered the present more wretched. I advanced towards the carriage, and the grand duke soon arrived. The door was opened, and I jumped in; the prince followed me. 'To Paris,' said he, and we rolled along with rapidity.

"When we had passed the barrier, Constantine said,—'My dear duke, this is quite a romantic elopement. The prettiest woman in France would not make my heart beat quicker than you make it at this moment. In the name of Heaven, tell me what I am to do with you?' added he, laughing heartily.

"In my state of vexation his gaiety was distressing. The merry laugh falls coldly on the afflicted heart. However, I could not fail to reflect that he was acting the part of a good and generous friend, and that the day so unfortunate for me was for him a happy one. When age shall have blunted his sensations—when time, which wears out the deepest impressions, shall have extinguished in him the joys of early life, the old man may feel proudly gratified at the recollection of his entrance into the capital of the formidable empire of France.

"'My dear duke, assist me,' continued he, with vivacity, 'I well know that I shall have rendered you only a useless service if I do not introduce you to my brother; but how is that to be done?'

"Tell him, prince, that Caulincourt invokes the recollections of four years of kindness and interest; that in the name of misfortune he solicits a few moments conversation; tell him that the favour I seek is more to me than life.

"'He must receive you. He must become my accomplice, for if our plot should be discovered, I know not what strange suspicions I shall be exposed to. There is much distrust amongst us. But never mind, the die is cast, so we'll leave the result to Providence.'

"I was in a sad perplexity. I felt that, setting aside the political position of the grand duke, the most profound secrecy was necessary to the success of my mission, more than doubtful as it was. If my presence should be suspected, the other sovereigns, instigated by Napoleon's enemies, would urge upon the Emperor Alexander my immediate dismissal, and the work of hatred would be completed before I could have the opportunity of saying a word in favour of the Imperial cause.

"Several plans were suggested and rejected. At last we agreed that I should remain in the carriage while the grand duke went to tell Alexander what had been done. We stopped in the *Allèe de Marigny*. Constantine having desired me to muffle myself up with his travelling cap and fur *pelisse*, alighted, shut the carriage door himself, and gave strict orders to his servants to allow nobody to come near the carriage.

"At this moment a neighbouring clock struck ten. I should in vain endeavour to relate what I felt during the three long hours I passed in the carriage. The most bitter reflections were accompanied by those stinging touches, which, like the tortures of the inquisition, seem to take life by fragments.

"A festive air reigned around the Palais Elysèe, The lamps at the principal entrance shed a brilliant light; carriages arrived and drove off in rapid succession. The neighing of the horses, the loud talking of the drivers, the noisy hurras of the Russian Imperial guard, were to me tormenting discordant sounds. At this moment, thought I, while I was waiting for an audience, perhaps the ruin of him who formerly reigned master here is decided. It was at the Elysèe that the emperor, then so powerful, formed his gigantic plan against Russia. From these terrible contrasts I drew a bitter reflection both on men and things.

"One o'clock struck, when the grand duke came and put an end to this torment of recollections. He said, 'the saloons were full, and the emperor, being in conference with the sovereigns, did not leave his cabinet until midnight. I had therefore to wait until everyone was gone. The Emperor Alexander is in despair at our prank, but he will receive you as a friend. Wear my cloak, and put on this uniform hat.'

"Constantine took my arm, and we proceeded on foot. We ascended by the interior staircase to Alexander's bedroom. The *Czar* received me with open arms. He had a truly noble heart."

CHAPTER 16

The Duke de Vicenza Proceeds to Fontainebleau

"'My dear duke,' said the Emperor Alexander, clasping both my hands in his, 'I feel for you with all my heart. You are the man I most esteem in all France. You may rely upon me as upon a brother. But what is your wish? What can I do for you?'

"For me, sire, nothing,—but for the emperor, everything.

"'This is precisely what I dreaded,' resumed Alexander, 'for I must refuse, I must afflict you. I can do nothing for the Emperor Napoleon. I am under engagements with the Allied Sovereigns.'

"But your Majesty's wish must have an immense weight in the balance of European interests; and if Austria should, as all considerations require, also interpose decidedly in behalf of France, it is still possible to conclude a peace which may insure general tranquillity.

"'Austria, my dear duke, Austria will not second me in any proposition having for its object to leave Napoleon on the throne of France.'

"But the Emperor Francis surely does not wish to dethrone his daughter and his grandson?

"'The Emperor of Austria will sacrifice all his personal affections for the repose of Europe. The Allied Sovereigns have resolved—irrevocably resolved—to be forever done with the Emperor Napoleon. Any endeavour to change the decision would he useless.'

"I was struck dumb. The formal declaration left me no hope. I expected to have to discuss very severe conditions; but the idea of the emperor being dethroned never had crossed my mind. It was only then that I perceived the magnitude of the danger which threatened the empire. Alas! we were no longer in a situation to attempt to enforce our demands.

"Events crowded upon us with overwhelming rapidity, and we had no power to evade any terms the conqueror might choose to exact. One proposition might still succeed, and I ventured to start the question of the Regency.

"Be it so, replied I; but is it justice and equity to include in the same sentence of proscription the Empress Maria Louisa and her son, the King of Rome? The latter at least, surely, is not an object of fear to the Allied Powers. It will be easy to preserve the incontestable rights of the son of Napoleon to the throne of France. A Regency—

"'We have had that under consideration,' said the Emperor Alexander, interrupting me, 'but what should we do with Napoleon? The father is an invincible object to the recognition of the son.'

"Sire, the emperor will make every sacrifice in favour of his son which the unfortunate circumstances of France demand.

"'My dear duke, you deceive yourself. At the present moment, doubtless, Napoleon will yield to the inflexible law of necessity. But restless ambition will soon rouse all the energy of his character, and Europe will be once more in flames.'

"I see, said I, deeply grieved, that the emperor's ruin has been resolved on.

"'Whose fault is it?' eagerly resumed the Emperor Alexander. 'What have I not done to prevent these terrible extremities? Do me the justice to allow that I did all in my power to open his eyes to the inevitable consequences of his unjust aggression on Russia. In the imprudent sincerity of youth, I said to him—"The Powers, wearied with insults and outrages, are forming alliances among themselves against your domination. One signature only is wanting to the compact, and that is mine." In reply to this frank communication, he declared war against me. He broke the bond of that pure and enthusiastic friendship which I had pledged to him.'

"A heavy sigh escaped my breast. I had not a word to reply to these accusations, which were uttered without vindictiveness or animosity.

"'Still,' continued Alexander, 'even yet I cannot find in my heart to cherish any unkind feeling towards him; I wish his fate depended on me alone.'

"Noblest of monarchs! I exclaimed; I feel assured that I do not vainly invoke your support for so great a man in adversity. Be his defender. Sire; that noble part is worthy of you.

"'I would wish so to be; on my honour, I wish it; but I cannot succeed. To restore the Bourbons is the wish of a very influential party here. With that family we should have no fear of the renewal of war.'

"You are misinformed. Sire; if some persons have dreamed of recalling the Bourbons, it is with a view to their own private interests, and not as a means of tranquillising Europe. The new generations can feel neither affection nor interest for that family. The Bourbons have nothing in common with France of 1814; time has consecrated the immense work of the revolution; the past now belongs to us no longer But, on the other hand, painful recollections remain with those whom the revolution overthrew. They will bring back from exile, court traditions and pretensions, hostile to the new interests of France. Believe me, Sire, from this monstrous junction of incompatible elements there will arise new torments and new misfortune for Europe.'

"'Your arguments would be perfectly correct, my dear duke, were it our intention to impose the Bourbons on the French people; but I at once declared against that. I do not make war on France. I am opposed only to the enemy of general tranquillity. My declaration secures full liberty for France to choose a sovereign. I am assured that the French nation desires the Bourbons, and if the public voice recalls them.'

"If your Majesty means by the public voice the machinations of a party of intriguers——

"'It is difficult to be judge and party in one's own cause. You are warm, my dear duke.'

"Sire, misfortune is susceptible, and——

"'Listen to me; hear me. Do not look upon me as the Emperor of Russia, but as a friend, willing to discuss the subject with perfect fairness; one who admires your attachment and the efforts you make in favour of your unfortunate sovereign. Be assured, then, that if I advance arguments adverse to your views, it is not with the sake of controversy, but for the purpose of placing the question on its true basis.'

"I cannot doubt your good faith, Sire, nor your wish to be impartial; but your Majesty is, against your will, subject to influences——

"'In short,' said he, interrupting me hastily, 'the Prince of Benevento attaches great importance to the assent of the senate of the great constituted bodies, and of the leaders of the army. This unanimity of wishes is of enormous weight in existing circumstances. It is said, and it appears to be true, that all have had *enough of Bonaparte*. I use the common expression. They wish at all hazards to insure tranquillity.'

"Fortunately, sire, those ungrateful men who owe everything to the emperor, and who now wish to get rid of him at all hazards, are not the nation. Will your Majesty be pleased to cause registers to be opened in all the municipalities of France? The true sense of the country would then be made manifest, and the Allies would see clearly whether the Bourbons are preferred to Napoleon, or to his son. If the Allied Sovereigns make it part of their policy to respect the rights of a great nation, an appeal to the majority of votes is the only means whereby they can prove that intention, and place the new government on solid bases. Europe took up arms to obtain peace. Be cautious Sire, lest ill-considered measures do not again endanger a dearly-purchased peace.

"The Emperor Alexander walked about for a quarter of an hour absorbed in deep thought. Then turning to me—'My dear duke, I am struck with what you have said to me. The method you suggest is, perhaps, the best for gaining the object we desire—a solid peace. But the course you propose would be attended with much delay, and circumstances hurry us on. We are urged, driven, tormented, to come to a decision. Moreover, the provisional government which is established reigns *de facto*. It is a real power round which ambition is rallying. Between ourselves, it is long since the schemes for this state of things began to work. The Allied Sovereigns are constantly surrounded, flattered, pressed and teased to decide in favour of the Bourbons; in fine, they have serious personal injuries to avenge. The cause you are defending includes a complication of interests which contribute to its ruin On the other hand, the absence of the Emperor of Austria is a fatality, and were I to attempt anything in favour of Napoleon's son, I should be left alone: none would second me.'

"Alas, Sire, the absence of the Emperor of Austria is indeed a Vitality; but your generous influence will suffice to counteract it. Declare yourself for the vanquished, and the cause of Napoleon's son will triumph.

"'They had good reason, my dear friend,' said Alexander, kindly giving me his hand—'they had good reason for making me promise not to see you This warmth of heart, which renders you so distressed, is infectious. You have roused every generous feeling within my heart. Well, I will try. Tomorrow, at the council, I will revert to the question of the Regency; every other proposition is impossible, so do not deceive yourself; and, *let us hope.*'

"This conversation," continued the Duke de Vicenza, "took place precisely as I have related it. That expression, *let us hope*, still vibrates in my ear, because in the mouth of Alexander it had a powerful meaning. I felt all its force, and my mind was filled with hope. Our serious dialogue was followed by a familiar conversation after the manner of former times. No one knew better than Alexander how to infuse into his manner that gracious ease which at once removes all embarrassment in interviews between persons of different ranks. Laying aside his Imperial bearing, he kept up a light conversation in his wonted lively style. We spoke of the *coquettish*, and delightful Antona,—still beloved, and still rebellious. 'She takes advantage of my weakness,' said he; 'I come to the best resolutions in the world, but they are all forgotten whenever I see her; in a word, my dear duke, I lose my senses.'

"Alexander was still distractedly in love with her, but there was a distance of seven hundred leagues between them; and Paris presented so many attractions, so many points of seduction, that I clearly foresaw that the reign of the fascinating Antona would shortly close. Alexander told me all that had taken place in his private circle since my departure. He recounted numerous anecdotes of the *elegants* of St. Petersburg; and I, though overwhelmed with sorrow, listened to these sprightly stories, in order that I might the more surely reach the heart of the only friend that was left me.

"It was now four o'clock in the morning, and Alexander seemed ready to fall asleep. Your Majesty, said I, would be glad to be rid of me; but that is no easy matter, for I have not the power to render myself invisible.

"'My dear duke,' said he, 'having entered secretly and in disguise, you cannot leave without compromising me; therefore stretch yourself in this easy chair.'

"I am no stranger here. Sire, said I, and I will go into the next chamber and remain there until your Majesty may be pleased to drive me out of it.

"The chamber in which I had the interview with Alexander," continued the Duke de Vicenia, "and in which the emperor was to repose, was the bedchamber of Napoleon when he inhabited the Elysèe. The room into which I retired had been his study. It contained a sofa, on which I flung myself, and during a short and disturbed slumber the events of the last two days recurred to my mind. I endeavoured from time to time to open my eyes in order to escape from painful slumber, but without success; and when at eight o'clock I found myself really awake, I fancied that I had lost possession of my senses. I had, indeed, passed a most frightful night."

The Duke de Vicenza here paused, apparently overcome by the

recollection of his sufferings. "I can conceive nothing more dramatic," I observed, "than the extraordinary position in which the Grand Equerry of the Empire, the envoy of the Emperor Napoleon, formerly so much feared, was placed. I can imagine all that you suffered, when concealed by the Emperor of Russia in the Palais of the Elysèe. . . How difficult would it be to give credence to such mysterious decrees of destiny, if they were not connected with that great and solemn catastrophe which has been accomplished under our very eyes."

"Doubtless," continued the duke, "the hidden causes which led the way to the fall of the empire have been kept concealed by the promoters of that event. Narrow-minded people regard it merely as a just punishment for the insatiable ambition of Napoleon; but it is always very convenient to judge of facts by results, I do not mean to deny that the emperor may have committed faults, but who was better qualified than himself to repair them? Is it possible to forget in a moment his vast glory, his great and noble actions? Ought France to have abandoned her hero at the moment of his misfortune? That fault exceeded any committed by Napoleon. When a few years shall have passed away, the conduct of the French people, during the terrible crisis of April, 1814, will be a problem incapable of solution. But to resume my narration:—

"I heard several persons passing in and out of the chamber of the Emperor of Russia. I stepped up to a window, and, looking through the curtains, I perceived that the garden was filled with troops, bivouacking, as they also were in our squares and in our streets. I could not bear this sight; and, retiring from the window, I again threw myself on the sofa, on which I had slept so restlessly. I reflected on the conversation which had taken place on the preceding evening, and endeavoured to find in it some cause of consolation. After a severe mental agitation, my powers of suffering seemed exhausted; and I was obliged to banish all thought from my mind to avoid falling into that feverish state of irritation which not unusually ends in madness.

"I occupied myself in examining the room in which I was. Nothing had been changed, not even the table, which was covered with maps of Russia, plans, and unfinished writings. Perhaps no one had entered the room since the departure of its Imperial occupant. I approached the table, and, impelled by an indescribable feeling, I pushed back the easy-chair, cut with a penknife in all directions, and concealed it behind the rest of the furniture. I then arranged the maps, and locked them up in the bookcase. The new occupants of the Elysèe might have there found matter for jests, and for mortifying comparisons between projects and results. . . . . The plans and writings were quickly made to disappear, for I tore them in a thousand bits, and buried them under the ashes in the fireplace.

"This being done, I seemed to breathe more freely. In the midst of the greatest trouble a mere trifle may afford relief to the anxious mind. If it only saves self-love from being wounded, it seems like a victory gained over misfortune. These details have, I am aware, no real interest, and I certainly shall not commit them to writing. Historical narrative demands conciseness, and affords little opportunity for the effusion of a suffering imagination. But, in talking with you, when in point of fact I only think aloud, I should find it quite impossible not to yield to the recollection of my emotions.

"About eleven o'clock I heard a knocking at my door. I opened it, and Constantine entered. 'Duke,' said he, 'the emperor sends you his compliments. He was unable to see you before leaving the palace; but in the meantime we will breakfast together. I have given orders to have it prepared in Alexander's room. We will shut ourselves up there, and endeavour to pass the rime until his return.'

"Only those who have sojourned at the Russian Court can form a just idea of the simplicity, of the familiarity, (never exceeding the limits of good taste,) which characterise the princes of the Imperial family in the relations of private life. At the French Court the etiquette is strict and formal. There we might suppose it likely for the sovereign to be complaisant with the functionary; but we never could imagine the possibility of the former cordially offering his hand to the latter. But at the Court of Russia, excepting on days of state and ceremony, the distinctions between the princes and the individuals whom they honour with their friendship are only observed by the latter.

"The manners of the Grand Duke Constantine are frank, natural, and easy. If his knowledge be superficial, his conversation is always agreeable and without pretension. He combines with a good deal of finesse the simplicity of a child. I recollect that one day in the empress's private circle we were bantering him on the elegance of his form, on the fine cut of his clothes, and a thousand other things. 'You may joke as much as you please,' said he, laughing; 'I have something in my favour reckoning from my neck down to my heels; and if Nicholas would only give me his head (Nicholas is handsome), I would give him in return all my rights of seniority.'

"'Would you indeed, Constantine?' said the empress, in her soft

177

tone of voice.

"'I would sign the contract at the feet of your Majesty.'

"'Poor fool! 'said Alexander; 'people do not exchange a crown for a handsome face.'

"'I would, though,' replied he, emphatically. This remark, and the naive manner in which it was uttered, diverted us during the whole evening.

"Constantine subsequently surrendered his right of seniority on the sole condition of being allowed to be happy in his own manner.

"But I must not wander back to the empress' parties," said the duke. "After breakfast, the grand duke and I returned and shut ourselves up in the cabinet: all these mysteries diverted Constantine greatly. Constantine said he wished to share the hardships and the dangers of my captivity. He related everything remarkable that had passed at St. Petersburg since I left it. I knew all the Russian society, and I was never done with questioning him. The war had made great voids among the many gay and happy young men whom I had known.

"In return, he wished to know everything about the Emperor Napoleon; his tastes, his habits, the most minute details of his camp life, were eagerly listened to. He paid a striking homage to the extraordinary genius of the great warrior, and cautiously avoided the slightest allusion that could be interpreted into direct blame. He spoke about my negotiations with the Emperor Alexander, who, he said, had only made me half his confidant, and though the result of the affair was to him, I must believe, a very indifferent matter, he had at least the courtesy to wish well to my efforts. I was unfortunate; he was affectionate and kind. These are the delicate shades by which a man is characterized.

"The Emperor of Russia did not return until six in the evening. 'My dear Caulincourt,' said he, while entering, 'I have been busy about your affairs. For your sake I have acted the diplomatist,—that is to say, I have been reserved and artful. I have avoided entering into serious discussion with the view of leaving matters pending. When pressed, I gave that sort of replies which bind to nothing. I entrenched myself behind certain powerful considerations, which did not permit us to decide rashly on a matter so important as the choice of a sovereign. Finding myself safe on that ground, I next made Schwartzenburg give way, and I resumed the question of the Regency. We had a warm discussion. I do not play the diplomatist with you, my dear duke, but I cannot tell you everything. Hasten back to the Emperor Napoleon, give him a faithful account of what has passed here, and return as quickly as possible; you understand me—as the official bearer of Napoleon's abdication in favour of his son.'

"Sire, said I, earnestly, what is to be done with the emperor?

"'I hope you know me well enough to be certain that I shall never suffer any insult to be offered to him. In whatsoever manner his destiny may be fixed, the Emperor Napoleon shall be properly treated. I give you my word for it.'

"When all was afterwards lost, I claimed this promise, and claimed it not in vain. It was to Alexander solely that Napoleon was indebted for the sovereignty of the Isle of Elba.

"Sire, I shall not endeavour to express my gratitude to you, it would be impossible for me to do it otherwise than by prostrating myself at your feet.

"'In my arms, my dear friend,' and he embraced me like a bother. 'Had I not wished to serve you, Caulincourt, I would have said so at once. Now we must part; I have my reasons tor urging you. Return to Fontainebleau as fast as possible.'

"The grand duke went downstairs to give orders about my departure; for it was necessary that I should leave Paris with the same precautions as I had entered it. At twilight we went out on foot, and found the carriage in the Champs Elysèes. An hour and a half afterwards we separated on the road to Essonne.

"Prince, said I, on leaving him, I carry with me a recollection which neither time nor circumstances can efface. The service you have rendered me is one which must bind a man of honour for ever and to death. In all places, in all circumstances, dispose of me, of my fortune, and of my life.

"'Yes, my dear duke, I rely on you, do you also rely on your Russian friends. Courage! you have my brother's support, so do not despair. *Adieu*, and return speedily.'

"Ill-informed persons, who have contracted unjust prejudices against the Russian Sovereign, will tax me with partiality for Alexander and his family. But I speak in truth and sincerity, and I fulfil an obligation of honour in rendering them that justice which is their due. The base alone disavow benefactors and benefits.

"Eighteen leagues separated me from the emperor; but I performed the journey in five hours. In proportion as I approached Fontainebleau I felt my courage fail. Heavens! what a message had I to bear! In the mission which I had just executed, I had experienced all the disgust

that could be endured by pride and self-love; but in the present business my heart bled for the pain I was about to inflict on the emperor,
who rose in my affections in promotion as the clouds of misfortune
gathered around him."

CHAPTER 17

Napoleon's Abdication

"The environs of Fontainebleau were filled with troops, who were bivouacking, full of impatience for battle. I know not how I was recognised, but I was surrounded and followed to the gate of the *château*, and cries of '*Vive l'Empereur!*' 'To Paris! to Paris!' resounded on all sides. The shouts of these brave men distressed me.

"When I alighted I saw the Prince of Wagram, who came eagerly up to me. 'Well, my dear friend,' said he, 'whereabouts are we now?'

"This question, and the tone in which it was uttered, displeased me. Where is the emperor? was my reply, uneasy at seeing the ground apartments all shut up.

"I found the emperor in the small apartments in the first storey, that run along by the gallery of Francis I.

"When I entered the cabinet he was writing. He rose instantly, and came to me. Ten years seemed to have passed over his noble head since last we parted. A slight contraction of the lips gave to his countenance an expression of indescribable suffering.

"'What has been done? Have you seen the Emperor of Russia? What did he say?' And, doubtless observing distress in my looks, he took my hand and pressed it convulsively, saying, 'Speak, Caulincourt, speak; I am prepared for everything.'

"Sire, I have seen the Emperor Alexander; I have passed twenty-four hours concealed in his apartments.

"'Ah, hah! Well?'

"The Emperor of Russia is not your Majesty's enemy (he made gestures expressive of doubt); no, Sire, in him alone your cause has a supporter.

"'To the facts—what is his wish? what do they intend?'

"'Sire, I replied, in a voice scarcely intelligible, your Majesty is required to make great sacrifices to secure to your son the crown of France,

"'That is to say,' replied he, in an accent terribly impressive, 'that they will not treat with me; that they mean to drive me from the throne which I conquered by my sword; that they would make a helot of me—an object of derision, destined to serve as an example to those who, by the sole ascendency of genius and superiority of talent, command men, and make legitimate kings tremble on their worm-eaten thrones.' . . . . He walked about for some instants in the greatest agitation. Then, turning to me, and crossing his arms—'And is it you, Caulincourt, who are charged with such a mission to me? ah!' He threw himself exhausted into a chair, and covered his face with his hands.

"I remained silent.

"He turned towards me. 'Have you not the courage to go on? Let me hear what it is your Alexander has desired you to say.'

"'Sire, said I, quite grieved and disheartened, your Majesty has no mercy. The stroke which is now felt by you lacerated my heart before it reached yours. For these forty-eight hours the torture has rankled in a thousand manners in my breast.

"'I am to blame, Caulincourt—I am to blame, my friend,' he said, with an irresistible accent. 'There are moments,' lifting his hand to his forehead, 'there are moments when I feel my brain beating within my head. . . . . So many misfortunes assail me at once. That powerful organisation, which so often sustained me amidst battles and perils, sinks under the repeated strokes which overwhelm me. I cannot doubt your fidelity, Caulincourt. Of all about me, you, perhaps, are the only one in whom I place implicit faith: it is only among my poor soldiers, it is only in their grief-expressing eyes, that I still find written fidelity and devoted attachment When happy, I thought I knew men; but I was destined to know them only in misfortune.' He paused, and remained plunged in deep thought, his eyes fixed on the floor.

"For my part, I was exhausted in body and mind. I happened to turn my eyes on a mirror in front of me, and I was appalled by my own looks.

"Sire, said I, I request permission to take a little rest. I am beyond measure fatigued. I have important communications to make to your Majesty, You must be correctly informed of the difficulties of your position before you can decide on the course to be adopted, and I feel that in my present state I am incapable of giving those detailed explanations which the importance of the subject demand.

"'You are right, Caulincourt; go and take some rest. I have a pre-sentiment of the subject about which we shall have to discourse, and it is necessary for me to prepare myself for the consequences. Go and repose awhile; I will take care to have you called at ten o'clock.'

"On reaching my chamber I fell down in a fainting fit. When I recovered my senses, I perceived Ivan near my bedside. He wished to bleed me, but I would not permit him. Had I not a reply to take back to Paris, where every instant a portion of the plank cast out for the shipwrecked was being carried away? I took a bath, and before ten o'clock I was in the emperor's presence.

"He was calm, but the look of care in his countenance bore witness to the anxiety of which he was the victim. 'Take a seat, Caulincourt,' said he, 'and tell me what they require—what is exacted from me.'

"I gave him a faithful account of my long conversation with the Emperor of Russia. Indignant exclamations frequently burst from his lips on hearing the baseness which I was obliged to describe. But when I came to the question which had been debated in the council of the Allied Sovereigns, relative to the restoration of the Bourbons, he sprung from his chair, and pacing rapidly up and down the room, 'Enough I enough!' he cried, 'they are mad! Restore the Bourbons! It will not last for a single year. . . . . The Bourbons are the antipathy of nine-tenths of the French nation:—and the army, whose leaders have fought against the emigrants—what will they do with the army? My soldiers will never consent to be theirs! It is the height of folly to think of melting down the empire into a government formed out of ele-ments so heterogeneous. Can it ever be forgotten that the Bourbons have lived twenty years on the charity of foreigners in open war with the principles and the interests of France? Restore the Bourbons! It is not merely madness, but it shows a desire to inflict on the country every species of calamity. . . . Is it true that such ah idea is seriously entertained?'

"I acquainted him unreservedly with all the machinations which were being carried on with that view.

"'But,' he observed, 'the Senate, the grand dignitaries, can never consent to see a Bourbon on the throne. Setting aside the baseness of agreeing to such an arrangement, what place, I should like to know, could be assigned them in a court from which they or their fathers dragged Louis XVI. to the scaffold! As for me, I was a new man, un-sullied by the excesses which defiled the French Revolution. In me there was no motive for revenge. I had every thing to reconstruct, and I should never have dared to sit on the vacant throne of France had not my brow been bound with laurels. The French people elevated me because I had executed with them, and for them, great and noble works. But the Bourbons! what have they done for France?—What portion of the victories, of the glory, of the prosperity, of France, belongs to them? What could they do to promote the interests or independence of the people—when, restored by foreigners, they will be forced to yield to all their demands, and, in a word, to bend the knee before their masters? Advantage may be taken of the stupor into which foreign occupation has thrown the capital to abuse the power of the strongest by proscribing me and my family; but to ensure tranquillity to the Bourbons in Paris! Never! Bear in mind my prophecy, Caulincourt.'

"How frequently," said the Duke de Vicenza, "have I for the last dozen years, as events successively passed before my eyes, reflected on the prescience of that mind, so prompt to perceive all the consequences of political changes.

"'Now,' resumed the emperor, after a pause, and in a more tranquil tone, 'let us return to the matter in question. My abdication is insisted on. Upon this condition the regency will be given to the empress, and the crown acquired for my son. I do not know that I have the right to resign the sovereign authority—that I should he justified in taking such a step until all hope was lost. I have fifty thousand men at my disposal. My brave troops still acknowledge me for their sovereign. Full of ardour and devotedness, my soldiers loudly call on me to lead them to Paris. The sound of my cannon would electrify the Parisians, and rouse the national spirit—insulted by the presence of foreigners parading in our public places. The inhabitants of Paris are brave; they would support me: and after the victory,' he added, assuming a more animated tone,—'after the victory, the nation should choose between me and the Allies, and I never would descend from the throne, unless driven from it by the French people. Come with me, Caulincourt; it is now twelve o'clock. I am going to review the troops.'

"Time will fail him, thought I; all is lost! and I followed him, a prey to the cruellest anxiety.

"The emperor inspected the line of his advanced posts, and at every moment the army was reinforced by the junction of dispersed bodies of troops, which were continually arriving. The artillery was directed on Orleans. The soldiers, delighted at again seeing the emperor in the midst of them, received him with acclamations of the most unbounded joy. 'Paris! Paris!' was the cry, and the officers, brandishing their sabres in the air, surrounded Napoleon, exclaiming, 'Sire, lead us on to Paris.' 'Yes, my friends,' replied the emperor, 'we will fly to the succour of Paris; tomorrow we will commence our march.' At these words *vivas* and shouts of all kinds rent the air.

"I confess," observed the duke, "that my heart beat quickly. At that moment I shared all the hopes of the emperor, and though success was far from sure, yet at least there seemed to exist some chances in its favour. Reduced as Napoleon was to such an extremity, it was necessary to attempt this *coup-de-main*.

"'Well?" said he to me, on dismounting from his horse in the courtyard of the *château*.

"Sire, I replied, this is your last stake; your Majesty ought alone to decide.

"'You approve of my determination,' said he, with a smile, 'that is clear;' and with an easy air be passed through the crowd of embroidered uniforms which still encumbered the saloons.

"There, various and conflicting comments were made upon passing events. The young generals, full of ardour, and regardless of fresh toils, embraced with delight the design of delivering the capital from the enemy; but among other groups, composed of persons who no longer had to make their fortune, dissatisfaction, though not loudly expressed, was plainly manifested. With them the idea of the misery which might result to individuals from a battle in Paris created alarm. The disposition displayed by the troops to go headlong forward, excited any feeling but confidence in those persons who were cool enough to reason. This *coup-de-tête*, for such was the expression used, might, it was said, in the event of success, save one individual, but it would be at the expense of all the rest.

"I was made acquainted with these observations by some persons distinguished by their generous feelings, and with whom honour had far greater influence than any personal considerations—men who never thought of balancing their fortune, or even their existence, against their duty to their country. I was tortured by anxiety, for I could not inform the emperor of these things, and yet on the following day the movement on Paris was to begin. In the evening, rumours of the abdication began to circulate. Napoleon, who had still something to learn of the perfidy and baseness of men, had confidentially disclosed to an old friend the communication I made him on the part of the

Emperor of Russia. 'The abdication is an advisable measure; it is the only means of putting an end to these eternal wars; it is now time to think of peace.'

"Such were the sentiments expressed by many, and in the event of Napoleon refusing to consent to the proposition, the expediency of forcing him was already spoken of by some. Be assured," continued the duke, "that all that I am relating is correct in every particular; at any rate, I speak with reserve rather than exaggeration. My heart swells with indignation at the recollection of those deplorable scenes; and it is with difficulty that I can persuade myself not to name those illustrious but ungrateful individuals; but it would not be right to put a brand on our former national glory. After this, events succeeded each other with irresistible rapidity.

"In the night, the emperor received an express from the Duke of Ragusa, who was encamped with his army at Essonne, communicating the *Senatus Consultum*, dated the evening before. The Senate had pronounced the forfeiture of Napoleon. The *aide-de-camp* who brought this intelligence had not been discreet, for it was at once known by every observing person at Fontainebleau; and it was the subject of conversation during the morning of the 4th.

"On the 3rd, orders were given to remove, on the following day, the imperial head quarters, which were to be fixed between Ponthierry and Essonne. Still it was easy to see that not a single dignitary was making any preparations to follow the movement. Napoleon was too much occupied to perceive, or at any rate he affected not to perceive, this absence of all activity. He went out as usual at 12 o'clock to review the troops, and all who had heard the news of the preceding night anxiously watched his movements; but Napoleon did not revoke the orders which he had before given.

"After the parade he was ushered into his apartments by all the marshals and dignitaries present. Then began at first insinuations; representations followed; then warm remonstrances; and at last a declaration that they would not march on Paris. It is impossible to describe what Napoleon suffered.

A few hours afterwards the emperor sent for me. His countenance was fearfully altered; but his expression was calm and his bearing firm. He took from off his desk a paper written entirely with his own hand, and presented it to me. He said,—'Here is my abdication, Caulincourt; carry it to Paris.' Never did Napoleon appear to me so truly grand as at that moment. Overcome by grief, the tears glistened in my eyes.

'Brave, brave friend,' cried he; 'but these ungrateful men!' he added, with strong emotion, 'they will live to regret me.' He then threw himself into my arms, and pressed me several times to his agitated breast. 'Depart, Caulincourt! depart immediately!' said he.

"Sire, I observed, upon an occasion of so much solemnity and importance, charged as I am to bear the official act of your Majesty's abdication, I request you to appoint two grand officers of the empire to accompany me.

"He reflected awhile, 'Ney and Ragusa—Marmont is my oldest companion in arms.'

"Sire, the Duke of Ragusa is not here: the Duke of Tarento will be a worthy representative of the army.

"The emperor was undecided, but the Duke de Bassano was consulted. He observed, that whatever might be the opinions of the Duke of Tarento, he was a man of honour, and would honourably execute his mission. Maret's opinion was well-founded; the demeanour and conduct of Macdonald were perfect.

"The powers were drawn up. A sombre melancholy was apparent on every countenance. Having given his last instructions, the emperor returned to his cabinet. I shall never forget the last look which he cast on me. Ney, Macdonald, and I, immediately stepped into a carriage; Rayneval and Rumigny accompanied us as secretaries."

"Alas!" said I to the Duke de Vicenza, who was rising to take leave, "what a sad termination of the bold project of marching on Paris!"

"All is not yet told. I was reserved for other sorrows; a few days after I was destined to support him expiring in my arms.....You will now understand how my life has been worn out with his."

"Ah!" thought I, "it may be easily foreseen that a few years hence you will both die the same death."

★★★★★★

The Duke de Vicenza, like the Emperor Napoleon, died of cancer in the stomach.

★★★★★★

CHAPTER 18

The French and the Tartars

"We arrived at Paris on the evening of the 4th, and I obtained a few moments' conversation with the Emperor Alexander before the meeting of the council of the Allied Sovereigns. 'Ah,' cried he, perceiving me, 'you have returned very tardily.'

"Sire, it did not depend on me.

"'It is a great misfortune!'

"Has your Majesty, then, changed your intentions?

"'I gave you my word, my dear duke; but events are beyond my control, and they proceed with such rapidity, that what was possible yesterday is today impossible.'

"But, Sire, I am the bearer of the act of abdication of the Emperor Napoleon in favour of the King of Rome. Marshals Ney and Macdonald accompany me as the plenipotentiaries of his Majesty. All the formalities are prepared; nothing can now impede the conclusion of the treaty.

"'My dear duke, when I told you to use haste I had my reasons for so doing. I knew the ground beneath your feet was slipping away. When you departed, the position of the Emperor Napoleon was still imposing, and might even become perplexing to us. The successive rallying of troops round Fontainebleau, their devotion to the person of the emperor, his address, his courage, were of a nature to create alarm. A *coup-de-main* might be boldly attempted on Paris, and a population of 700,000 or 800,000 souls was to be kept in check; all these things rendered our position difficult. These were grave considerations, and I gave them their proper value. But today the position of the Emperor Napoleon is not the same.'

"Your Majesty deceives yourself; the Emperor Napoleon has at his command, within, at most, the circle of a few leagues, 80,000 men, who loudly demand to be marched upon Paris, who will suffer them-selves to be cut in pieces to the last man, and whose example will electrify the capital.

"'My dear duke,' interrupted Alexander, 'I am truly sorry to cause affliction to you. You are in complete ignorance as to what is going on. The senate has declared the forfeiture of Napoleon.'

"I know it, Sire; but the army?

"'The army! the adherence of the commanders of corps are pour-ing in from all parts. They disguise, under the pretext of submission to the mandates of the great body of the state, their eagerness to absolve themselves from allegiance to a sovereign who is unfortunate. Thus to their personal interests is united the legality of the act. Such are mankind, my dear duke.'

"Sire, I blush for those of my countrymen who have thus tarnished the honour of their past lives. But, Sire, these shameful exceptions will find no echo in the army, which remains devoted and faithful to its sovereign.

"'Again you are mistaken, duke. At the very moment in which we speak, Fontainebleau is uncovered, and the person of Napoleon is in our power.'

"What say you, Sire? cried I. Still fresh treasons?

"'They who are anxious for the triumph of a different cause from yours, my dear duke, have the power in their hands. They labour to detach from the party of Napoleon the most influential generals; and as every man looks to his own fortune, every man is eager to secure it. The camp of Essonne is raised.' I recoiled in dismay.

"'The camp of Essonne is raised,' repeated Alexander; 'the Duke of Ragusa has sent in his adherence, and that of his division of the army. The troops which compose it, commanded by General Souh—..., are in full march towards Versailles—what more shall I tell you?

"In spite of the many bitter deceptions I had witnessed," added the duke, "the intelligence struck me like a thunderbolt. A most singular fact was connected with it. The man who thus deserted, who was marching his troops on the road to Versailles, and delivering the em-peror to the mercy of the enemy; this General Souh— ..., had come the evening before to Fontainebleau, and, under pretexts of losses and pecuniary embarrassments, extorted from the emperor two thousand crowns.

"I need scarcely tell you," pursued the Duke de Vicenza, "that the secret of this base conduct did not escape from my lips. A feeling of national honour withheld me from betraying to a foreigner such base conduct on the part of a Frenchman.

"Sire, I replied, in the face of such facts, I foresee but too plainly the dispositions I shall find in the council. I have no hope but in the magnanimity of your Majesty.

"'I am hurried along by circumstances,' replied Alexander. 'The abdication has been too long delayed. In politics, three days are three ages. As long as the Emperor Napoleon found himself supported by an army united in resolution to march to Paris, powerful considerations balanced the schemes proposed by the adversaries of the Imperial cause. But now, when the army appears to abandon its chief; when the marshals and generals are leading away the soldiers under their command—now, I repeat, the question is entirely changed. Fontainebleau is no longer an imposing military position. In addition to this, all the persons of note at Fontainebleau have sent their submissions, and have here in Paris an emissary who treated in their names? Now, judge for yourself what I could do.'

"I raised my hand to my burning brow, and in the stupor into which this communication had thrown me I had no power to express a single thought.

"'During your absence,' continued Alexander, 'a discussion arose on the subject of the Regency. Recriminations go for little when an idea arises in my mind, and the carrying it into execution appears just; but, my dear duke, your antagonists are skilful persons. Some very curious things have taken place. A droll sort of comedy was acted in our presence the day before yesterday. Whether anything had transpired which took place at our conference; whether the Emperor Napoleon had made any confidants at Fontainebleau, I know not; but the fact is, that the affair of the Regency and your promised arrival were known, and everything around us was in motion. The day before yesterday, Messrs. de Talleyrand, d'Albert, de Jaucourt, the Abbés Louis and de Montesquiore, introduced the question of the Regency, and contended against it with all their might.

"'There was no want of complaints and accusations against your emperor; and M. de Pradt declared, that neither Bonaparte or his family had any partisans; that all France earnestly demanded the Bourbons. I made some observations. Then General Dessolles, addressing me personally, said, in an impressive tone:—"Sire, you promised, on your arrival in Paris, not to treat with Bonaparte, and, acting on that promise, we have not hesitated to declare him deposed, and to recall the Bourbons. Now to declare for the regency would be to decree the continuation of the men and the dynasty of the empire. The members of the provisional government would then have nothing to do but to demand of the Allied Powers an asylum in their dominions." I tell you, my dear friend, the men who manage the affairs of your country are very clever, they manoeuvre well. The adherences of the civil and military bodies are pouring in. Amidst the manifestations, whether spontaneous or advised, my position is the more difficult, because, instead of being supported by my allies, I meet on their part an active resistance.

"'It is not,' added Alexander, with kindness, 'it is not with the intention of breaking my word, Caulincourt, that I present to your eyes so many miseries; it is to make you appreciate the difficulties, or, let us speak plainly, the impossibilities which masters my good wishes.'

"The Emperor Napoleon, I exclaimed, is betrayed, basely abandoned, delivered to the enemy by the very men who ought to have made for him a rampart of their bodies and their swords! This, sire, is horrible! horrible!

"Alexander's countenance assumed an expression of bitter disdain, and, placing his hand on my arm, he said—'And add, duke, that he is betrayed by men who owe him everything, everything—their fame, their fortune. What a lesson for us sovereigns! Take courage, Caulincourt, I will be at the council before you. We shall see what can be done.'

"In leaving the house of the Emperor Alexander, I met in the court-yard M. de Pradt. He was incessantly hovering around the sovereigns, and never left the saloons of the Allies. I knew his underhanded practices, and did not wish to speak to him. He, however, came up to me, and, with the easiest air in the world, said, 'I'm charmed to see you, duke.' I looked at him without returning his salutation. 'Duke,' added he, rubbing his hands, (you know that is a habit he has got), 'your affairs are not going on very well. You are sinking fast!' I was no longer master of myself. You are a villain, said I, seizing him by the collar and taking him roughly. But what could I do with a grey-headed *abbé*? I comprehended how ridiculous it would be to vent my fury on this man, and I satisfied myself with pushing him from me and making him pirouette. And," added the duke, shrugging his shoulders, "That was as much vengeance as he was worth."

"The Abbé de Pradt," said I, "has not revealed this episode in his famous revelations of April, 1814; and yet I must do him the justice to own that he has shown great candour of cynicism in the account he has given of his own feats."

"He neither forgot nor forgave the *pirouette*," continued the duke, "and when all was lost, he pursued me with his venom and malice. It was a matter of glory and profit to him to persecute the advocate of the Bonapartes. It was a title by which favours were to be obtained; and, apropos of that, is it not one of the most revoking scandals inflicted by the restoration, that the dignity of Grand Chancellor of the Legion of Honour should have been conferred on the Abbé de Pradt?—The Abbé de Pradt, perjured in all his oaths, become the most bitter enemy of his benefactors! The Abbé de Pradt, in short, is Grand Chancellor of the Legion of Honour! But let us leave these miserable creatures. It is really impossible to touch upon that epoch without exhumating something disgraceful to human nature.

"Whilst yet excited by this absurd *rencontre*," continued the duke, 'I rejoined Macdonald and Ney; I did not tell them what I had learned from the Emperor of Russia. Our mission was sufficiently thorny, and I refrained from lacerating the feelings of two men charged with me to defend the interests of Napoleon.

"We betook ourselves to the council; I wish I could carry you with me into the saloon of the Allies; give you an exact idea of the assembly, composed of our enemies, and of those base Frenchmen who, having mounted the cockade of foreigners, aided them in their efforts to enslave France. But why should I attempt to describe that which is beyond all description: the mute play of the faces, the attitudes, the gestures of the different actors; and yet, therein lies the whole spirit of a great drama.

"When we entered, the Emperor of Russia was talking earnestly with the King of Prussia, in the embrasure of a window. On the left hand of William, and a little behind him, stood General Beurnonville. The discussion appeared animated. The King of Prussia, in replying to Alexander, appeared always to summon his acolyte, who, with an obsequious bow, approved his words, spoken, doubtless, in opposition to those of the *Czar*. I understood afterwards that General Beurnonville, when he carried to the King of Prussia the important news of the defection of Marmont and of his division, prevailed on his Majesty to reject with firmness the regency which was about to be proposed to the council by the plenipotentiaries of Napoleon. Matters were so managed that each sovereign, or each representative of a power, was circumvented, besieged, and harassed by one of those men whose names have acquired so miserable a celebrity.

"A little further off, Schwartzenberg, Nesselrode, Licbtenstein, and Pozzo di Borgo, were grouped together. This last-mentioned personage made himself remarkable by the vivacity of his gestures; be talked with warmth, and this could only arise from his urging measures of rigour against Napoleon. Near this group the partisans of the royalists were buzzing about and fidgeting. From an air of joy on their faces, the arrogance and self-possession of their manner, it was easy to judge that they were well assured of the success of their intrigues, and had no doubt respecting the issue of the conference about to be opened.

"Our arrival put an end to the separate conversations. The Emperor of Russia and the King of Prussia approached a large table covered with a green cloth, which occupied the middle of the room. They sat down, and each person took his place.

"I laid before the Emperor Alexander, in the name of the Emperor Napoleon, the act of abdication in favour of the King of Rome, and of the Empress Maria Louisa, Regent.

"King William spoke first, and coolly observed that subsequent events no longer permitted the Powers to treat with the Emperor Napoleon. The wishes of France for the return of her ancient sovereigns was manifest on all sides. The first body in the state, the senate, supported by the assent of the citizens, having declared Napoleon deposed from the throne, the Allied Sovereigns could not mix themselves up in the affairs of the French Government, and recognise, contrary to the declaration of the Senate, the dethroned emperor's right to dispose of the crown of France.

"Marshal Macdonald exposed with force the high political considerations which ought to induce the Allied Powers to realise the act of abdication in favour of the empress and her son. 'The emperor,' said he, 'holds the crown from the French nation; he resigns it for the purpose of obtaining general peace. The Allied Powers having declared that he was the only obstacle to peace, he does not hesitate to sacrifice himself when the interests of his country are concerned. But if they deny him the right of abdicating in favour of his son, great misfortunes may result therefrom. The army, entirely devoted to its chief, is still ready to shed the last drop of its blood in support of the rights of its Sovereign.'

"A smile of disdain followed this declaration; in a certain part of the room whisperings were heard; at the same moment Marshal the Duke of Ragusa was announced. He entered holding his head erect, and with a smile upon his lips. Shaking of hands and congratulations were exchanged between him and some personages who went to meet him.

"The effect which his presence produced is not to be described. There is, in the contemplation of a bad action, something revolting to generous minds. Thus a sensation of stupor pervaded the majority of the assembly. It may be said, that in the presence of this incarnate treason, there was not strength to add insult to the misfortunes which pursued the vanquished hero.

"But personal interest soon banished these generous emotions, and this was natural enough. The occasion was so favourable for the Allies! France was surrendered, and delivered over to their mercy. Our very enemies had never dreamed of so easy a conquest. The Emperor Alexander said to me one day, 'I truly believe that if we had wished to place Kutusoff upon the throne of France, they would have cried out *Vive Kutusoff!*'

"Really," said I, to the Duke de Vicenza, "in that idea the Tartar expressed a good deal of contempt for us."

"Alas! there is no Tartar, be he serf or prince, who would not shrink from the baseness which dishonours this passage of our history. Recollect the noble blind peasant, Petrowisk; think of Moscow and its magnificent palaces, burned as a sacrifice to the country, and between those savages, inspired with sublime patriotism, and ourselves, you will make a most sorrowful comparison.

"I continually run away from my subject," pursued the duke; "it is because, when I talk on these matters, I feel, in spite of myself, those emotions revive over which years have rolled.

"The arrival of Marmont rendered it unnecessary to resume the subject under discussion. The considerations we had attempted to establish no longer existed, and on both sides explanations had become idle. In fact, the defection of the camp at Essonne, the advanced guard of the army of Fontainebleau, delivered the emperor bound hand and foot to his enemies. Already one corps of the Russian Army, by a movement combined with the retreat of the French troops, was echeloned from Paris upon Essonne, and covered all that bank of the Seine. In this state of things a conditional abdication was no longer to be thought of. Napoleon was said to be deposed from the throne by the wish of the nation and the army. The powers could not mix themselves up with the internal affairs of France in anything. An unconditional abdication must be sent to Paris as quickly as possible. Such was in substance the declaration to which it was our business to submit. Every instant dispatches arrived, which were joyfully transferred from hand to hand—they were adherences. Thus to all the humiliations of defeat was added the inexpressible disgust caused by the presence of certain Frenchmen assisting as conquerors in the disasters of their country.

"We retired in consternation. Our duty was not now to dispute for the throne, but to watch for the personal security of the emperor. This idea prevailed over every other: it pursued me without intermission. The only means of preserving the emperor was to place him, by a treaty, under the safeguard of the Powers. What a sad alternative!

"An unconditional abdication was the sacrifice for which the future fate of Napoleon, and that of his family, would be guaranteed. Time pressed. But, said I, who amongst us will take upon himself to be the bearer of this fresh blow?

"'You,' answered Ney, with a tone of sorrow, 'you are the friend of his heart, and you can, better than any other, soften the bitterness of this news For my part, I have no courage but in the presence of an enemy. I can never, never go and say coldly to him—' (Poor Ney! But his admirable military career, his lamentable end, should cover all his faults.)

"Macdonald, filled with grief, kept a mournful silence. At length, taking my hand, which he pressed with affection,—'It is a sorrowful, a most sorrowful mission, but you only can fulfil it to the emperor, whose entire confidence you possess.'

"Macdonald appreciated the difficulties of this terrible task which devolved on me. He was of opinion that the emperor, exasperated by this last exigency, would resume the project of continuing the war.

"I departed. The distance from Paris to Fontainebleau appeared to me so short, that when my carriage entered the court of the castle I was struck with it as with a thing unexpected. I remained, as it were, transfixed in my seat, the prey of despair. Was I, then, destined only to approach the emperor to give him torture? I revolted at the misery of my destiny which forced upon me the office of inflicting pain on him whom with my blood I would have ransomed from his sufferings. For a week I had a hundred times defied fate to make me more wretched, and fate unrelenting appeared every hour to throw back my defiance. I sprang from my carriage, and reached the cabinet of the emperor almost running. I know not how it happened that there was no one there to announce me. I opened the door. Sire, it is Caulincourt, said

I, and I entered.

"'Already!' and his penetrating and rapid glance appeared to wish to pluck my thoughts from my lips.

"He was seated at a window looking out upon the gardens. His livid complexion, the disorder of his dress, made me fearful that he had been watching all night, and I could not find courage to commence the sad subject which had brought me back. 'The defection of Essonne,' said he, with an effort, 'has served as an excuse for new pretensions, is it not so? Now that I am abandoned, openly betrayed, there are other conditions? Let me see, what do they now demand?'

"I explained the changes which had taken place in his military and political position, through the defection of his troops. I related my conversation with Alexander, and all that had passed in the council, except the arrival of Marmont in the saloon of the Allies—Marmont, whom he called his oldest companion in arms, and whose name had sprung spontaneously from his lips when he was selecting plenipotentiaries to entrust with the care of defending his interests. I could not in truth speak of that man. Napoleon, too, disdained to pronounce a name now sullied with odious treason.

"I had ceased to speak, and the emperor, struck with a stupor, remained absorbed in his reflections. 'We must break off these negotiations, which have become so humiliating,' said he, at length, in an altered tone. 'War and its hazards offer nothing worse than such conditions. I will not accept them.'

"But it was not in the ardent and fiery organisation of Napoleon to reason coolly, when he could pour forth the feelings of his heart. A first impression almost always found him master of himself, after that the lava which flowed in his veins made his imagination burst like a volcano, and cast forth fire and flames. Then his eyes flashed, the tones of his voice became awful, the expression of his face became lofty and terrible, and all the force, all the energy, all the power of human intelligence appeared concentrated within him in his nature in gigantic proportions.

"All at once, thrusting aside with violence the stool on which one of his legs was resting, he arose and rushed towards his desk, on which were opened maps stuck full of pins.

"'Do they suppose,' cried he, in a voice of thunder, 'do these arrogant conquerors suppose that they are masters of France because treason has opened to them the gates of Paris? If a handful of vile conspirators have planned my destruction, the nation has not ratified the infamous deed. I will summon my people around me. Fools! they cannot conceive that a man like me only ceases to be formidable when he is laid in the tomb. Tomorrow, in one hour, I will shake off the fetters with which they have bound me, and rise stronger and more terrible than ever, at the head of 130,000 warriors.

"'Attend to my calculation, Caulincourt: I have here around me 25,000 men of my guards. Those giants, the terror of the legions of the enemy, shall form the nucleus round which I will rally the army of Lyons, 30,000 strong. These, with Grenier's corps of 18,000 just arrived from Italy, Suchet's 15,000, and the 40,000 scattered under the command of Soult, make altogether an army of 130,000 men. I am master of all the strong places in France and Italy, though I know not as yet whether they contain aught but felons and traitors. I am again upon my feet,' said he, raising his head proudly, 'assisted by this same sword which has opened to me every capital in Europe. I am still the chief of the bravest army in the whole world—of those French battalions of which no portion has suffered a defeat. I will exhort them to the defence of their country by the principles and in the name of liberty. Above my eagles shall be inscribed "Independence and our country," and my eagles will again be terrible! If the chiefs of the army, who owe their splendour to my conquests, wish for repose, let them retire. I will find among those who now wear worsted epaulettes, men fit to be generals and marshals!'

"During this vehement sally the emperor strode up and down his cabinet with quick steps. All at once he stopped, and said, 'Be seated, Caulincourt; write to Ney and Macdonald to return directly; all is broken off.'

"Sire, I pray your Majesty to take time to reflect before you adopt an extreme measure.

"'All has been reflected upon,' replied he, drily; 'I have not the choice of means.'

"Your Majesty has given way to natural irritation; but, Sire, circumstances have acquired a weight which does not permit a step to be taken before having confronted in every aspect the chances which may ensue.

"'I renounce all negotiation. They have rejected the personal sacrifice which I imposed upon myself for the sake of purchasing the peace and the repose of France. They have insolently refused my abdication, and I retract it. I will prepare for the conflict; my place is marked out above or below the surface of a field of battle. May the French blood, which is again about to flow, fall upon the wretches who wish the ruin of their country !'

"It was useless at that moment to attempt to enter upon a calm and dispassionate discussion. I knew the emperor. He would firmly resist opposition long sustained; bat he would yield to It great misfortune, and attempt to resume at a later opportunity these distressing questions. I asked his leave to retire. 'We are most unfortunate, Caulincourt, for I and you are one. Go, and we will speak of this when I see you again.'

CHAPTER 19

Napoleon Signs the Act of his Abdication

"When I got to my own quarters," said the duke, "I threw myself upon my bed. All that the emperor had uttered entered deeply into my heart. I could have shed tears on beholding the powerlessness to which such means and such energy were reduced; but there is at the bottom of our hearts something which revolts at the idea of insult offered to our country. I trembled at the resolutions of the emperor. Doubtless he could for some time have prolonged the war, but the best blood of France would have been shed in useless victories. Six hundred thousand foreigners covered the soil; their reserves, collected upon the frontiers, waited but the signal to pour themselves upon our provinces. Rebellion was in the heart of France, in the capital of which one hundred thousand bayonets protected treason, and supported an illegal government *de facto*. Though convinced by these considerations, go pregnant with misfortunes and disasters, yet I could not approve the projects of the emperor.

"My duty imposed upon me the unpleasant task of opposing them,—of pointing out to him the dark picture of the calamities which he would bring upon our country by carrying into execution such desperate measures. I knew that I had but little time left. Hours and minutes were vanishing rapidly. Now that I am in cold blood, I cannot comprehend, I cannot conceive, how I resisted, during twenty days, the fatigue of body and the torment of mind which assailed me. My position in relation to Napoleon was completely different from that of others. No person partook, or could partake, his grief to the same degree as I did; and when he said 'You and I are one,' he expressed in a few words the communion of feeling between us.

"Nothing can describe the confusion which reigned on all sides, and in all things, during this episode of the abdication. I will tell you at the proper time a very curious trait which relates to the brave General Leval; but let us return to the Castle of Fontainebleau, where so many sufferings were forged by evil passions.

"The emperor, who possessed great nobleness of sentiment, could not comprehend baseness and perfidy. Thus it never entered his thoughts that he was surrounded by people who waited with impatience to be released from their various obligations to him, to run to Paris to carry the assurances of their devotion to the new government Napoleon confided in one or two of his old acquaintances, whom he thought devoted to him, the news which he had received, the bad success of our negotiations, and his projects: he unbosomed himself without distrust, and, in retiring from the cabinet of the emperor, these confidants went and spread alarm and irritation amongst the impatient

"The rupture of the negotiations produced a general explosion of outcries, reproaches, and fury, throughout the gilded galleries of the palace. If the cabinet and the waiting hall were deserted, everybody had at his own abode his *coterie* and his adherents eager to bear news from Paris, and all were of one mind to reject the determination of Napoleon, which tended to prolong the war. Since he had become unfortunate, he was only thought capable of committing errors.

"It was not to his regal circle that Napoleon should have confided his projects. He should have entered sword in hand the chamber in which his mournful and silent officers were grouped together, and have said to them, 'To us, my friends, belongs the honour of avenging France!' At a few paces distant, at the bottom of the staircase, he would have found his soldiers; and, saluted by their acclamations, he should have rushed with his cohorts from the Castle of Fontainebleau upon the field of battle. He would have hurried along with him all those brave men. whom the feelings of youth and pure courage render always ready to rally round their country's banners!

"General Bonaparte would have done so. The Emperor Napoleon was influenced by the habits of a throne. He sought for support in the great functionaries of his crown, and these men, enervated, shrunk from adversity. The empire was falling to pieces! what matter if the commotion touched not their hotels and their *châteaux!*

"On my first return to Paris they were beginning to murmur, but silently! They were, however, increasing; the time for caution was past.

200

They were able to express their thoughts without danger, and they expressed them loudly. They had had enough of the empire. If Napoleon was unfortunate, who's fault was it? Was that a reason why men were to sacrifice themselves, their situations, the interests of their families, to extravagant projects? The new revolution was a grand event, affecting every French interest; and if one single person were sacrificed, there would be but a single misfortune to deplore. Others called to mind, that the Bourbons were old Frenchmen—that they reigned over our fathers. These particulars, which for a long time I had forgotten, came all at once into my recollection!

"New vacancies were perceptible every hour. It was, who shall find a pretext to go to Paris. They quitted their posts without permission, forgetting the wants of the service, indifferent about pleasing or displeasing him from whom they no longer expected anything. But why, said they, is the abdication so long delayed? When will this end? At length each became master of his own actions. His indecisions, his slowness, his warlike notions, compromised the position of the whole world. The, new government received with welcome all who arrived from the army. What would be left for the last comer? This state of things was intolerable, and the burden of the song in every mouth was, 'This must come to an end.'

"These base feelings were openly expressed. The mask was raised; the Regency was rejected; the son of Napoleon was expelled the throne. It was nonsense to remain in the ante-chambers of Fontainebleau when favours were showered down at Paris."

"Heavens!" I exclaimed; "what a hideous picture do you draw of the baseness of the world. In your place, duke, I do believe I should have fled from Fontainebleau, and, avoiding every human being, have stopped not till I had reached the retirement of the forests."

"But," continued the duke, sorrowfully, "this picture which brings the tears of indignation into your eyes, is but a sketch. Ask those men of honour who were still to be found at headquarters,—they will relate to you unheard of things.

"You will readily suppose that the time I did not pass with the emperor I passed in my own quarters. I need scarcely assure you," added the duke, with animation, "that no treasonable language was uttered within the threshold of my door. I would have thrown out of the window the first person who should have dared to say a word hostile to the emperor. They knew it: thus I was assailed by their anathemas and their rage. They pretended that if, through false pity, I could not soften to the emperor the sentiments which prevailed in respect to him in Paris, yet if, in a few words, I should tell him the truth, and threaten no longer to mix myself in his affairs, he would soon hasten to sign the abdication. Thus they pretended that I was the indirect cause of the delays which deferred the abdication of Napoleon. They took it very ill of me, and as I was deeply compromised in the cause of the vanquished, and pleaded his cause with all and against all, I had already become a man whom they avoided; some through fear of being compromised, and others because they knew that in my presence they could not but blush. Thus, when we met face to face, the most generous of them affected an interest and a solicitude about my health—it seemed much altered by my continual fatigues and journeys. Some *esprits forts* carried their magnanimity so far as to offer me their hands. You know me," said he, laughing. "You can figure to yourself with what an air I received these marks of kindness."

We all laughed. Those who knew the air of dignity, and the polished stateliness of the Duke de Vicenza, may form an idea of the manner with which he could reduce these poor fools to their proper places. The Duke de Vicenza, who was tall and erect, possessed an elegance and dignity of manner which rendered him imposing to his superiors, and amongst his equals classed him by himself. I know no one, not even the emperor, who could have conceived the idea of treating him with anything approaching to disrespect.

"Nevertheless," continued the duke, "it was but too true that the refusal of the emperor to abdicate rendered his personal portion most critical. For my part, I felt a mortal inquietude. The provisional government, which wished the complete ruin of Napoleon, and the Allies, who feared some desperate enterprise on his part, were made acquainted with all that was passing in the cabinet of the emperor. They dreaded one of those bold determinations which oftener than once had astonished Europe.

"The time which had passed since my departure from Paris had been usefully employed. They had not lost an hour. When I arrived at Fontainebleau I directed a confidential officer to send out scouts. He returned in the evening, and announced that foreign troops occupied all the avenues round Fontainebleau. The Russian Army was spread over the right bank of the Seine, from Melun to Montereau; another force had taken up its position between Essonne (abandoned by our troops) and Paris; other divisions barricaded the roads to Chartres and Orleans; others, again, which had pursued us almost step by step upon the roads of Champagne and Burgundy, had formed military establishments in the whole country between the Yonne and the Loire. In short, a vast net was spread round Fontainebleau, and at the first signal one hundred and fifty thousand men could rush upon the little army which yet guarded Napoleon.

"This information was correct. It was obtained by an intelligent officer, on whose fidelity I could rely. I ran to the emperor. He reflected a few moments. 'Not an hour is lost by these people,' said he; 'but a road which is closed against couriers can soon be opened by fifty thousand men. Ah, *parbleu!* this is what will give an advantage to the councillors of peace at any price. If this news be known, we shall see many more of them.'

"This news, sire, is as yet known only to yourself, and to two men of honour, who will keep the secret. But, after all, its publicity would add nothing to the real dangers which surround your Majesty. I conjure you, sire, decide—

"'——Dangers!' he exclaimed, 'I fear them not. A useless life is a heavy burden! I will not long support it. But before I decide, before I come to a terrible decision, Caulincourt, I wish to consult with the marshals; I wish to know if my cause, if that of my family, is no longer the cause of France, and then—then I will decide.'

"At this moment the Prince de Neufchatel and several marshals entered, Their countenances were embarrassed. The conversation commenced with some commonplace expressions. Berthier, biting his nails, muttered some words. He had, he said, sent some orderly officers to several points. All their reports were unanimous; the enemy was advancing, and taking up his position round Fontainebleau.

"'I know it,' interrupted the emperor, drily.

"But they had not come merely to announce this bad news. Very soon each of them gave his opinion, and if they did not yet dare to give decisive advice, they discussed the dangers which menaced Fontainebleau. During this conversation the emperor evinced admirable dignity. He adverted to the two conditions imposed by the Allies. The personal sacrifice which they required of him he was resigned to, but to consent to the deposition of his wife and son from the crown which he, Napoleon, had conquered by his own deeds,—that he refused.

"A mournful silence succeeded this communication.

"The emperor calmly enumerated the forces which remained to him, and which he could make use of, not to render the war eternal, but to avenge the honour of France, to restore her independence, and enable him to treat for peace on conditions less humiliating. Should he be obliged to renounce the defence of France, Italy, he observed, still offered to the army and to its chief a retreat worthy their misfortunes and their glorious recollections.

"I had taken no part in the general conversation. I had listened to the emperor's noble and dignified appeal to the hearts, to the honour, of his ancient lieutenants. But those hearts remained cold, and honour consisted only in repose. To this address of the emperor they opposed the interests of France—a useless civil war,—the country ravaged by invasion. But they found no word of sympathy for the frightful misfortune which fell upon the benefactor, the sovereign, who during twenty years had been the glory of France.

"Woe to these ungrateful men!

★★★★★★

Berthier, Murat, Ney, Massena, Augereau, Lefevre, Brune, Serrurier, Kellerman, Perignon, Clarke, Beurnonville, and many others, preceded Napoleon in the tomb.

★★★★★★

"Unable to repress my feelings, I was proceeding to leave the apartment. The noise I made attracted the attention of the emperor. Our eyes met; we understood each other: and as I opened the door, he said:—'Stop, Caulincourt.' He sat down at his desk, and wrote at full length the act of his abdication, put his signature to it, and then, proudly raising his head, said, 'I wish to be alone,' and when all but myself had left the room, he added, 'Those men have neither heart nor conscience. I am less conquered by fortune than by the egotism and ingratitude of my brothers in arms—this is hideous! Now all is consummated. Leave me, my friend.'

"I shall never," added the duke, in a tone of deep feeling, "forget those scenes at Fontainebleau.

"There is nothing in history," said he, "to be compared to these last convulsions of the French Empire, to the tortures of its chief to this agony of hours, of days!

"Six years have passed away, and the horrible rock of St. Helena has received the last breath of the greatest man of ancient or modern times.

"'And to our eternal shame,' observed Colonel de R——, 'the horrible rock of St. Helena possesses the ashes of the hero of France.'
"

We remained some minutes under the impression of these cruel thoughts. The duke thus resumed:—

"At six in the morning I entered Paris. In the course of the day we presented to the council of the Allies the abdication of the emperor. I demanded that all hostilities should be suspended, and that the different army corps of the foreign troops should cease to move upon Fontainebleau. Orders were dispatched instantly to all points, and conferences were held to determine what should be done with the emperor and his family.

"I am bound in justice to acknowledge that we were seconded with energy by the Allied Sovereigns in everything that we believed it was our duty to demand for the Imperial Family. Alexander said, 'in the pecuniary arrangements to be made with the Emperor Napoleon, it was proper that he should have sufficient to remunerate his military household, and secure the fortune of his servants. If, ultimately, these articles of treaty were evaded or forgotten, it is to those who inherited the empire that this odious violation of justice is to be attributed.'

"The question of the residence of the emperor was discussed with great animation. The French councillors wished him to be sent to a distance. At length they named St. Helena; then they hesitated between Corfu and Corsica; they spoke of the isle of Elba, and eulogised its fine climate—that it was, in short, superior either to Italy or France! I seized this opening to make a special demand. Complaints and perfidious insinuations arose. Elba was too near. Italy was still under the spell of Napoleon. But the Emperor Alexander, with whom I spoke a few moments, supported me with spirit, and decided that the principality of the island of Elba should be conceded to the Emperor Napoleon, to enjoy for his life, with the title of sovereignty and proprietorship.

"Whilst these conventions were under stipulation, I received a courier from Fontainebleau; the emperor wrote to me:—

Bring me back my abdication—I am, conquered—I yield to the fortune of arms; a simple cartel should be sufficient.

"In another letter, brought in the evening, he said:—

Why do you speak to me of conventions of a treaty? I want none. Since they will not treat with me, and only employ themselves about the disposal of my person, to what purpose is a treaty? This diplomatic negotiation displeases me; let it cease.

"About five in the morning I was awakened by a fresh courier. He was the bearer of the following message:—

> I order you to bring back to me my abdication. I will sign no treaty; and in all cases I forbid you to make any stipulations for money—that is disgusting.

"I received seven couriers in twenty-four hours. I was perfectly bewildered. I knew what he was ignorant of. I had a dreadful announcement to make. The emissaries of the provisional government were collecting around Fontainebleau. M. de Maubreuil, in 1817, at the time of his disgraceful process, had the incredible courage to reveal for what purpose they were there.

"It was, then, most urgent to bring matters to a conclusion, and I pressed, with all my might, the completion of the conventions. On the evening of the 14th of April, all was ready. We returned to Fontainebleau, bearers of the definitive treaty, to present it to the emperor. Clearly as I foresaw the difficulties of his accepting it, I hoped to conquer them by force of perseverance.

"The glance of Napoleon, when he perceived me, was like lightning.

"'Do you at length bring me back my abdication?'

"Sire, said I to him, I beseech your Majesty to hear me before yon address to me unmerited reproaches. It was no longer in my power to send back to you that act. My first care, on my arrival at Paris, was to communicate it to the Allied Sovereigns, for the purpose of obtaining a cessation of hostilities. It has served as the basis to the negotiations of the treaty. The official document of the abdication of your Majesty is already inserted in the journals.

"'And what is it to me that they have made it public, that they have inserted it in the journals, if I do not choose to treat in these forms?'

"I endeavoured to inform him with exactness of what was passing at Paris. I was forced to recall to his recollection the circumstances by which he was surrounded. To all I said, he replied, 'I will not sign—I want no treaty.'

"A part of the day was spent in these painful debates.

"During this, all was rumour throughout the Castle. The saloon adjoining the emperor's cabinet was filled with groups who discussed the news received from Paris. They were indignant that Napoleon had not yet signed, since everything had been definitively concluded. 'What does he wait for?' Every time the door of the cabinet opened, heads were thrust forward; they were so near that they could hear what passed within. The asylum of misfortune was violated by the barbarous curiosity of courtiers.

"When I quitted the emperor, I left the treaty upon his desk. I had not even been able to prevail upon him to read the whole of it. I returned to my quarters. I had need of rest; my energy was exhausted in this incessant struggle. I almost gave myself up to despair; but my thoughts returned to the sufferings of this great and noble victim, and I found the will and the power to attempt to alleviate them. My efforts and my devotion were still necessary to him. In the evening I returned to the emperor, and I found him profoundly dejected. The irritation of the day had produced a cruel apathy. I strove to rouse him from this state. He replied in monosyllables, but his thoughts were elsewhere.

"Sire, said I to him, in the same of Heaven, in the name of your own glory, come to some determination, whatever it may be; circumstances do not admit temporizing. Sire, I cannot express the agony which preys upon me; but when Caulincourt, your faithful, your devoted friend, conjures you, begs of you on his knees, to consider the position in which your Majesty is placed, there must be reasons most imperative which urge his perseverance.

"'What would you have me do?'

"And as he uttered these words he looked mournfully at me.

"I kept silence. He arose, and walked about slowly for a long time, his hands crossed behind his back; at length, as if waking from a painful dream, he said to me, in a calm voice—'It must come to an end; I feel it: my resolution is taken.'

"These last words were pronounced with an inflection of voice which chilled my heart.

"'Tomorrow, Caulincourt.'

"My presentiments seldom deceive me; they are the revelations of the soul, they are the reflections of what is to come. That evening, when I took leave of the emperor, I felt an indescribable feeling of anxiety. I could not prevail on myself to leave him. As we separated, he took me by the hand; his hand was burning, mine was like ice; and when the door of the cabinet shut upon me, with an inexplicable sensation, I seized the key. I wished for a pretence again to enter. At length I moved away. My heart felt heavy, my ideas were confused, and I sought sleep in vain. A few hours later this internal anguish was explained. I will recount to you this horrible scene, but at present—"

"No, no, not at present," repeated I, as I remarked the altered expression which overspread the pale countenance of the Duke de Vicenza. Though weak, and suffering myself, I could have passed the whole night in listening to the sad narrative.

Chapter 20

Napoleon Takes Poison

"Yesterday evening," said the duke, when we met together on the following day, "I could not describe to you the dreadful night at Fontainebleau. I found myself so ill, and the recollection of it is agonising!

"I had not been long in bed when Pelard or Constant, I now forget which, knocked loudly at my door, telling me to come with all speed to the emperor, who wished to see me. A fearful presentiment shot through my heart; and before five minutes elapsed I was by the bed on which the emperor, a prey to frightful convulsions, seemed on the point of expiring. It was a horrible sight! His face was of a livid paleness, his lips were contracted, his hair matted to his forehead by a cold perspiration, his eyes dull and fixed. Oh! the rigidity of that look made me shudder!" (and the duke by an involuntary movement covered his face with his hands, as if to avoid a fearful vision.)

"Racked by a horrible suspicion," continued the duke, "I wished, but I dared not, I could not, question him.

"'Duke,' said Ivan to me, in a low voice, 'he is lost if he do not drink; he refuses everything; but he must drink—he must vomit. In the name of Heaven, persuade him to drink.'

"I snatched the cup from the hands of Ivan; it contained tea, I believe. I presented it to the emperor, who pushed it from him. 'I die, Caulincourt—to you I commend my wife and son; defend my memory—I can no longer support life.'

"I was choking; I could not speak. I presented again and again the cup: he again and again pushed it aside: this struggle drove me mad— 'Leave me alone! leave me alone!' said he, in a dying voice.

"Sire, said I, excited by my grief, in the name of your glory, in the name of France, renounce a death unworthy of you.

"A deep sigh escaped from his heaving breast. Sire, cannot Caulin-court obtain this favour of you?

"I was bending over the bed, my tears fell upon his face; be fixed his eyes upon me with an indefinable expression. I held the cup to him; at length he drank. A vomiting, accompanied with violent spasms, threw all of us into a mortal fear. Exhausted, he fell back almost lifeless on his pillow,

"Ivan, with a distracted air, said 'He must, he must drink again! he is lost—he is lost if he does not drink,' I again commenced my entreaties, and he resisted them. At length, by dint of supplications and prayers, he drank at intervals, and repeated vomitings brought some relief. The cramp in the stomach became less violent, his limbs became more supple, the contraction of his features ceased by degrees. He was saved!

"During the two hours that this alarming crisis lasted, not a single complaint escaped his lips. He smothered the cries which his agony drew from him, by grinding a handkerchief between his teeth. What fortitude that man possessed!

"The interior of this chamber of death, this agony, by the pale light of the tapers, cannot be described. The silence was uninterrupted but by the sobbings of those present. There was no witness of this terrible scene present who would not have given his own life to have saved that of Napoleon, who in his domestic retirement was the best of men, the most indulgent of masters. The regrets of all who served him survive him.

"A short calm succeeded. He slept for half an hour. During that interval. Constant told me that whilst be was in bed in the entresol beneath, he had heard a noise in the chamber of the emperor. He ran to him, and found him in violent convulsions, his face turned upon the pillow to stifle his cries. He refused all the assistance poor Constant strove to give him. Ivan was called. When the emperor saw him, he said 'Ivan, the dose was not strong enough.' Then it was they acquired the sad certainty that he had taken poison. 'Let the Duke de Vicenza,' added he, in a voice scarcely intelligible, 'be called.' The fearful crisis seized him, and at that moment I arrived.

"Alarmed for the result of the action of the poison upon the health of the emperor, I turned to consult Ivan, whom I thought to be still in the chamber. He had disappeared. I sent in search of him; he was nowhere to be found. This disappearance at such a moment was inexplicable. I learned at length that Ivan, alarmed at the responsibility which the words of the emperor—'The dose was not strong enough'—might bring upon him, had taken the first horse he found in the courtyard of the castle, and set off for Paris. We saw no more of him. The emperor was lying in pain. I threw myself upon a chair; my mind took a review of the series of disasters of all sorts, which, within a month, had succeeded each other without intermission. The palace of Fontainebleau had become hateful to me. It represented to me the scenes of horror and blood of which that place had been the theatre. I called to my recollection that these same walls had witnessed another murder, and I thought I still heard groans, imprecations, prayers, and death rattle, of another victim.

"The emperor awoke. I drew towards his bed; the attendants retired—we were alone.

"His eyes, sunk and dull, seemed seeking to recognise the persons by whom he was surrounded; a world of tortures was revealed in their expression. 'Heaven has forbidden it,' said he, as if applying to some inmost thought; 'I could not die.'

"Sire, your son—France, in which your name will live for ever, impose upon you the duty of supporting adversity.

"'My son! my son! What a sad inheritance I leave him—a child born a king; today without a country. Why did they not let me die?'

"In this scene there was a contrast that startled the imagination. Napoleon poisoned, deploring the destiny of his only child. That Napoleon—he, the sovereign whose sway had extended from the north to the south—Napoleon, the giant of battlefields, who had planted his victorious eagles on all the capitals of Europe!

"Sire, replied I, you must not die thus. France must deplore you living!

"'France? She has abandoned me; and you, Caulincourt—you, in my place, would have done what I did. When fortune smiled on me, have I not often faced death in the field of battle?'

"Ah, the circumstances in which your Majesty is placed are deplorable; but—

"'It is not the loss of the throne,' interrupted he, with vehemence, 'which renders my existence insupportable. My military career is sufficient for the glory of a man; and,' added he with emphasis, raising himself on his side, 'a crown of laurel is less fragile than the jewelled diadem which encircles the brows of the most powerful monarch. . . . But do you know what is more hard to bear than the reverses of fortune? Do you know what it is that pierces the heart most deeply? It

211

is the baseness, the hideous ingratitude of man. I turn my head in disgust from their cowardice and selfishness. I hold life in horror; death is repose—repose at last. What I have suffered for the last twenty days cannot be comprehended.'

"Whilst he spoke I regarded him with an inexpressible regret. Exile was about to hide the meteor which then shone so brightly. Its first rays enlightened, vivified France; and France suffered it to disappear.

"At this moment the clock struck five; the rays of the sun, shining through the red curtains, coloured with a deep tint the serene and expressive face of Napoleon. There was so much grandeur, so much power, in this man, that it seemed he could be destroyed but by a phenomenon.

"He raised himself up, drew back the curtain, and said, passing is hand across his forehead—'Caulincourt, there have been moments in these last days when I thought I should go mad—when I have felt a devouring heat here. Madness is the last stage of human degradation; better to die a thousand times. Do you remember our visit to Charenton?'

"I trembled. The impression of that visit to Charenton, in 1807, was not effaced; and from that day, perhaps, a fixed idea, unchangeable as his resolution, made him prefer death to the possibility of such a calamity. Sire, I cried, banish these dreadful thoughts. Your lofty mind will never bend. Your courage ought to equal your renown. The secret of this night most not pass these walls. Europe contemplates the great Napoleon on the pedestal of his high misfortunes.

"'I comprehend you. In resigning myself to life I accept tortures which are nameless: it matters not, I will support them.' He remained thoughtful for some moments. At length he resumed—'I will sign the treaty today. Now I am well, my friend. Go and rest yourself, Caulincourt.'

"He wished, in sending me away, to repossess himself of the energy of which he stood in need to finish the sacrifice. I was not deceived. He appeared calm, but the calm was fearful.

"At ten o'clock the emperor asked for me. I found him up and dressed. His face was greatly altered, but he had resumed his self-control, and nothing in his manner bespoke the convulsion of his mind. Every now and then he fixed his eyes on mine. This silent interrogation expressed his thoughts; he spoke them not—he uttered not a single word which bad relation to the scenes of the past night.

"We discoursed of many points relative to the treaty. 'These pecuniary clauses,' said he, 'are humiliating: they must be cancelled. lam now nothing beyond a soldier: a *louis* a-day will be sufficient for me.' We discussed warmly this question; I appreciated and approved his refinement of feeling; nevertheless, the maintenance of a military establishment, his state as a Sovereign, would not permit that the stipulations in question should be suppressed. He concluded by yielding, and resigned himself to ratify the treaty—that last link which yet united him to the sovereign power he had exercised with so much glory.

"'However,' added he, 'hasten the conclusion of the whole; place the treaty in the hands of the Allied Sovereigns, Tell them, Caulincourt—tell them in my name, that I treat with a conquering enemy, and not with this provisional government, in which I see nothing but a committee of factions men and traitors.'

"The two plenipotentiaries, Ney and Macdonald, were directed to come to the cabinet of the emperor. He affixed his signature to the treaty His ruin was consummated. All that remained of the most powerful of monarchs was the immortal man!

"With a firm voice he gave us his last instructions; he then added, 'My abdication and my ratification of the treaty cannot be obligatory, unless the Allies shall keep the promises made to the army. Do not let the documents go out of your possession until that be done.'

"Our return to Paris excited transports of joy amongst the contrivers of the enterprise. They were about to enjoy the fruit of their labours.

"The Council assembled, the sovereigns and members of the provisional government were present. We officially presented the abdication and the treaty of the 14th of April, ratified by the emperor. The discussions were adjourned till next day for divers points to be established. After the exchange of congratulations and compliments, usual in such cases, at the moment we were about to retire, the members of the provisional government, with whom in every circumstance I had carefully avoided coining in contact, solicited our adherence. General Dessoles approached me, and begged me, in flattering terms, to adhere to the new order of things, inasmuch as all the dignitaries and nearly all the generals of the army had done so.

"Sir, answered I, in a firm voice, I regulate not my conscience by that of others. I am the plenipotentiary and the subject of the Emperor Napoleon. I shall not cease to be so until he has no more occasion for my services, and has released me from my oaths. Macdonald, with noble firmness, made a similar reply to a request of the same sort addressed to him. Freed at length from the presence of certain persons, we retired.

"On my return home, I felt something like an interval of happiness. After the cruel shocks my feelings had sustained, a respite was comfort. My mind was in a state of perplexity. The events of the few last days recurred successively to my thoughts, and I could scarcely put faith in their reality. I repeatedly fancied myself to be under the illusion of ideal events. I felt in my waking moments that peculiar sensation of anxiety and uneasiness which assails us in sleep, during troublesome dreams.

"Paris, at that period, was a nameless something which baffles description—a scene of disorder which overthrows all received ideas, all rules of justice and injustice, of honour and dishonour. In times of reaction, men, characters, and events, suddenly rise up and appear to be exclusively the offsprings of the temporary commotion. Society seems to be in a state of dissolution. A vertigo assails the public mind; and everyone yields to the impulses of passion, without consulting either conscience or dignity. The convictions of today will not be those of tomorrow. A visionary state of existence usurps the place of reality, and imparts a false colouring to all opinions. When this overexcitement subsides, we blush to find that we have been espousing the cause of rogues or fools, and made ourselves parties in iniquitous intentions. We are astonished and indignant at discovering that we have been playing the part of dupes in a comedy, in which honest men are the tools of intriguers.

"Nothing can better prove the absence of all governmental legality, and above all, the incredible confusion which prevailed in Paris in 1814, than the following anecdote, which was related to me by one of the actors in the burlesque scene. It is perfectly characteristic of the time.

"As soon as the abdication and treaty were signed, every individual of note who had accompanied the emperor to Fontainebleau left him and proceeded to Paris. With the exception of the Duke de Bassano, who never for a moment quitted his post, I do not think that a single minister or great dignitary remained at Fontainebleau, It was advisable to ascertain whether the bulk of the army would, with equal complaisance, adopt the new order of things; accordingly, each of the marshals was requested to obtain as many adherences as possible from the troops under his command. A wish expressed by the dispensers of favours and places then sufficed to stimulate zeal and *patriotism*; and the question was, who should be most active in enrolling under the new banner the generals who yet remained faithful to their old colours.

"The brave General Leval commanded a division of ten thousand men, whom he had valiantly brought from Spain to the succour of France, when she was invaded by foreign troops. His division, which arrived in the course of February, had distinguished itself in several engagements on the plains of Champagne, and was now encamped within twelve leagues of Paris, It formed part of the army corps commanded by Marshal ———.

"Instead of following the example of many other military commanders, General Leval remained with his troops, and did not come to beg favours in Paris. You know the General," pursued the duke. "He is not a man of elegant appearance, or showy manners; on the contrary, he might, in a drawing-room, be considered vulgar. But in his military capacity he was a very distinguished man, and was highly esteemed by the emperor. In short, General Leval, who was universally respected for his talents, integrity, and courage; who was idolized by his troops, and who enjoyed the rank of Grand Officer of the Legion of Honour, was not a recruit to be disdained, and his silence perplexed the friends of the provisional government. They could not conceive why a man, having an endowment of one hundred thousand *livres* to preserve, should hold himself aloof, and not come forward to tender his allegiance and his services. At that time such conduct was perfectly inexplicable.

"Marshal ——— dispatched one of his *aides-de-camp* to General Leval with a letter, advising him as a friend to delay no longer sending to the provisional government his adherence and that of his corps of officers.

"The officer," pursued the duke, "who was sent with this errand to General Leval, was M. de C———, who gave me an amusing account of this affair.

"General Leval read and re-read the marshal's letter. 'I cannot comprehend this,' said he to himself 'What is the meaning of it?' Then, with his accustomed coolness, addressing himself to M. de C———, 'Pray, Sir, can you explain this?'

"'Explain what, general?'

"'The marshal writes to request my adherence and that of my officers; but he does not state what we are to adhere to! Will you have the goodness, Sir, to tell the marshal that I can only answer his letter by inquiring, what we are to adhere to, and why? (*Adherer à quoi? Adherer pourquoi?*)'

"'You know,' said M, de C——, when he related his story, 'that General Leval is not a man whom I should take the liberty of laughing at; yet, on hearing this *à quoi?* and *pourquoi?* I confess I found it not a little difficult to restrain my risibility. Not that the words conveyed to me any other meaning than the general in his soldier-like honesty meant to imply; but because I could not imagine any satisfactory answer that could be given to his questions. The truth was, I had never myself thought about the meaning attached to the word *adherence*, which had been for some time resounding in my ears.'

"M. de C—— returned to Paris at full speed. 'Well,' said Marshal ——, 'you have lost no time,' and he held out his hand in expectation of receiving General Leval's letter.

"'Marshal,' said M. de C——, 'I have brought only a verbal answer.'

"'How!' said the marshal, frowning; 'does he realise his adherence?'

"'The general read your Excellency's letter once or twice over—'

"'Well?'

"'Well, marshal, he says he does not understand it; and he has desired me to ask your Excellency why he is to adhere, and what be is to adhere to?'

"'What he is to adhere to?' repeated the marshal, as if an idea had suddenly flashed across his mind. 'True—I never thought of that. General Leval's question is very natural. He is quite right—Hark ye! M. de C——; go immediately to the Prince de Benevento, and tell him that I sent to solicit the adherence of General Leval. Repeat to him the answer which the general sent to my letter, and request him to give you the explanation which the general wishes. It is a singular affair! *à quoi? pourquoi?* I will be hanged if I can answer the question.'

"On arriving at Prince Talleyrand's hotel, M. de C—— sent in his name, and was immediately admitted.

"'Prince,' said he, 'Marshal has sent me to consult your Excellency relative to General Leval's adherence.'

"'What about it. Sir; I suppose the general has sent it—'

"'Prince, the general declares that he does not understand what is required of him. When he read the marshal's letter, he said, with astonishment—*Adhere to what?—Why are we to adhere?* The marshal has now sent me to request your Excellency to—'

"'You are the son of M. de C——, the master of the ceremonies, I

216

believe,' said Prince Talleyrand, interrupting the young officer.

"'I am. Prince ———. The marshal requests that———'

"'Ah! and how is your father? Is he in Paris?'

"'He is very well. Prince ———. The marshal begs—'

"'I should be delighted to see him.'

"With these words, Prince Talleyrand rose from his seat, and hobbled towards the door, with a cool *marquois* sort of air, peculiar to himself. 'Pray present my compliments to the marshal.—Tell him the provisional government will profit by his advice—and is obliged to him.'

"M. de C—— declared that he laughed all the way from the Rue Saint Florentin to the marshal's hotel. The answer I had now to deliver was almost as good as the general's.

"'Well, what says the prince?' inquired the marshal, eagerly.

"'He sends you his compliments, and the thanks of the provisional government,' replied M. de C——.

"With this sort of levity," added the Duke de Vicenza, "affairs the most important to the country were frequently treated."

"It was truly pitiable," observed I; "but nevertheless, the story you have just related is exceedingly amusing. Certainly M. de Talleyrand is the cleverest man in the world for getting out of a difficulty."

"A few days afterwards," resumed the Duke de Vicenza, "I heard the counter-part of the anecdote from General Leval himself. With that blunt simplicity of manner which characterises him, he thus narrated the affair:—

"'I was quietly established at headquarters and instead of orders, the most absurd reports were transmitted to us from Paris. I could perceive that some fermentation was rising up; but I remained firm at my post. I assembled my troops, and passing along the front ranks of each regiment, I declared that the first man, whether officer or private, who dared to flinch from his duty, I would run my sword through his body. Aye! and they knew I would keep my word; for every man kept firmly to his post, I assure you.

"'When Marshal ——— wrote to me, I saw clearly how affairs were going on; but would it have become me, overwhelmed as I was with the emperor's favours, to have put his cockade is my pocket, and have forsaken him. All my promotion, from the rank of sergeant, has, it is true, been earned by my blood on the field of battle; but my titles and endowments, to whom do I owe them? To the emperor; and certainly be never owed me anything. It would be the vilest ingratitude in me to have forgotten his benefits and betrayed him.

"'When the emperor released us from our oaths; and when his abdication was officially communicated, then I did as others had done. Then, and not till then, I sent this much-talked of adherence. But tell me, duke, don't you think I had good reason to be offended at the marshal's letter?—Was it not a shameful proposition to make to a man of honour—an old general who has grown gray in the field of battle?'

"There is something soothing to the feelings," said the Duke de Vicenza, "in the admirable conduct of General Leval, contrasted as it is with the prevailing turpitude of the time. Unfortunately I had not to treat with the army, which offered more than one consolatory example; and the duties of another kind, which I continued to discharge till the emperor's departure, have left behind them only afflicting recollections.

"However great the activity I used after my return to expedite the arrangements for the departure of the emperor, I did not proceed sufficiently fast for his wishes. He sent courier after courier to me to hurry the arrangements. 'Caulincourt,' he wrote to me in one of his short notes, 'I wish to depart. Who would have ever supposed that the air of France would become heavy and suffocating to me? The ingratitude of mankind kills more surely than steel or poison. It has rendered my existence a burden. Hasten, hasten my departure.'

"It was decided that the four great powers should each send a commissioner to the emperor. Alexander sent General Schouwaloff, to whom he gave particular instructions; Austria, General Koller; England, Colonel Campbell; and Prussia, General Valdebourg Truchssefs.

"As I did not fear the sight of these commissioners would be disagreeable to the emperor, I had urgent reasons to wish they should immediately betake themselves to Fontainebleau. They arrived there on the 16th, in the morning. I put off other discussions relative to the treaty, and hastened to rejoin Napoleon. What a life was mine in those days of desolation!

"When I arrived at Fontainebleau I passed through the small number of troops yet remaining with the emperor. Nothing can express the grief which was depicted in the countenances of these soldiers. Their looks sought in mine the nature of the sentiments I felt for the emperor. They had seen so many cowardly defections. When they beheld me, cries of 'Long live the Emperor!' overwhelmed me. I comprehended their feelings, and this recompensed me for the many cruel and disgusting scenes I had witnessed. The sympathy which existed between these brave men and me was highly gratifying. In the midst of the general perversity there were some who knew that honour consisted in fidelity to misfortune.

"But this good impression was very soon superseded by one of a different nature. The galleries and the saloons adjoining the apartment of the emperor were deserted. With the marshals had disappeared the officers of their respective staffs. The blast of adversity had passed over, and the gilded mob had vanished. This solitude was striking. The redoubtable chief, who never moved without a magnificent retinue,—the great monarch, who had seen kings at his feet,—was now nothing more than a private individual, disinherited even of the friendship and care of his own friends! Everything in this splendid palace inflicted wounds and horror. I was in a fever of impatience to withdraw the emperor as soon as possible from this torture.

"On my arrival, I found him alone in the little garden, between the Galerie des Cerfs and the chapel. The sound of my footsteps roused him from his reverie. He turned his head quickly—a ray of joy brightened his countenance. When I got close to him, he took my arm, and, continuing his walk, said, 'Is all ready for my departure?'

"I answered, Yes, Sire; seeking to allay my emotion.

"'Tis well, Caulincourt. You exercise for the last time the functions of grand equerry near my person.' (There was a most distressing allusion in this phrase.) 'Can you believe that Berthier has departed—departed without wishing me farewell?'

"Sire, said I, overcome by the indignation I had for many days repressed, Berthier has no importance but by the predilection of your Majesty. Under your orders any man of punctuality and memory would have made a good major-general. This is essentially the negative merit of Berthier. His conduct towards your Majesty in these last days will establish justly the part which belongs to him in the immortal campaigns of the grand army. The Prince of Neufchatel, Sire, has descended from the pedestal on which your friendship had mounted him.

"'Berthier,' said the emperor, 'was born a courtier. You will see him begging an employment of the Bourbons.'

"He afterwards spoke to me with dignity of the shameful conduct which the great officers of the empire had shown to him. 'I was,' said he, 'mortified to see men whom I had raised so high in the eyes of Europe bringing themselves so low. What has become of the halo of glory which encircled them? What now must Sovereigns think of all these illustrations of my reign? I have done well,' added he, smiling bitterly, 'I have done well. Caulincourt, this France is mine; everything by which it is disfigured is to me a personal affront, I am so identified with it But I must go in and sit down; I feel fatigued. Have you seen the commissioners?'

"No, sire; I came immediately from my carriage to your Majesty.

"'See them, Caulincourt. Hasten, hasten my departure. It is too long delayed.'

"Just as we left the garden, a *cuirassier* of the guard, in great agitation, came from the Gallerie des Cerfs, where he had probably been watching an opportunity of speaking to the emperor. He ran towards us.

"'What do you want?'

"'Please your Majesty, I demand justice,' said he, in a supplicating voice.

"'What has happened?'

"'An odious act of injustice has been done to me. I am thirty-six years old; twenty-two years I have been in the service. I have my decoration,' said he, striking roughly his broad breast, 'and yet I am not in the list of those who are to go with your Majesty. If I am thus sent to the right about, blood shall flow for it. I will make a vacancy amongst the privileged. This affair shall not pass thus.'

"'You have, then, a strong desire to go with me?'

"'It is not a desire, my emperor, it is my right, my honour, which I claim, and—'

"'Have you well considered this ?' said Napoleon, with kindness—'that you must quit France, your family, your promotion? You are a quartermaster.'

"'I relinquish my promotion,' said he, bluntly. 'I have my *galons* and my cross; they will suffice. I will pass over the rest. In such a time as this, our country is our regiment, the steeple of the parish church our standard. As to my family, you have been my family these two-and-twenty years—you, my general. I was a trumpeter in Egypt, if you can but remember.'

"'Very well, you shall go with me, my good man. I will arrange it.'

"'Thanks, thanks to your Majesty! I should have done some mischief, that is certain, if I had not been permitted to go.' And the poor fellow retired with pride and happiness.

"'Caulincourt,' said the emperor, with emotion, 'I can only take with me four hundred men, and the whole of my brave guard wish to follow me. Amongst those *courtiers*, the question is which shall be most ingenious in finding in the antiquity of his services, and the number of his armorial bearings, claims to share with me my exile? Brave, brave men! why cannot I take you all with me?' and he pressed my arm convulsively.

"His departure was fixed for the 20th; two days only remained. Every moment I could snatch from the business of preparation I passed with the emperor, whose days flowed on in desponding uniformity. Not a visit of duty, not a recollection of gratitude, broke in upon the solitude. The emperor did not complain; but he suffered. Every time the sound of a carriage interrupted the silence of the courts of the palace anxiety was visible in his looks. He seemed to listen unconsciously. Some name escaped him—'Molé,' 'Fontanes,' 'Berthier,' 'Ney,' and nobody, nobody came. Little disappointments thus continually repeated are dreadful—they wear out resignation and courage.

"Montholon, who had been on a military reconnaissance, arrived from the banks of the Haute Loire. He spoke with enthusiasm of the feeling which animated the people and the soldiers. 'By rallying the troops of the South,' said he, 'a formidable force might still be assembled.' 'It is too late,' replied the emperor, with an indescribable expression, 'they would not——'

"A second time this reproach fell from his lips, and in these words a terrible accusation was contained. But men and fortune would have been wearied before the genius of the hero!

"The preparations were completed by the morning of the 19th. The moving about, the occupation of looking to everything that could render the journey less painful—in fact, my agitation supported me. But when all was done, and I could no longer render myself insensible to the termination of these cares, I felt my heart rent at the idea of a separation so close at hand. I shut myself up and tried to calm myself. My grief could only increase the agonies of the emperor. I had yet duties to fulfil, orders to receive; he relied on me, and it was not fit my courage should fail.

"In the morning he sent for me. He appeared resigned, but his air of dejection, the haughty expression of his eyes, the unusual slowness of his movements, evinced the violence of his efforts to smother his excruciating sorrow. As a man, he suffered a thousand deaths. What matter? That was his secret; and he kept it to himself; he was to render to no one an account of it. As a sovereign, it was his duty to show himself dignified and composed in the presence of misfortune.

"'Caulincourt, is all read?' I made a sign in the affirmative. 'Tomorrow, at twelve o'clock, I shall step into my carriage,' he added, in a hurried tone.

"I could not utter a word. He looked at me for a few moments, and held his hand to me. 'Caulincourt, I am heartbroken. We ought never to part.'

"Sire, cried I, in despair, I will go with you; France has become hateful to me!

"'No, Caulincourt, you must not quit France with me: you may still be useful to me here. Who is to look to the interests of my family, and of my faithful servants? Who is to defend the cause of those brave and devoted Poles, of whom the 19th article of the treaty guarantees the rights acquired by honourable services! Think well. It would be a shame for France, tor me, for all of us, Caulincourt, if the interests of the Poles were not irrevocably secured.

"'In conformity to the right which the 19th article gives me, I have caused a statement to be prepared—I have fixed the sums which I wish to be paid to my guard, my civil and military household, and to my attendants. Fidelity cannot be recompensed with money; but at present it is all I have to give. Tell them it is a remembrance which I leave to each individually, as an attestation of their good services. Be on the watch, Caulincourt, till these arrangements are fulfilled.'

"I assured him his commands should be religiously obeyed.

"'In a few days, I shall be established in my sovereignty of the Isle of Elba,' resumed he, with bitterness. 'I am in haste to get there. I have dreamed of great things for France. Time failed me—the concurrence of all was requisite—they have refused me. I told you, Caulincourt, at Duben, the French nation knows not how to support reverses. This people, the bravest and most intelligent in the world, has no pertinacity but in flying to the combat—defeat demoralises them. During sixteen years the French have marched with me from victory to victory; a single year of disasters has made them forget everything!'

"He sighed deeply. 'The way in which I have been treated is infamous—and, what!' said he, with animation; 'they separate me violently from my wife and child! In what barbarous code do they find the article which deprives a sovereign of his rights as a father and a husband? By what savage law do they arrogate the power to separate those whom God has joined? History will avenge me! It will say

"Napoleon, the soldier, the conqueror, was clement and generous in victory. Napoleon, when conquered, was treated with indignity by the monarchs of, Europe.'"

"Large drops of perspiration were on his forehead, his agitation increased every moment. He gave me the most dreadful pain. Sire, interrupted I, all my zeal, all my efforts, shall be exerted to put an end to this impious separation. It is the cause of all fathers and all citizens——

"'—It is a planned thing. Do you not see, that because they dare not blow my brains out with a pistol, they assassinate me by slow degrees? There are a thousand means of causing death.'

"Sire, in the name of Heaven, be calm; your Majesty may rely on me. I will see the Emperor of Austria on his arrival at Paris. The empress will second me; she will wish to rejoin you. Have hope, Sire, have hope.

"As I spoke, his aspect brightened. His heart, dead to soft emotions, began to resume hope.

"'You are right, Caulincourt, my wife loves me; I believe it she has never had cause to complain of me. It is impossible that I have become indifferent to her. Louise is amiable in her disposition, and simple in her tastes. She will prefer her husband's home to a duchy granted in charity; and in the Isle of Elba I can yet be happy with my wife and my son.'

"The emperor walked quickly up and down his cabinet; a fixed idea was impressed upon his mind, and his impressions, always quick and ardent, readily adopted the projects to which his imagination gave birth. Who knows, if Napoleon had been united to his wife and son, that France would have had to deplore the misfortunes of the hundred days, and subsequently the captivity and death of the hero?

"But this hope, which for a moment soothed his grief, I shared not in. I tried the negotiation; I pressed it; I supplicated; I was not seconded nor aided by anyone.

"The irritation of the emperor was calmed; he spoke to me without asperity of the state of affairs. He defined the difficulties which would render the stability of the new order of things impossible. He analysed what was likely to ensue from the absurd combination which would re-establish the Bourbons on the throne. 'Between the old Bourbons,' said he, 'and the present generation of Frenchmen, there is an incompatibility of feeling. The future is big with events. Caulincourt, write often to me; your letters will make some amends for your absence from me. The remembrance of your conduct towards me will reconcile me to the human race. You are the most perfect of my friends.' He held out his arms to me, I embraced him.

"'My friend,' pursued the emperor, 'we must separate. Tomorrow I shall have occasion for all my courage to quit my soldiers. My brave guard! Faithful and devoted, in my good and in my bad fortune! Tomorrow I take my last farewell. This is the final struggle that remains for me to make.' He then added, with an accent broken with emotion, 'Caulincourt, we shall meet again one day, my friend,' and he rushed out of the cabinet.

"I was a league from Fontainebleau, on the high road to Paris," continued the Duke de Vicenza, in a faltering voice, "before I felt conscious as to how and why I was there. On quitting the emperor's cabinet, scarcely knowing what I did, I threw myself into my carriage, which was waiting at the entrance to the grand staircase.

"I could no longer deceive myself; all was now over! At that moment I was a prey to the most poignant grief. It seemed to me as though I had never before measured the full depth of the abyss. Certainly I had never before so highly appreciated the personal merits of Napoleon;—he had never appeared to me more great than at the moment when he was about to depart in exile from France. . . . I regarded him as the expiatory victim, chosen from among us all to redeem the crime of our twenty years of glory and conquest. My thoughts followed him to his miserable sovereignty of Elba.

"I was independent in my fortune on the overthrow of the empire. I was tired of men and things. I wished for repose; but repose without him. . . . It was the ruin of all the delightful illusions which gave a value to life. I did not comprehend how I should henceforth drag out my colourless existence. I dreamed of travels into remote lands, of mental occupations, which should fill the measureless void of my days to come. I questioned the future, and in the future was written, in letters of blood, 'Waterloo.'"

Chapter 21

Napoleon's Return from Elba

"After the departure of the emperor, I devoted my attention to everything that could promote the immediate execution of the treaty. I even went beyond zeal in the fulfilment of this duty. In addition to the continued pertinacity with which I urged forward my melancholy task. I had an actual necessity for something to occupy my thoughts. I felt that fever of the soul which only finds relief in an absorbing activity. My most doleful forebodings had not prepared me for the deplorable change of fortune which had annihilated the edifice reared by so many marvellous exploits!

"For those who, through ambition or affection, attached themselves to the new government, there was no change in France beyond a name, a man. To me, this name, this man, were the personification of regenerated France. I could not understand a state of things in flagrant opposition to all our interests, to all our sympathies. I could not consider any longer as my country the land crowded with innumerable armed foreigners, who made themselves masters in our cities, in our streets, in our fields, in our villages, in our *châteaux*, in our cottages. This occupation of the country by six hundred thousand enemies banished the last illusion with respect to the opinion which had presided in the choice of the Bourbons to govern France. We were no longer anything but tributaries at the mercy of a coalition, intoxicated with their late easy successes. The government *de facto,* and that which had succeeded the empire, were but, according to my notions, a transition to I know not what kind of constituted authority. In a word, it was difficult to regard in a serious light, this great comedy of the restoration.

"I had on this subject some curious conversations with the Emperor of Russia. Alexander readily allowed the person with whom he conversed the liberty of expressing his opinion; and we sometimes laughed heartily at the conceits given as food for the *gobemouches*. Unfortunately in this parade of government all was not a matter of joke.

"The Emperor of Russia possessed an enlightened understanding. Moreover, he was young, and his ideas were suited to the age in which he lived. He had admired the good faith and the genius of Napoleon; our army had been the model upon which he strove to form his own, and in the heart of Alexander, in spite of everything, a generous regret arose when he compared what he now saw with what he had seen.

"Certainly, strange things were passing before our eyes. We saw Louis XVIII. make his entry into Paris in an open carriage. His dress was curious. It was a costume that belonged to no country: two enormous epaulettes, however, denoted a wish to give it somewhat of a military character. Beside the king sat the Duchess d'Angoulême. His feelings were excited, and she was bathed in tears, evidently wrung from her by bitter recollections. On the opposite seat, were the Prince de Condé and the Duke de Bourbon, both in old-fashioned military uniforms, such as were worn at the time of their emigration.

"Heaven forbid that I should say anything which may seem to cast ridicule on old age or misfortune! If the carriage had passed through the streets of Paris escorted by the friends and servants of the restored family, the whole procession would have been perfectly consistent and in keeping. It would have presented to the eyes of the multitude a living tradition of the old regime personified by the Bourbons; there would have been no deviation from good taste and propriety. But the carriage being preceded, surrounded, and followed, by the Imperial guards, was one of those paradoxes, the explanation of which baffles common sense.

"Louis XVIII. entered Paris escorted by the faithful and devoted guards of Napoleon, whose worn uniforms bore evidence of the toils and dangers they had encountered in the conflict in which they had fought so nobly to repel all that they were now forced to accept.

"What dark and threatening looks they cast around them! What an expression of proud disdain was depicted on those warlike countenances in answer to the frenzied demonstrations of Parisian inconstancy.

"In ancient Rome the triumphal car of a conqueror, decorated with spoil, was oftener than once seen surrounded by the guards of a conquered foe. But we were not in Rome; we were in Paris, where the conqueror had conquered no one. At no very distant time, these facts will perhaps appear fabulous!

"Alexander was struck with the incongruity between the places and the persons; the disparity between the old and the new, with the mixture of what was with what had been. Time, in a period of twenty-two years, had remodelled men, their opinions, their ideas, their interests, and their institutions. Thus the old king, when he awoke in Paris, gazed around with astonishment, recognising neither men, opinions, things, interests, or institutions. 'Give me,' said he to himself, 'those good, old, well-beloved countenances, which do not regard me as a foreigner in my kingdom of France. Give me the good old uniforms, the *gardes de corps*, with their laced clothes, the noble livery of my ancestors, the red *mousquetaires*, or the gray, or the black, who were distinguished under my forefathers. Those splendid uniforms would bring repose to my eyes, wearied with these blue satellites of the republic and the empire, who for twenty years have shut me out from my dominions.'

"The army, *en masse*, was dishonoured, ill-used, and disbanded. Its glory was repudiated; its best services forgotten: its noble wounds were despised. Those who had conquered millions for their country were delivered up to misery. Before the eyes of the fierce grenadiers of Napoleon, they paraded the gay household troops of the king.

"But in these indignant bosoms the hearts of lions were beating, and the month of March dispersed in its hurricane the gilded doves which served to ornament the court of the old king!

"At the second entry of the Allies, in 1816, we often spoke of 1814, with the Emperor Alexander. 'Many faults were committed,' said he to me one day.

"Yes, sire, replied I, quickly, and one person has paid for all.

"'My dear duke,' interrupted he, with an air of solicitude, 'everyone will pay his share, I fear. These people are incapables. We are deceived. May it please Heaven that the peace so dearly purchased be not again broken.'

"I have told you," continued the duke, "that I owed to the Emperor of Russia, in 1814, and afterwards in 1815, my escape from the persecutions of which I was the object. I had never claimed his protection. It was known that he accorded me his favour and friendship, and they did not dare to pass certain bounds. He had on more than one occasion to explain himself bluntly with *qui de droit*, when after the hundred days violent measures were resolved upon against me.

"'Sire,' said he to Louis XVIII., 'I have proposed to the Duke de

Vicenza, in testimony of the peculiar esteem in which I hold him, a brilliant settlement in my dominions; he has declined it. "They will believe," replied he, "that I flew from the dangers of my new position, and that after having devoted myself to the cause of Napoleon, I recoiled from, the consequences of my conduct. I wish to live as I have done, to hold my head high among my fellow-citizens. Public approbation indemnifies me for the injustice of power."

"'It is curious,' said Louis XVIII., pretending to laugh, 'that the grand equerry of Bonaparte (for so he always designated me) should believe that we owe him our acknowledgments.'

"'Your Majesty,' replied Alexander, piqued, 'knows that the gospel informs us *no man can serve two masters.* The duke is only ambitious of the acknowledgments of the master to whom he has been faithful.'

"'Much good may they do him, then,' replied the king, drily.

"I have been well attacked and well defended, said I, laughing, to the Emperor Alexander; and I begged that he would not, on my account, carry on this little warfare with his brother of France, of whom I sought neither favours nor good graces. Hereafter I will tell you how Alexander himself had reason to be dissatisfied with Louis XVIII.

"'It is because, my dear duke,' replied he, 'there is in me something that revolts against stupid prejudice. Are attachment and devotion to an unfortunate sovereign such common things that we monarchs ought not to be profoundly moved by them?'

"Sire, your Majesty preaches in a desert; they do not comprehend you. My conduct during the proceedings at Fontainebleau is a fault which can never be overlooked. I have too much pride to seek an absolution which I do not require.

"But let us return,' said the duke, "to 1814, when, after disgusts and bickerings of all kinds, I obtained, step by step, the execution of those articles which were capable of being immediately acted upon, whether in respect to the brave Poles, or in respect to Napoleon and his family. Besides this, I claimed such guarantees as I could get; but what were guarantees in opposition to dishonesty? Engagements the most sacred were basely violated.

"I frequently received news from the Isle of Elba. The emperor supported with heroic courage the loss of the greatest throne in the world. In one of his letters he said to me:—

It is less difficult than people think to accustom one's self to a life of retirement and peace, when one possesses within one's self some resource to make time useful. I employ myself much in my study, and when I go out I enjoy some happy moments in seeing again my brave grenadiers. Here my reflections are not continually coming in contact with painful recollections.'

"In another letter I find the following passage, which bears the stamp of the wonderful nature of Napoleon:"—

The lot of a dethroned king, who has been born a king, and nothing more, must be dreadful. The pomp of the throne, the gewgaws which surround him from his cradle, which accompany him step by step throughout his life, become a necessary condition of his existence. For me, always a soldier, and a sovereign by chance, the luxuries of royalty proved a heavy charge. The toils of war and a rough camp life are best suited to my organisation, my habits, and my tastes. Of all my past grandeur I alone regret my soldiers; and of all the jewels of my crown, the French uniforms which they allowed me to take with me are the most precious I have preserved.

The duke ceased speaking for a few moments. I understood the sacred impression of his recollections!

He resumed: "I was not in the secret of the intended return from Elba, and from the knowledge I have of the character of Napoleon, I am convinced that that daring project was executed as soon as it was conceived. The emperor was deceived by statements, not wilfully false, but made without reflection, by persons who were not so situated as to be enabled to judge of the fitting opportunity for this extraordinary act.

"The government took a false course. It lost its way amidst mixed institutions which were neither of the old or new regime. It ought to have been left to wear itself out in its own incapability. The Allies would have appreciated the dangers menaced to the tranquillity of Europe through the nullity of the rulers they had given to France.

"The Bourbons did not comprehend what Henry IV. comprehended so completely, that they had nothing to fear from their friends, and everything to dread from their enemies; and of these enemies they were every day, with incredible blindness, increasing the numbers.

"I here express conscientiously my opinion, free from all resentment. As private men, the Bourbons possessed elevation of mind, nobleness, and a great fund of goodness. As sovereigns, their name is worn out, their race is exhausted.

"Had the Bourbons been destined to reign in Holland or Germany, they might have reigned peaceably over a quiet and religious people. The Bourbon family, in the condition in which it finds itself placed, in reference to France, will never permanently establish itself there.

"In 1814, I followed attentively the march of power, and it was easy to foresee that in a short time they must fall beneath their own blows. The news of the landing of the emperor alarmed me. It was too early! This fault destroyed my last hopes. The emperor said to me on the 20th of March, at the Tuileries, 'that the success of his temerity was a return of that mysterious destiny which had spoiled him during so many years.' I regarded it only as the accomplishment of those terrible decrees of fate which overthrew thrones, kings, and nations.

"I received by a courier, who came in thirty-two hours from Lyons, a short note from the Emperor. It was as follows:—'Success has justified all. I have re-conquered France and the French. In eight days I shall be in Paris. Lyons, March 10.'

"I must say, in spite of my sombre apprehensions, that I was happy, truly happy! The triumphant inarch of Napoleon through France made the hearts of his friends swell with pride. He was still the chosen of the people! the man of miracles, whose delusive presence worked prodigies!

"History, in narrating this phasis of the life of Napoleon, can never rise to the height of the subject. In characters of fire must be recorded the magnificent popular ovation which bore the exiled monarch from the gulf of Juan to the palace of the Tuileries. Future ages will behold kings pass away without emotion. Love, devotion, admiration, whatever the French nation could render to its sovereign, is buried in the tomb with Napoleon!

"I went to meet the emperor, whom I rejoined near the barrier, at Fontainebleau. He was escorted by the population, and by the troops who had been sent to fight against him. It was a touching spectacle, that *cortège* for which no preparation had been made, which was joined by all the military he met on his way. All faces were beaming with delight, and never did the physiognomy of Napoleon in the very last days of his triumphs express so much happiness. Perceiving me, he held out his hand quickly. 'Caulincourt! Well, you see me!' I could not speak. 'Go, and wait for me at the Tuileries,' added he, with emotion. 'Go, Caulincourt.'

"I joined the *cortège*, and a little before we arrived at the Carrousel I got before the emperor. It was not easy to get through the mob, which rushed towards the *château*. He was carried by the multitude to the top of the great staircase.

"It was a curious thing to find in the saloons of the Tuileries the greater number of those persons who had deserted the saloons at Fontainebleau. Almost all the old ministers, almost all the marshals, thronged around the emperor. Apart I reflected that in many circumstances impudence supplies the place of an impossible justification.

"I looked at the countenance of Napoleon; there was a cloud of disdain in its expression, yet his tongue uttered nothing but kind words. His theme had been prepared, he had *forgotten* that which he could not pardon.

Queen Hortense and her lovely children met him at the *château*. Tears of joy inundated the face of the queen. Amiable Hortense! the united to the charming qualities of a mother, a quick and penetrating mind, and a powerful understanding. The emperor tenderly cherished Hortense and Eugene—the noble Eugene, whose unblemished life, whose conduct towards Napoleon, before and after his reverses, ought to be cited as a model of dignity and propriety, opposed to so much base ingratitude.

"After the first moments given to the effusion of feeling, the emperor, with his usual activity, was occupied all night in expediting orders, reorganising the offices, and composing his cabinet. This was prodigious; but we were accustomed to find him indefatigable. When engaged in mental occupation he neither felt fatigue nor the want of sleep. He used to say that twenty-two hours out of twenty-four ought to be usefully employed.

"At the moment I took my leave, he said, 'Early tomorrow, Caulincourt;' and these words in a tone as if we had to terminate a business commenced the day before.

"At nine o'clock in the morning, the garden, the courts, the staircases, the rooms, were filled with a joyful throng. There was a deafening clapping of hands. From without, the people with frantic acclamations called for the emperor, who showed himself from time to time; but there was something constrained in his countenance. He was not fond of these revolutionary parades.

"The grenadiers of the Isle of Elba, who had marched nearly two hundred leagues in twenty days with Napoleon, arrived in succession at Fontainebleau, where the emperor ordered them to rest, on the night of the 20th. They bivouacked in the court of the Tuileries, and nothing can paint the proud expression spread over the warlike faces of these men. The emperor was to review them at noon, and although harassed with fatigue, and for the most part without shoes or stockings, their feet lacerated, they were to be seen busying themselves to appear smart.

"At this review a little episode occurred, which, though unnoticed by many, struck me very much by the local colouring which imparted to it an infinite charm.

"All the neighbourhood of the palace was covered with troops. It seemed as if, by the wand of some great magician, they had risen out of the earth. The regiments sent to oppose Napoleon, and which the day before were twenty or thirty leagues from the capital, arrived in succession every moment, with colours flying, and music playing. They took their places in the square of the Carrousel, now occupied by the army of Paris, which two days before was commanded by the Duke de Berry.

"Napoleon, attended by an immense retinue of staff-officers, came down at twelve o'clock. He harangued the troops, and passed along the front of all the regiments assembled. He had for all of them those ready words which never fail to produce a marked impression on the persons to whom they are addressed. In one corner the grenadiers of Elba were grouped together, in their tattered uniforms. Exhaustion was imprinted on their manly countenances, as they awaited their turn to pass in review before their emperor. When Napoleon drew near them, a burst of shouts impossible to describe overwhelmed him. He answered only with smiles, and with an affectionate nod of the head. An old soldier, whose eyes glistened beneath his worn-out cap, and who appeared to be dissatisfied with the silence of Napoleon, grumbled out, 'The devil! this is short work; he has grown so hoarse with talking to the rest that he has nothing to say to us!'

"'The emperor heard him. He turned back, and stopped short, and with an air, an accent, and a manner which cannot be described, he said: 'What reason have you to complain? Have you not returned with me from the Isle of Elba?' and he continued to walk on.

"Caps were thrown up, and deafening shouts and hurras followed him til he was out of sight.

"In this simple trait is shown the fabulous power which he exercised over the army, and the inexhaustible enthusiasm which is attached to the recollection of him.

"The emperor employed the whole day in dispatching couriers in reconstructing the government; 'for,' said he, 'they have overturned everything—everything is to be begun again.'

"In the evening he was compelled by lassitude to take some repose. He shut himself up in his cabinet, and for the first time since his return we were alone. He sat close to the fireplace, with his feet upon the fender, and his arms crossed. He was in an excellent humour. He said, jokingly,

"'You must be astonished, Mr. Diplomatist.'

"Yes, Sire.

"'I am concerned for your Excellency; my poor Caulincourt, you see ambassadors cost a good deal of money, and do very little good. It is better for a sovereign to manage his affairs himself;' and he rubbed his hands together in a bantering manner.

"I replied, laughing, Your method. Sire, is more expeditious.

"'All is going on very well, but we have plenty of work upon our hands. First of all it is decided you must resume the portfolio of foreign affairs,'

"Sire, I have requested to be employed in the army. I fear circumstances will place your Majesty under the necessity of—

"'You spoke to me of Molé,' interrupted he, pursuing his idea, 'I do not wish to appoint him, and probably he himself does not care about it; he is not sufficiently compromised in my cause to plunge himself into it up to the neck, at least up to the new order of things. He would in foreign affairs be good for nothing. He does not know the foreign cabinets, and they do not know him. That notion of yours is ridiculous.'

"'It is only you, Caulincourt, who can be of service to me in this post; the last negotiations of Fontainebleau have in every respect placed you in a favourable light, and, *par dieu!* you never really ceased to be my monitor for foreign affairs! Metternich must be written to; negotiations with Austria must be renewed. It is from that quarter we must expect some facilities in arranging our affairs with Europe.'

"Sire, you need my services. I will again take the portfolio, but I do not share your Majesty confidence with respect to the assistance which Austria will accord.

"'Ah, bah; is that your hobby-horse,' said he, rising up impatiently; 'why should not Austria assist me? I have proclaimed peace throughout my march. I have promised peace, and as far as depends on me, my promise shall be fulfilled. Circumstances are imperative. I will recognise the treaty of Paris. I can now accept what I could not accept at Châtillon without tarnishing my glory. France was obliged to make sacrifices. The act is done; but it did not become me to strip France to preserve the crown. I take the affairs of the country as I find them; I wish the continuation of peace. It is the sound policy of the Powers not to rekindle the torch of war.'

"'I have written to the empress,' (I was surprised at this unusual designation from the mouth of the emperor, who constantly said my wife or Louise;) 'she will prevail upon her father to rejoin me—what reason can he have to oppose it? I do not return with hostile intentions. I have marched throng France without firing a shot I do not wish to re-commence war.'

"Sire, it will be necessary to impress this conviction on the minds of the Allied Sovereigns. This is the difficulty which prevails throughout the question, and Europe is still in arms.

He reflected. 'I comprehend you—I comprehend you, Caulincourt. My return, believe me, is not the result of a sudden and unpremeditated whim. Certain persons thought I was too near to them—and the rock of St. Helena is a sure place. Did you know nothing of these projects?'

"No, Sire; and I will lay a wager that the atrocious idea took birth only in the heads of those miserable creatures whom nothing can convince. There is an atrocious design in the snare spread for your Majesty.

"'——A snare! a snare!' As he repeated these words he walked hastily up and down the room. 'Is France, then, become a den of thieves?' After a few minutes of meditation he resumed, 'The die is cast! I am not come back to overturn, but to restore. I wish to give France solid institutions, in harmony with modern ideas, Utopian visions have taken possession of the public mind during my absence, and it is remarkable, that under the reign of the Bourbons the revolutionary factions have revived those fallacious theories which put words in the place of things. These English kings (*rois Anglaises*) have made me lose in ten months the ten years I employed in subduing the revolution; they have rendered all government in the hands of a single individual impossible, and yet it is only in that way that a sovereign, be he king, emperor, or dictator, can provide for the glory and the prosperity of the country. Is not that your opinion, Caulincourt?'

"Sire, your position is surrounded with great difficulties, the Bourbons have spoiled France, which you had fashioned for absolute domination, though it was skilfully concealed by the operation of the miracles you wrought. Now-a-days the prison which produced submission

234

is broken, and, as your Majesty foresees, obstacles are to be overcome on those very points on which it was customary to decide the question without even the necessity of submitting it to public opinion.

"He replied quickly, 'He who takes the helm must support the weight of it; everything will be made right in a state of peace. We must attend to that which is more pressing. Write to Austria. Your participation in these negotiations is an authority. They know you were always inclined to peace. It is neither your fault, nor mine, if things come to extremities.'

"This conversation," continued the duke, "is very remarkable, inasmuch as it triumphantly refutes the absurd calumnies which you have read and heard of the warlike intentions of Napoleon on his entry into France. The recital I have given you is in the spirit, and I can almost say, the precise words, of the emperor. When I left the cabinet I wished that I could have placarded them upon all the walls of Paris, that I could have published them by sound of trumpet through the squares and streets. If the whole nation had been convinced of the sincere desire of Napoleon for peace, it would have been impossible for the Allies to have refused it, under pain of having to contend against a population of 32,000,000! This is positive. Unfortunately, with the exception of the army and of the people, amongst those who count as nought the national interest when it opposes their private interests, nothing but the return of war was seen in the return of Napoleon. This panic, treacherously fomented by an anti-French party, established an incessant opposition of inertness, against which the energy and the devotion of the army were broken.

"In the interior of the cabinet some curious things took place. The march of the emperor had been so rapid, that many addresses to the king arrived at the same time as the addresses to the emperor. Napoleon took a malicious pleasure in examining the signatures of prefects, and other authorities, who formerly had been loaded with benefits from him. 'Look at these men,' said he, with a smile of pity; 'one must laugh at them to avoid feelings of indignation and regret.'

"Independently of official correspondence, a great quantity of letters arrived, some filled with advice and warnings, others disclosing plots against the emperor's life, others containing declarations of love. The first were, without pity, consigned to the waste paper baskets; Napoleon did not often attend to advice which he did not ask for. He took no heed of the denunciations of attempts against him. 'Whoever stakes his own life against mine will make no confidants,' said he, shrugging up his shoulders; 'the hour of my death is written above.'

"But when he was in good humour he would amuse himself with the *billets doux*. On one occasion, a little perfumed letter, elegantly written, with large armorial bearings on the seal, attracted his attention, and, *ma foi!* it had the honour to be read all through to the signature. In reading it, the physiognomy of Napoleon assumed an air of irony, which excited my curiosity. I avow my indiscretion, and over the shoulder of my honoured master I read also. I will not tell you the name of the fair writer, and that is generous on my part, for afterwards her beautiful mouth uttered, in resentment, a shocking piece of blasphemy. I am assured, that on learning the death of the emperor, Madame de —— said, drily, '*Morte la bête, mort le venin*' This old proverb, by its forced application to circumstance, gained the lady great honour to certain saloons. If I had had the letter of 1815 in my hands, I will not say whether I might not have been tempted to have inserted it in the journals, in form of a corollary to the lady's witty *jeu de mots!*

"But I return to the emperor, who, contrary to his custom, read and re-read the letter. He appeared flattered, but undecided: at last he threw it in the fire. 'Ah, bah!' said he, laughing, 'I have not an hour to lose;' and it was because the emperor had not an hour to lose that a grudge was cherished against him.

CHAPTER 22

The Emperor Alexander and the Bourbons

"I had sent the emperor's propositions to Vienna," said the Duke de Vicenza, "and he impatiently looked for an answer to them. He was also anxious for a letter from Maria Louisa.

"Napoleon and I were completely at variance with respect to the hopes he entertained in reference to Austria; and he had great difficulty in repressing his displeasure at finding himself unable to bring me to his way of thinking. There was also another circumstance which annoyed him.

"After a very animated discussion on the subject of Austria, he exclaimed, 'Well! I am on the right side in this dispute. He must be right who invokes peace for his country,—peace for Europe. If they reject my proposition, they must submit to condemnation at the tribunal of humanity.'

"Sire, observed I, since it is my task to proceed with these negotiations, permit me to call your Majesty's attention to the decree, dated from Lyons. That decree orders the assembling of the Electoral Colleges in Paris, for the purpose of assisting at the coronation of the empress and the King of Rome. The last paragraph in particular is very impolitic.

"'What do you mean? said he, rising from his chair petulantly, 'Do you constitute yourself a censor on my acts?'

"This is harsh language, Sire, to a man who has never feared honestly to speak his mind, even at the risk of displeasing your Majesty.

"'What, then, is your opinion of this decree? said he, with an air of anxiety which he could not conceal.

"It appears to me, sire, to place your Majesty in a false position.

First, with respect to Austria, who cannot but feel compromised in reference to the Allied Powers, for they must suppose her to be on a footing of good understanding with you. Next, it places you in a false position with respect to France, if the empress should not be in Paris at the expiration of a week.

"'*Parbleu!* I know it. But do you imagine that in so bold an enterprise as that of reconquering a kingdom with six hundred men, something must not be left to chance—that Providence of adventurers? A thousand reasons prompt me to maintain an appearance of perfect confidence in the arrival of the empress. Can you not guess those reasons?'

"Pardon me, Sire. I admit the almost inevitable necessity which led you to risk this course; but if it be not justified by success, it may be attended by fatal consequences.

"'Then,' resumed he, hastily, 'To refuse me the empress, would he equivalent to a declaration of deadly war between France and the Allied Powers. The French people will see that I am not the aggressor this time. They know too well what the first invasion cost them, and France, though momentarily degraded, will recover under my banner energy and courage to avenge her humiliation and her injuries. Do you know the idea that occurred to me on the very night of my arrival. I was thinking whether with thirty-six thousand men, whom I can assemble in the twinkling of an eye in the north, I should not commence hostilities by marching straight on Brussels. The Belgian Army awaits only a signal to rally round my eagles.'

"A gesture of incredulity escaped me.

"'The accuracy of my information cannot be doubted,' pursued Napoleon. 'The old animosity of Belgium is roused against England. Holland is merely the instrument of England, whose policy has been to sequestrate Flushing and Antwerp, for the purpose of destroying them. Belgium also rises against Prussia, from old national antipathy. In this state of things, the Belgians will help me to drive those powers from the Rhenish provinces, and I shall maintain a position purely but redoubtably defensive behind the Rhine.'

"Do you recollect, sire, the conduct of Belgium during the events of 1813? The Belgians had no ground of complaint against the French, with whom, for the space of twenty years, they had shared all public appointments and emoluments; yet in the days of our disasters they called Prussia *to their deliverance*, and opened for her an entrance into Flanders. The Belgians mercilessly drove the French inhabitants from their towns, insulted the French authorities, and pursued them to the frontiers. Belgium basely renounced and forsook France. From time immemorial the Belgians have been a people devoid of nationality, always rebelling against their rulers, and without stability, either in their affections or their political opinions.

"Confidence in the fraternity of the Belgian nation was one of the generous errors of France. The natural turbulence and inconstancy of the Belgians render them dangerous auxiliaries in any cause in which they may be engaged. In the circumstances in which your Majesty is placed, I conceive that the alliance of Belgium would, at least, be of doubtful advantage. If the French Army could subjugate the country without the aid of its inhabitants, then, indeed, those who might have refused to take part in the contest would gladly rally round the standard of victory. But to trust to this ephemeral alliance would, I fear, be an error.

"The emperor had allowed me to speak on without interruption, which was contrary to his usual custom when we were discussing any contested point. He seemed to reflect earnestly on the remarks which had fallen from me, and, after a pause, he said, 'You are right, Caulincourt; the Belgians behaved shamefully to me in 1813 and 1814, and, as you have justly observed, I had done everything for their country. The public works executed in Belgium by my orders were worthy of ancient Rome. The dykes, Flushing, Middleburgh, the basin of Antwerp, on which such vast sums have been expended, are all due to France. I had attached to my court the principal families of the country, to prove that I regarded the Belgians as a portion of the great French family; and yet, in the days of our disasters, they basely forsook us. I have less reason to complain of the Dutch, for they owed me nothing. But we must look upon things as they are, and not as we would wish them to be.

"'I am thoroughly convinced that Belgium would unite with us as a *pis-aller*, rather than with England or Prussia; and what does it signify if we profit by the alliance? Wellington is at Vienna, Blucher at Berlin; the English and Prussian forces are feeble, and scattered over the banks of the Rhine; they have neither commanders nor fortresses. There are chances, and very great chances, of success. I may enter Brussels on the 1st of April, and make myself master of all Belgium, before the Allies, thus taken by surprise, can be in a condition to resist me And, nevertheless, I sacrifice this grand scheme to the general wish. I offer peace. Future generations will decide whether my inspirations or the

239

cold calculations of positive prudence promised the best chance of extricating France from the embarrassments in which she has become involved.'

"The time was passed," added the Duke de Vicenza, "when Napoleon, the sovereign arbitrator of the affairs of France, could decide on them singly. He had now all the responsibility, but he had no longer the power of acting. His genius was cramped by the most insupportable of tyrannies—necessity. Necessity constrained him to sue for public approbation, so variable in its Judgments; necessity obliged him to substitute the will and the intelligence of several individuals for the firm will and high intelligence of a single one.

"In a the extraordinary circumstances in which be was placed in 1815, Napoleon, the dictator, the adored chief of the brave and most devoted army that ever existed, might have performed inconceivable prodigies. Napoleon, the constitutional emperor, tied down by law, and held in check by the hesitation and lukewarm caution of secondary powers, was doomed to fall!

"The emperor has often been reproached for having given only *an additional act* to the constitution of the empire, instead of the new constitution which he had promised along all his route from Carnes to Paris. Nothing can be more absurd than this reproach. In the first place, on his arrival he had no time for legislating; and, even if he had, all the constitutions in the world could not have prevented fools from losing precious time in idle discussion, or knaves from betraying France a second time, whilst Napoleon and the army were making heroic efforts for her defence at Waterloo.

"Experience will demonstrate the fallacy of all those theories whose practical application, in a universal sense, is impossible. Russia, Prussia, and Austria, are well governed states without constitutions. England and France are the very antipodes of each other in manners and character. Can a system of government suitable to the one country be equally appropriate to the other? Time will decide this great question.

"I am well aware," added the duke, smiling, "that the profession of faith will expose me to the charge of being an absolutist, an imperialist, and I know not what. The fact is, that the impressions I received from the emperor corroborated my opinions, but did not form them. I found myself admirably situated for the opportunity of studying and judging governments; and I am convinced that the causes of their prosperity, of their stability, and of the happiness of nations, are to be

240

traced, not in the form of their institutions, but in the wisdom which directs them.

"I was at the Tuileries when the telegraphic despatch arrived, announcing the capitulation of Pallu. Almost at the same moment a second despatch announced that the Duke d'Angoulême was a prisoner. It was said that the emperor was with difficulty prevailed on to ratify the convention, because be wished to retain the prince as a hostage. This is untrue. The emperor, with his usual nobleness of feeling, wrote to Grouchy, directing him to watch over the safety of the prince, and to protect him against any ill treatment until he embarked at Cette, whither he was proceeding. 'I should be sorry,' said Napoleon, 'to hear that any harm has befallen him. He has done his duty as a prince.' He said no more on the subject. Fouché took to himself all the credit due to this generosity. He opened a negotiation under the pretext of recovering some diamonds, which, being the property of the state, were to be surrendered up by the Royal Family. There was no necessity for Fouché's interference in this business; but it enabled him the more easily to correspond with Ghent. Fouché was Napoleon's evil genius.

"I was entrusted, by order of the emperor, with two very difficult negotiations. Neither Baron Vincent, the Austrian Minister, nor M. Boudiakine, the Russian Chargé d'Affaires, had yet left Paris. The truth is, there was no great hurry manifested in delivering their passports. I arranged to have an interview, in the house of a third party, with Baron Vincent, with whom I was acquainted. The baron was a mild and moderate man, and had there been any possibility of coming to an understanding, he would have promoted it. But be assured me from the first that the Allies were averse to Napoleon's continuing on the throne, and he never encouraged me to hope that this feeling would undergo any modification in the cabinet of Vienna.

"'Nevertheless, he pledged his word to me that he would make the Emperor Francis acquainted with Napoleon's wish to maintain peace. In compliance with my urgent entreaties he undertook to convey to Maria Louisa a letter from Napoleon. Baron Vincent is a man of honour, and I felt confident that the letter was delivered. The answer was not received.

"This was all I was able to effect my interview with M. Boudiakine gave rise to a very interesting conversation. M. de Jancourt (who did us so much mischief at the time of the negotiations of Fontainebleau) forgot, at his departure, to withdraw from the portfolio of foreign affairs a treaty secretly entered into between England, Austria, and

France, and by which those powers pledged themselves to oppose the dismemberment of Saxony, meditated by Russia and Prussia. This was a very curious document. I laid it before the Russian Minister, adducing it as a manifest proof of the ingratitude of the court of the Tuileries towards the Emperor Alexander. Boudiakine could scarcely believe his eyes, and after an effort to repress his indignation, he said to me, 'It must be confessed that the Bourbons owe but little gratitude to the Emperor of Russia. They well know that he warmly pleaded the cause of the regency; and had he been seconded by Austria, it is probable Louis XVIII. would never have quitted Hartwell.'

"The *liberal Autocrat*,' replied I, (for this was the title by which Alexander was designated in the little *coterie* of the faithful,) though he was so caressed and *fêted*, was nevertheless a visitor whom they were very glad to get rid of.

"'No doubt of that,' said M. Boudiakine. 'But my sovereign was never deceived by the demonstrations of friendship with which he was overwhelmed, and nothing was ever more amusing than the conversations between the Emperor Alexander and Louis XVIII. The latter was ever intent on producing effect by dint of wit and talent, whilst the emperor, whose conversation was always characterized by exquisite good taste, constantly maintained a firm footing, which admitted of no misconstruction. I promise, duke, to report faithfully to my Sovereign the conversation I have had with your Excellency, and to acquaint him with the 'wish expressed by the Emperor Napoleon to preserve peace, and to become the Ally and friend of Alexander.'

"When, at a subsequent time," added the duke, "I mentioned this treaty to Alexander, he said:—'Boudiakine did inform me of it, and the affair rather surprised me; but the fact is, there was no great deal of sympathy between my *Brother of France* and myself. But what could I have done, my dear Caulincourt. I should have stood alone; and I must confess that your emperor's last achievement sufficiently proved to me how much he was to be feared.'

"You may now understand," pursued the duke, "the cause of the coolness between the two sovereigns.

"On another occasion we were discussing the conduct of the English cabinet towards the captive of St. Helena; and Alexander said to me, in a tone of voice indicating deep emotion:—'It would have been very embarrassing to me had Napoleon consigned his fate to my hands, for I would rather have declared war against every power on earth than have betrayed the confidence of a vanquished enemy.'

242

"What fatality could have led Napoleon to distrust the only one of the sovereigns in whom feeling was not utterly blunted by the interests of policy?

"The declaration of the Congress of Vienna cut off all hope of treating with the sovereigns. The couriers whom I had sent off with the despatches could not reach their destination. In every direction communications were intercepted. The emperor, on his arrival, had found himself compelled to suppress the censorship, and to concede full liberty to the press. The consequence was, that Paris was inundated with pamphlets, which, on the one hand, spread alarm and disaffection, and, on the other, made the public perfectly well acquainted with all that was going on abroad. All eyes were turned towards Ghent, and few persons ventured to compromise themselves in the Imperial cause. The government was thus left to its own resources, and wanted support.

"But, in spite of this unfortunate state of things in the capital, the provinces enthusiastically rallied round the emperor. The south was now tranquillised and manifested the best feeling. Paris was one of the greatest embarrassments of the moment; it was the seat of intrigue, and the nucleus of contending factions.

"The Royalists, secretly supported by Fouché, having money and promises of favour to distribute in the name of the Bourbons, directed their attacks on the wavering, the timid, and the ambitious, whom they succeeded in detaching from the Imperial cause. The liberty of the press was a powerful engine, which the Royalist party set in motion. They were informed of all the proceedings in the Congress of Vienna, and they actively circulated the intelligence they obtained. It frequently happened that we were made acquainted with the most important events only through the medium of pamphlets. It was by one of those channels that we heard of a furious declaration of the Congress. That declaration will remain an historical monument of the ingratitude and insult cast on a sovereign whose victories had always been marked by mercy and generosity. Napoleon never insulted a conquered king.

"Independently of the Royalists, there was another party, who, being fired with mistaken and extravagant notions of patriotism, gave considerable cause for alarm. I allude to that set of men who formed themselves into clubs, associations, and confederations of various denominations. This party contained within itself elements which might have been turned to the best account, had they been directed to a truly useful and practicable object, that of heartily uniting to repel the invaders. This national duty might have been accomplished with the concurrence of the people, who certainly evinced an earnest disposition to unite in it But as it too frequently happens, ambitious brawlers took the lead in the associations and perverted their real objects. Instead of organizing a force to defend the country, attention was solely directed to plans of government. Whilst these plans were the subject of discussion, Europe in arms was debating at Vienna the question of dismembering France!

"That was a melancholy period of our history! Foreign enemies were not the authors of all our disasters. We ourselves blindly dug the grave in which we buried our national sympathies and our prosperity.

"The emperor determined to review the National Guard of Paris; and many of his friends endeavoured to dissuade him from this measure. It was represented to him that the Royal Volunteers, incorporated with the National Guard, openly menaced his person and his life. But the emperor, who was inaccessible to fear, replied to these warnings— 'I have been too long acquainted with foreign balls to stand in fear of a French ball.' The review was ordered.

"The emperor refused to have any escort; he would consent only to be accompanied by his staff, and that at a distance. Meanwhile sinister reports had spread among the Guards. Without the emperor's knowledge, and indeed without orders from anyone, some grenadiers of the Island of Elba had joined us. When we approached the front line of the legions, the emperor made a sign directing us to keep back, and he commenced the review. The emperor advanced a short distance, at a slow pace, along the front of the ranks, without knowing that he was followed by the grenadiers, who however were pretty close behind him. But in a few minutes he spurred his horse to a gallop, and then, turning suddenly round, he beheld to his astonishment his unexpected escort. He was not only surprised, but a little irritated at this infraction of his orders, and he said, in an angry tone, 'What do you do here? Where is your commanding officer?'

"There was no commanding officer, neither had any order been given; it was merely the spontaneous act of ten or a dozen brave fellows, anxious to watch over the safely of their sovereign. They made no reply to the emperor's questions, but hung down their heads and looked confused. Napoleon understood all, and he said, in a milder tone of voice, 'Begone, begone.' The grenadiers showed no disposition to move. The emperor then rode up to one of them, and shaking him by the arm, said, 'It is my desire that you should all begone. Do you hear, *old moustache?* Why do you not obey? I am surrounded here by good Frenchmen. I am as safe with them as with you.'

"The effect of these words were quite electrical. 'Yes, yes. Sire, you are safe,' exclaimed the National Guards. 'We will lay down our lives to defend yours!' They rushed from their ranks, surrounded the Emperor, and kissed his hands. The enthusiasm vented itself in exclamations, in which various shades of opinions were expressed, such as '*Vive l'Empereur!—Vive l'Empire!—Vive Napoleon!—Vive la Nation!*' Cries of '*Vive la Garde Imperiale!*' were responded to by shouts of '*Vive l'Armie Nationale!*'

"Among the malignant reports industriously circulated at this time, there was one which attributed a feeling of animosity on the part of the Imperial Guards towards the National militia. The alleged ground of this ill feeling was said to be, that when the National Guards defended Paris in 1814, they did not hold out long enough to enable the army to arrive and engage the enemy before the walls of the capital.

"This report having come to the ears of the emperor, he issued orders for a dinner to be given by the Imperial Guards to the National Guards after the review of the Champ-de-Mars. The dinner was gay and social, and friendly feeling was restored between the two corps. In the evening, the troops, headed by their officers, defiled in front of the windows of the Tuileries, bearing the emperor's bust, which they afterwards deposited at the foot of the column.

"A year previously, the vile parasites of foreign invaders had torn the statue of the great man from its patriotic pedestal.

"Napoleon was eminently gifted with a consciousness of his own dignity. He gave orders for the removal of the bust during the night. 'It is not,' said he, proudly, 'at the close of an orgy that my bust must be restored to its place on the column. The day will come when France will remember me, and will avenge, by a national act, the contemptible insult of a hireling mob.'"

CHAPTER 23

The Hundred Days

"Every hour of that short interval called the *hundred days* brought about a disenchantment, and defeated some of the hopes which the emperor's return had kindled in the hearts of his friends. The chambers were about to open, and it was indispensable that the head of the state should govern without opposition, and devote all his energies, all his intelligence, to the object of paramount importance,—namely, the defence of the country. Nothing but united efforts to repel the enemy could save France from a second defeat.

"The emperor was exceedingly anxious. His eagle glance enabled him at once to perceive the inextricable difficulty into which France might be plunged by imprudent resistance. I, too, was not without my share of anxiety. I was very uneasy respecting the probable results of the Champ-de-Mai.

"'Caulincourt,' said the emperor to me, 'I have yielded to public opinion, but I am convinced that this measure is ill-timed. The French people have so much ardour of imagination, so much changeableness of feeling, they are so prone to mistake effects for causes, and to deceive themselves respecting their rights, that they cannot with safety be trusted all at once with absolute liberty. The Utopians will ruin all. The opposition which is inherent to representative governments will be ill understood. It will degenerate into absurd obstacles, and will paralyze the action of government. To deprive royalty of its supremacy is to take from it its moral force.'

"Under the influence of these gloomy forebodings, the emperor, with indefatigable activity, employed himself, night and day, in preparing for the approaching war. Every thing was to be reorganised and re-established. The *materiel* of the army no longer existed. The store-houses and arsenals were empty, and it seemed as though a vast conflagration had destroyed all the military resources of France. It is impossible to convey any idea of the utter neglect of all business in connexion with the war department. It must, however, be confessed that in the military preparations the emperor was ably seconded. The reorganisation of the national guards and of the army was accomplished with admirable enthusiasm. Manufactories of arms and ammunition, and establishments for military clothing, were all put into active movement from one end of France to the other. The spirit of the people was excellent, and but for impediments, which emanated from the very centre of the government, the immortal work would have been brought to a glorious completion. France presented to Europe the imposing spectacle of thirty-two millions of people rising in defence of their native soil.

"I need not," pursued the Duke de Vicenza, "speak of the Champ-de-Mai, nor of the official acts. With those matters you are, of course, acquainted. Less generally known, but not less interesting, are the private details which throw light on the gloomy picture. On the rare occasions on which I advert to this subject, I am scrupulously careful to assign to each one his proper part in the grand historical drama. I was a member of the government. I saw with 'my own eyes,' and no consideration shall withhold me from speaking the truth. It is not my fault if truth conveys a terrible accusation against men, who, in their insane presumption, fancied themselves capable of saving France in their *curule* chairs.

"It is false and wicked to attribute our disasters to him whose genius might have repaired them, could he have acted in conformity with his own inspirations. But those persons who would have appropriated to themselves the honour of the triumph, evaded the responsibility of the defeat. I accuse no one. I wish only to claim for all, equally, the application of the axiom, let each man have the merit or the blame of his own works. Napoleon is no more, and the hero who shed so much lustre over France must not be disavowed by his country. He is still too near to us to be judged fairly. To judge Napoleon must be the task of posterity.

"The appointment of Carnot to the office of minister of the interior, was much censured. The past conduct of that celebrated man, and his well-known republican opinions, filled the Imperialists with alarm. My political creed was totally opposed to that of Carnot; but his conduct at Antwerp, in 1814, assured me that he would do nothing that did not tend to the interest of his country. In ordinary times Carnot would not have accepted office under a system of government adverse to that which he conceived indispensable to his country's welfare; but in the fearful circumstances in which we were placed, he lost sight of his own personal opinions, and cordially supported the Emperor, whose cause he identified with the cause of France. Carnot's conduct in 1815 was highly honourable.

"The honest frankness of his nature rendered him incapable of dissembling, and from him the Emperor sometimes heard language to which he had not been accustomed. One day, when I was present, Carnot said to him—'Sire, your *acte additionnel* has displeased the nation. It does not answer the wishes of the people. Permit me to modify it. I have courage to tell you the truth, because your welfare and ours depend on your deference, . . . (Here the emperor made a gesture indicative of displeasure.) . . . The word offends you, Sire; but I know of no other which so well expresses my meaning. I say, therefore, your deference to the wishes of the people.'

"'But,' replied the emperor, endeavouring to check his impatience, 'the enemy is at our gates. Let us first repel him, and when we obtain peace we shall have time to think of liberal institutions.' After Carnot's departure the emperor said to me—'That man is certainly animated by the best intentions; but the house is on fire, and instead of endeavouring to extinguish the flames, he is thinking about new arrangements and alterations to render it more convenient. Carnot is one of those men whose minds seem to be in a state of vertigo.' . . . He walked about the room for some time, agitated and thoughtful, and then he seated himself at his writing-table, which was covered with pamphlets and journals of every kind. 'Look here, Caulincourt,' said he; 'just see how the organs of different factions understand what Carnot terms *deference to the will of the people.*

"'The old revolutionists wish me to abolish the empire, and to establish a republic; without that, say they, there is no safety. The partisans of the regency reproach me for not having proclaimed Napoleon II. The pure liberals are of opinion that I ought to resign the crown, and leave to the *sovereign nation* the right of restoring it to me, or of offering it to one who may be deemed more worthy. Truly, if I have abused the *canon law,*' pursued he, shrugging his shoulders, 'these scribblers cruelly abuse the right of discussing their absurdities. . . . All this would be merely laughable if we were not surrounded by a million of armed men.'

"A few days afterwards," continued the Duke de Vicenza, "the chambers met, and we had a fair opportunity of seeing the feeling which animated the representatives. Nothing could have been more proper and desirable than that Prince Lucien, a man of talent and firmness, should have been chosen president of the chamber. The *acte additionnel* conferred on the chamber the right of electing its own president, and Languinais was chosen. This man was a reformer by principle, a *frondeur* by temperament, and he had been the uniform opponent of every form of government which had been established since the year 1793.

"On hearing of this nomination the emperor said, bitterly—'Well done! This is the first use that has been made of the franchise I granted.'

"It was, I think, in the second sitting that the advocate, Dupin, proposed that the chamber should not proceed to business until the demand of the representatives should be conceded: the demand in question was, that they should be furnished with a list of the new peers. This was merely the prelude to other proceedings of the same sort; and in the following sitting the same deputy, Dupin, endeavoured to carry a measure destructive of the established government.

"He alleged that the oath to be taken to the sovereign by the nation, (represented by its deputies,) in order to be valid and lawful, must not be taken in virtue of a decree emanating from the will of the prince, but in virtue of a law which should be the will of the nation constitutionally expressed.

"This captious proposition was supported by another advocate named Roi, but was rejected by the unanimous accord of the rest of the chamber. Its real tendency was to declare null and void the oath which had just been taken at the Champ-de-Mai, by the nation and the army to the emperor, and the constitution of the empire. That oath being the bond which united the army to the emperor and the emperor to the nation, the consequence of its annulment must have been to deprive Napoleon of the attributes of sovereignty and legitimacy with which he had been invested.

"Could the man who proposed this measure 'be conscious of the full extent of its mischief? Or was his object merely to call public attention to his first steps in the career of politics?

"The emperor, on being made acquainted with this proceeding, said, indignantly—'I perceive that the deputies, instead of uniting with me to save the country, wish to withdraw from my cause, and to gain popularity at my expense. . . . Do they mistake me for a Louis XVI.?

Do they imagine that I will submit to be ruled or to have my throat cut by a set of factious brawlers? My blood shall be shed on the field of battle, but never on the scaffold?'

"The shrewd and correct judgment of Napoleon scanned, with its usual clearness, the consequences of the proposed measure. He saw that it was more than an insult to his person; it was a direct attack upon his throne.

"'What motive,' pursued he, in a more subdued tone, 'can instigate such conduct on the part of an unknown individual, who received, only yesterday, the honour of being chosen to represent a portion of his fellow-citizens? He has commenced his career by an attempt to stir up anarchy. Does be imagine that be is fulfilling the duties consigned to him, by thus appealing to the passions of the evil-disposed? Surely he ought to know that a war cannot be national unless the people are united heart and soul with their sovereign. What has the advocate Dupin to complain of? Have I done him any injury? Why does he thus furiously assail the man who, during the space of twenty years, has led the French to victory, sharing alike their hardships and their glory? The conduct of Dupin is not that of a man who wishes to serve his country.'

"I followed the emperor to his cabinet, where we sat writing during the remainder of the evening. But occupation had not the effect of diverting away the sad impression caused by the proceedings of the day. He was anxious and agitated. After some time he laid down his pen, and throwing himself back in his armchair, he said to me, in a desponding tone,—'Caulincourt, we are wasting time. Fate is hurrying France to destruction. In present circumstances, the best devised plans must fail. These men are themselves working the ruin of their country. By alienating from me the affections of the people, they are demoralising public feeling, and damping public energy. At this moment, when I am about to join the army, I am alarmed at the thought of leaving the government *de facto* (for so it really is) in the hands of a turbulent chamber, eager for the exercise of authority, and heedless of the critical position of the country.

"'When the conflict has fairly commenced, the presence of a deliberative body cannot fail to be mischievous, perhaps even fatal. Turbulent and ambitious men, thirsting for popularity and power, set themselves up as advocates of the people, advisers of the sovereign, and defenders of things which are not attacked. If their advice be not followed, they lay aside the character of counsellors and become censors. They next turn from censors to rebels. Such is the course of all deliberative assemblies, composed, as they are now, of a majority of intriguing, dishonest, and ignorant men. The last class are always the dupes of the two former, and they become unconsciously their instruments and accomplices. The bold rule the timid; and weak persons, whose terrors have been worked upon, soon find that they have only been helping others to mount the ladder of ambition.'

"Your Majesty has, observed I, recapitulated in a few words a whole catalogue of those illusive theories in which ideologists love to indulge. All that I see passing around fills me with sad forebodings. We must fall.

"'There is still hope,' eagerly interrupted the emperor. 'The first cannon balls that are fired for the independence of France will restore the true spirit of patriotism in her representatives. The game is begun, and it must be played to an end.'

"Next day the emperor received the deputation with the address. I never shall forget the look which accompanied that part of his answer, in which he uttered the words,—'*Let us not imitate the Lower Empire.*' Some of the promoters of discord seemed abashed by the reproach which this expression conveyed.

"I could mention a thousand traits indicative of the bad feeling which pervaded the chamber; and not one of those traits escaped the penetration of Napoleon. He could see through every dark manoeuvre, and he clearly perceived the hostile attitude of that great power which was rising up in opposition to the throne. 'The honest members of the chamber,' said he, 'do not see that they are being mystified and duped by the royalists, who have many artful and able leaders among their party. Under the mask of the love of liberty, they insinuate themselves into the favour of the patriots, and with the *acte additionnel* in their hands, they delude them into disastrous measures under the pretext of reining in my tyranny. Ask these new converts, on the day when the royal cause is triumphant, what they mean to do with the men they have misled? They will answer, to send them into exile to reflect on the dangers of democracy.'

"In this state of anarchy the emperor left the capital to make head against the overwhelming force arrayed against our unfortunate country."

"I asked the Duke de Vicenza, whether it was true that General Bourmont had solicited leave to enter the emperor's service, and that it was on the application and guarantee of General Gerard that the emperor consented to employ him.

"Your question," replied the Duke de Vicenza, "brings to my recollection one of those acts over which, for the honour of human nature, one would fain draw the veil of oblivion.

"General Bourmont was well treated by the Bourbons in 1814, and he might, like many other general officers, who conceived it to be their duty to espouse the royal cause, have remained faithful to the white cockade. Immediately on the emperor's return, the general became assiduous in his attendance at the Tuileries. At one of the receptions, the emperor was making his usual tour through the saloons, and addressing a few gracious words to those present. Suddenly he perceived Bourmont, and he passed on without speaking. The general followed him, and said,—'Sire, the Allies have declared war against France. I entreat your Majesty to accept my services.'

"The emperor turned round, and looking steadfastly at the general, said, in a very decided tone of voice, 'No, General Bourmont, no.'

"Sire, I have been guilty of nothing which should make me forfeit the honour of serving in the army. The favour which I solicit '

"'Bye and bye.—Bye and bye, I will think of it.'

"'Sire,' replied Bourmont, with deep emotion, and placing his hand on his heart, 'I should have thought that a man like me had no need to perform quarantine.'

"'We shall see—we shall see,' said the emperor, and he passed on.

"There was a report in circulation that Gerard had influenced the emperor in thus slighting Bourmont; but I have heard a very different account,—*viz*. that Gerard expressed his admiration of Bourmont's conduct. At all events, the general got a command—you know the rest."

"I heard," replied I, "though without believing it, the story of General Bourmont's application to the emperor. It was one of those things to which one finds it difficult to give credit."

"The emperor," pursued the duke, "consigned the management of the government to a council, composed of his two brothers, Lucien and Joseph, the four ministers of state, Defermont, St, Jean, d'Angely, Boulay de la Meurthe, Merlin, and several other ministers. He wound up his instructions with these words:—'I depart tonight. Do your duty—the army and I will perform ours. I recommend you to act with union, zeal, and energy. Be careful, gentlemen, not to suffer liberty to degenerate into licence, or anarchy to take place of order. Bear in mind that on unity the success of our exertions must depend.'

"After the emperor retired to his cabinet, where be had numerous orders to dispatch, I once more earnestly renewed my request to be permitted to accompany the army. 'No, Caulincourt, no,' replied he; 'it is impossible. Do not think of it.'

"I represented to him that the post of minister for foreign affairs was at that moment merely nominal, and that I could be of no use in Paris.

"'Say no more of this—it cannot be; and on my still urging him to consent to my going, he added,—'I am going to take Maret with me, and if I were not to leave you in Paris, who would there be here on whom I could rely,'

"The emperor then proceeded to arrange some business connected with the different ministerial departments. He gave me his private instructions with the most unlimited confidence. He foresaw many misfortunes; but be trusted with perfect reliance to his devoted army.

"The clock struck three, and daylight was beginning to appear. 'Farewell, Caulincourt,' said the emperor, holding out his hand to me. 'Farewell—we must conquer or die.' . . . With hurried steps, he passed through the apartments, his mind being evidently absorbed by melancholy ideas. On reaching the foot of the staircase, he cast a lingering look around him, and then threw himself into his carriage.

"When the carriage was out of sight, and the rattling of the wheels was no longer audible, the most gloomy feelings overwhelmed me. The silence which pervaded the capital seemed to bode evil. I went down into the garden, and walked about, but without being able to calm the inward agitation that preyed upon me. A mass of flame seemed to be gathering on the horizon; I heard the howling of the storm, and my eyes involuntarily turned towards the opposite bank of the Seine. From that direction came the thunderbolts which dealt destruction on France."

CHAPTER 24.

The Disasters of Waterloo

"On the day after the emperor's departure, I proceeded, in company with the minister of the interior, to the chamber of peers. Carnot presented an accurate report of the true situation of the country. He announced that the emperor wished, in concurrence with the Chambers, to give suitable organic laws to France. With praiseworthy courage and candour he acknowledged the fears excited in the friends of the government by the manifest progress of demagogic spirit. He concluded by observing that on the union of all depended the safety of the state.

"The boldness of this avowal gave umbrage to some; but Carnot carried along with him the authority of his own example. He was a sincere republican; and yet he refrained from the declaration of his opinions, in consideration of the dangers which menaced his country. There was only one man who could save France, and Carnot devoted all his energies to aid that man, zealously and loyally,

"Carnot's address was followed by the report of the Minister of Foreign Affairs. I represented, without reserve, our position with Europe in arms against us, and I stated that it was the fixed determination of the Allied Powers not to grant any truce, nor to accede to any treaty with France. I described the fruitless efforts made by the emperor to bring the Allied Sovereigns to pacific sentiments, by making every concession compatible with national honour. I observed that France, being menaced on all sides by warlike preparations, was under the necessity of striking the first blow in the conflict, under pain of compromising her dignity and her interests by protracted hesitation. I concluded by appealing to the enlightened patriotism of the representative powers, and imploring them to aid and support the emperor, who was himself on the frontiers, fighting in defence of the independence of the country.

"My address," pursued the duke, "excites some sympathy. I am inclined to believe that the majority of the assembly were actuated by good intentions, but energy was wanting. Foreseeing a defeat, all suffered themselves to be influenced by personal considerations—all were anxious to be saved from foreign domination, provided they could be saved without detriment to their possessions and interests. Selfishness, that scourge of society, was destined to prevail over generous resolves. How very little great political characters appear when we have a close view of them.

"Communications, similar to those made to the Chamber of Peers, were presented to the Chamber of Deputies by two ministers of state: they elicited unequivocal demonstrations of dissatisfaction from the representatives. In the interval between the departure and the return of the emperor, the Chambers, instead of devoting attention to measures of defence, resumed their discussions on the *acte additionnel*, and launched into theoretic dissertations, of which untimeliness was their least objection.

"On perceiving the spirit evinced by the Chambers, I could not help calling to mind the words of the emperor, which were impressed with that correctness of observation which characterized him. How perfect was his acquaintance with the machinery of government! To what a degree of prosperity would he not have brought France, if, instead of directing all his efforts to her aggrandisement, he had confined his attention to her internal government. But his volcanic temperament, which for the space of twenty years made him regard nothing as impossible, could not be satisfied with anything short of conquests and wonders. He could not brook the thought of seeing ardent and intellectual France, without preponderance, without domination, over the European equilibrium. He resolved to see her unrivalled in glory, respected and envied by all the nations of the earth. The year 1815 closed this brilliant dream. Terrible reality superseded the noble illusions of a noble heart. France destroyed the existence of her hero, before his last sigh was breathed at St. Helena!"

"Even now," said I to the Duke de Vicenza, "whenever I pronounce his name, a bitter regret attaches itself to a painful recollection——. Did Napoleon often speak of his son and Maria Louisa?

"Of his son sometimes; but of the empress never. It is not a little remarkable that he never alluded to the negotiations which I was to have undertaken in 1814, for reuniting him to Maria Louisa. Having been deceived in his hopes of possessing the affections of the woman to whom he was so much attached, he was, no doubt, anxious to avoid a useless explanation. He was too proud to complain, and he disdained to reproach.

"I will mention to you," continued the duke, "a circumstance characteristic of that strange period called the Hundred Days, during which the government had no positive or palpable existence. An occult power ruled the public mind, and directed the public resources. Honest men found themselves betrayed and mystified. They beheld scenes and deeds of darkness which they could not bring to light,—they saw mischief which they could neither prevent nor denounce.

"It was midnight, I was sitting alone in my cabinet writing, when my attention was suddenly diverted from my occupation by a loud knocking at the door of the hotel. In a few moments I heard hurried footsteps approaching my apartment. The usher entered and presented to me a note which was scarcely sealed. It contained only the following words, written in Latin:—

The army has been destroyed at Waterloo.

I was for a moment petrified.—But a rapid reflection brought me to myself. This, thought I, is the work of some demon, and the intelligence here communicated is intended to be circulated through Paris. I rang the bell violently. Stop the bearer of this note, I exclaimed. Do not let him leave the house.

"'Sire,' replied the usher, 'I was in the porter's lodge, when a gentlemanly-looking man entered. He appeared rather agitated, and he said, hurriedly,—"Here is a letter for the minister, and here is a twenty-*franc* piece for anyone who will deliver it to him immediately, wheresoever he may be."—Having uttered these words, the person disappeared as hurriedly as he had entered,'

"I could not, I would not," continued the duke, "believe what I saw written, and yet, thought I, it is very improbable that anyone would give twenty *francs* for the sake of a silly hoax. I instantly ordered a coach, and proceeded straight to Carnot. I showed him the billet, and expressed my fears respecting machinations hatched by the emperor's enemies.

"'The last telegraphic intelligence, which was received today at noon,' said Carnot, 'was satisfactory. The Haie Sainte and Mont-Saint-Jean had been carried by our troops.'

"That is true, replied I, but how happens it that we have no later

256

news?

"'That may be easily accounted for. Supposing the telegraph nearest to the theatre of war to have gone wrong; it would be sufficient to interrupt the communications along the whole line.'

"'I am exceedingly uneasy . . . . If the fatal news be true, it must have been transmitted this evening by the telegraph. The signals are visible until three-quarters past eight.

"'No dispatch has arrived this evening,' said Carnot, emphatically; 'of that I am certain.'

"You mean to say, my dear Carnot, that you have received none?

"He immediately seized the idea which my words were intended to convey.

"'If,' said he, 'your suspicions were just, he would certainly deserve to be hanged. . . . But let us go, without delay, and clear up this affair.'

"We shall not get at the truth, said I.

"'Carnot speedily dressed himself, and we both proceeded to the hotel of the Duke of Otranto. It was now two o'clock in the morning.

"'We will not give him time to invent any falsehoods,' said Carnot. 'We will follow the servant into his bedroom, and take him by surprise.'

"However, our nocturnal visit put Fouché sufficiently on his guard. He raised himself up in his bed, and gazed at us with an air of astonishment.

"'Colleague,' said Carnot, in a sharp tone, 'you have received intelligence from the army which has not been communicated to us.'

"'What do you mean ?' said he, evidently disconcerted. 'I have received none.'

"'We have sustained terrible disasters. The army is stated to have been destroyed at Waterloo.'

"'How did you hear this? No doubt it is all an absurd invention.' As he uttered these words his voice faltered.

"Duke, said I, the report is either true ,or false. If this speaks truth, said I, presenting to him the note, the news must have been communicated by telegraph, for there has not been time for the arrival of a courier.

"'What do you infer from that?' said he, drily.

"'*Parbleu!*' exclaimed Carnot; 'what we infer from it is, that we are delivered up, bound hand and font, to the enemy; and that there is among us a traitor—a Judas!'

"'Have you come here to insult me?' said he, hastily jumping out of bed, and throwing on his *robe de chambre*.

"'There can be no insult,' rejoined Carnot, sternly, 'except for one who feels that the epithets of traitor and Judas are applicable to himself.'

"*Monsieur*, said I, addressing myself to Fouché let us not quarrel about words; we have come here to discuss a fact . . . You affirm that you have received no news?

"'I do, positively.'

"Then it follows that the intelligence announced in this anonymous billet is false?

"'I cannot say whether it be false or true?'

"Well, the telegraph of this morning will, I hope, prove that I have been misinformed.

"'And, even supposing the telegraph were to confirm this sinister news! do I command the telegraph? Besides, what motive could I have for suppressing dispatches and delaying their communication ?'

"We felt that it was useless to make any reply to these remarks, and we accordingly took our leave.

"'What do you think of this?' said Carnot to me, after we came out.

"'I think,' replied he, 'that he knows all, and that the disaster is but too certain. . . . We are lost.'

"'I fear so. . . . He has spies and agents everywhere. He has received the news, no matter by what means; and his object is to devise some diabolical plan for repressing the national feeling which would be excited by the loss of the battle.

"The most curious part of the whole affair was, that at six o'clock in the morning the telegraph announced the fatal catastrophe, and that the tenor of the dispatches evidently denoted that there was a deficiency in the last correspondence communicated to the council.

"The person who communicated this information never made himself known. How he obtained his information I am unable to guess.

"In the course of the day several couriers arrived. It was determined in the council that the fatal telegraphic dispatch should not be made known, and that the most perfect secrecy should be observed until the receipt of further intelligence. Nevertheless, in the evening the news was whispered in some of the fashionable *salons*, . . . and it was easy to read in the triumphant looks of the royalists the disasters of Waterloo.

"Next day, alarm began to take possession of the public mind. The interruption of the bulletins created fear; and the populace evinced symptoms of that sort of suppressed agitation which always precedes a crisis. Some disturbances also took place in the theatres. The pit called for the performance of the *Marseillaise* Hymn, and turbulent groups assembled in the *coalisses* and green-rooms.

"The emperor's expected arrival was announced to me during the night by a courier from Laon. I immediately proceeded to the Elysèe to receive him. Scarcely six days had elapsed since I bade him farewell, and those six days had obliterated the past, and sealed the doom of the present and the future.

"The emperor arrived early in the morning, overcome by grief, and exhausted by fatigue. He endeavoured to give vent to the emotions of his heart, but his oppressed respiration permitted him only to articulate broken sentences—'The army,' he said, 'has performed prodigies of valour! .... inconceivable efforts! .... What troops! ... Ney behaved like a madman He caused my cavalry to be cut to pieces! ...All has been sacrificed! ... I am ill and exhausted I must lie down for an hour or two... My head burns ... I must take a bath!'

"He took the bath, and retired to bed; but he continued restless and feverish. He asked me many questions, but I was so fearful of increasing his excitement that I absolutely refused to speak of the affairs of Paris. I had none but disheartening communications to make to him. The altered expression of his countenance sufficiently indicated the sufferings of his mind; but nevertheless he could neither divide his thoughts from the fatal field which he had just quitted, nor subdue his anxiety for the course of affairs in Paris.

"'It is grievous !' he exclaimed, 'to think that we should have been overcome after so many heroic efforts. My most brilliant victories do not shed more glory on the French Army than the defeat of Mont St.-Jean. ... Our troops have not been beaten; they have been sacrificed, massacred by overwhelming numbers. ... My guards suffered themselves to be cut to pieces without asking for quarter. ...I wished to have died with them; but they exclaimed— "Withdraw! Withdraw! You see that death is resolved to spare your Majesty." And opening their ranks, my old grenadiers screened me from the carnage, forming around me a rampart of their bodies. ..... My brave, my admirable guard has been destroyed and I have not perished with them!'

"The emperor paused, and heaved deep sighs. I listened to the sad recital with agonised feelings.

"'I had,' resumed the emperor, 'combined a bold manoeuvre with the view of preventing the junction of the two hostile armies. I had combined my cavalry into a single corps of twenty thousand men, and ordered it to rush into the midst of the Prussian cantonments. This bold attack, which was executed on the 14th, with the rapidity of lightning, seemed likely to decide the fate of the campaign. French troops never calculate the number of an enemy's force. . . . They care not how they shed their blood in success. . . They are invincible in prosperity; . . but I was compelled to change my plan! Instead of making an unexpected attack, I found myself obliged to engage in a regular battle, having opposed to me two combined armies, supported by immense reserves! The enemy's forces quadrupled the number of ours. I had calculated all the disadvantages of a regular battle. The infamous desertion of Bourmont forced me to change all my arrangements. To pass over to the enemy on the eve of a battle! Atrocious! The blood of his fellow countrymen be on his head! The maledictions of France will pursue him.'

"Sire, observed I, on a former occasion you rejected that man; how unfortunate that you did not follow your own impulse!

"'Oh! this baseness is incredible. The annals of the French Army offer no precedent for such a crime. Jomini was not a Frenchman. The consequences of this defection have been most disastrous. It has created despondency in the minds of those who witnessed the paralyzing effects of previous treasons. My orders were not properly understood, and consequently there was some degree of hesitation in executing them. At one time. Grouchy was too late; at another time, Ney was carried away by his enthusiasm and intrepidity. He exposed himself to danger like any common soldier, without looking either before or behind him; and the troops under his command were sacrificed without any necessity.

"'It is deplorable to think of it! Our army performed prodigies of valour, and yet, we have lost the battle. Generals, marshals,—all fought gloriously,—but nevertheless an indescribable uncertainty and anxiety pervaded the commanders of the army. There was no unity, no precision, in the movements——and,' added he, with painful emotion, 'I have been assured that cries of *sauve qui peut* were uttered. I cannot believe this. What I suffered, Caulincourt, was worse than the tortures of Fontainebleau. I feel that I have had my death wound. The blow I received at Waterloo is mortal!'

"What could I say in reply to this?" said the duke. "What consolation could I offer to his wounded spirit?

"I retired to the emperor's cabinet, where he rejoined me in about half an hour after. His pale countenance and sunken eyes bore evidence of his mental suffering; but he had recovered some degree of calmness.

"'My intention is,' said he, 'to unite the two Chambers in an imperial sitting. I will faithfully describe to them the misfortunes of the army, and appeal to them for the means of saving the country. After that, I will again return to the seat of war.'

"Sire, said I, the intelligence of our disasters has already transpired; and there is considerable agitation in the public mind.

"'My first intention was,' said he, 'on my arrival in the capital, to alight at the Chamber of Deputies; and whilst yet covered with the dust and smoke of the field of battle, to unfold the danger of the country. I was dissuaded from this design.'

"I feel much grieved. Sire, in being compelled to add to your unhappiness; but It is incumbent on me to make your Majesty acquainted with the truth. The feeling of the deputies is more hostile than ever.

"'Nevertheless,' he exclaimed, 'they must yield to conviction.'

"They knew before the meeting of the council, resumed I, the extent of our disasters, and yet no sympathy for your misfortunes was manifested previously to your return. The machinations which ruined us in 1814, are renewed in 1815 under new forms.

"'Treachery, treachery everywhere! Where is the heroism of '93, when all France arose as one man to repel foreign invasion? Can these men have French blood in their veins?' His eyes' beamed with extraordinary lustre.

"Sire, said I, deign to listen to me! The Chambers never deserve your confidence, nor, will they answer to your appeal. Permit me likewise to say that I regret to see your Majesty in Paris. It would have been better, sire, if you had not separated from your army, which was your strength, your safety. In the midst of your troops, you are inviolable. They are *courtiers* who will never betray or forsake you. With them you are still a redoubtable chief; without them you are a powerless sovereign.

"'I have no longer an army,' said he, mournfully. 'I may find men, but how are they to fight? They are without arms or ammunition. However, by dint of patriotism and unity all may yet be repaired. You are low-spirited, my dear Caulincourt. You view things through the

261

veil of disappointment. After all, the deputies are the representatives of the nation; we must not despair of their patriotism at the present moment; the question at issue is, not opposition to. me personally, but the salvation of the country; and they must second me. They feel the weight of the awful duty that hangs upon them, and they know that they are responsible to their fellow citizens. Three months ago France greeted my return with enthusiasm. Is that forgotten?'

"Lucien and Joseph entered, and the emperor anxiously questioned them respecting the course which the Chambers were likely to adopt. Their answers confirmed the opinion which I had expressed, and they advised him to defer the convocation for the imperial sitting. They added, that it appeared to them most advisable to allow the ministers to take some previous measure.

"The emperor gave me some orders, which I retired to execute. I was glad that he had consulted his brothers before he came to any determination. Lucien is a man of judgment and resolution. He knew, as well as I, the real state of things, and he was certain to give none but good advice.

"In passing through the apartments, I found them filled with all the great functionaries and dignitaries, who had hurried to the Elysèe on hearing of the emperor's arrival. The *aides-de-camp* and officers who had returned from Waterloo, were eagerly interrogated. The terrific spectacle of the route and destruction of the army was still present to their eyes; and the details they gave filled with dismay all who heard them. The *scenes of Fontainebleau* were re-enacted at the Elysèe. The actors were the same, and their conduct no less shameful.

"As I was coming out, I met the Duke de Bassano, who had not left the emperor. 'All is lost !' said he, pressing my hand. He was over-whelmed with grief, as he narrated to me some particulars which had come to his knowledge. I could not help repeating with him. 'All is lost!'

"Ever since the emperor's arrival, I had been in a state of mind which I cannot attempt to describe. At Fontainebleau I thought I had suffered every extreme of mental agony. But I was deceived. My torments were now renewed under a still more painful aspect. In 1814, foreign conquerors within our walls dictated laws to us. We had to submit to the fete of the vanquished. But now, the government was our own; the emperor was in Paris; public feeling in the provinces and in the capital was hostile to the enemy and to the second restoration. With the active and intelligent concurrence of the constituted authorities, the country might be saved. Who was the person who intervened between the nation and her sovereign? Who consummated our ruin?

"I withdrew to my own apartments to console myself. These successive trials had almost exhausted my firmness. I am not of a temperament to fall lukewarmly; and I felt my strength sinking beneath this tenacity of misfortune.

"After the lapse of about two hours, I returned to the Elysèe, where the council was convoked. All the ministers were present. The Duke de Bassano read the bulletin of Mont St.-Jean. To that sentence of death the emperor, with dignity, made the following reply:—'The army is covered with glory. Desertions, misunderstandings, and an inexplicable fatality have rendered unavailing the heroic exertions of our troops. Our disasters are great; but they are still reparable if my efforts are seconded. I returned to Paris to stimulate a noble impulse. If the French people rise, the enemy will be subdued. If, instead of resorting to prompt measures, and making extraordinary sacrifices, time is wasted in disputes and discussions, all is lost. The enemy is in France—in eight days he will be at the gates of the capital. To save the country, it is requisite that I should be invested with vast power, with a temporary dictatorship. For the interest of all, I ought to possess this power. But it will be more proper, more national, that it should be conferred on me by the Chambers.'

"No reply was made to this address, to which all listened with downcast eyes; or, to speak more correctly, I should say all, with the exception of Fouché, who darted oblique glances on the countenances of his colleagues, as if to watch their feelings.

"The emperor called upon Carnot to deliver his opinion, which he did frankly and energetically. He spoke as follows:—'It is necessary to declare that the country is in danger; to summon every French patriot to take up arms. Paris must be placed in a state of siege, and defended to the last extremity, or we must retire behind the Loire, recall the army of La Vendée, with the corps of observation of the south, and hold the enemy in check, until it be possible to collect or organise sufficient forces to resume the offensive, and to expel the enemy from France.'

"I did not share Carnot's opinion, as to the expediency of the retreat on the Loire. I called to mind the events of 1814, and I maintained, with all the earnestness of positive conviction, that the occupation of the capital by the enemy would, a second time, decide the fate of the Imperial throne. The safety of the country, said I, must not depend upon isolated measures, or on the good or bad intentions of the Allied Powers. (Here I fixed my eyes on a certain personage.) It is indispensable, Sire, that your Majesty should be invested with an absolute dictatorship. The nation must make a great effort. The Chambers must do their duty by not separating the cause of the country from that of its sovereign. These are the conditions on which the safety of France depends.

"Whilst I was speaking, Fouché was evidently revolving in his mind the course which it would be most expedient for him to adopt. My proposition was calculated to subvert his intrigues, and to thwart his plan of deposing Napoleon. He had too much tact to oppose me openly, and he accordingly expressed his concurrence with those of our colleagues who were unanimously of my opinion. He eulogized the wisdom of the measure which Carnot and I had proposed. He dwelt on the justice of my observation respecting the occupation of Paris by the enemy; and he artfully added,—'Nevertheless, I think these measures ought to be referred to the Chambers. By showing them good faith and implicit confidence we shall convince them that their duty is to unite with his Majesty the emperor in energetic measures to save the independence of the nation.'

"As he concluded his address, he cast a sinister glance at me, which seemed, as it were, a defiance to outwit him. I saw through his artful design in proposing the sanction of the Chambers. His looks seemed to say, 'You may spare yourself all further trouble; affairs are entirely at my control.' Between Fouché and me there existed one of those antipathies which resolve into hatred on the one part, and hatred mingled with contempt on the other.

"Decrès protested against Fouché's suggestion, and declared that it was useless to hope to gain over the deputies, who, he said, were disposed to go to the most violent extremes.

"Regnault added, that he did not believe the representatives would consent to second the emperor's views; and that they openly declared he could do nothing more for France.

"'Speak candidly,' said the emperor; 'it is my abdication they wish for, is it not?'

"'I fear it is. Sire, and though it is deeply repugnant to my feelings to tell your Majesty a painful truth, yet it is my belief that if you were not to abdicate voluntarily, the Chamber would require your abdication.'

"'Well, Duke of Otranto,' sold the emperor, directing at Fouché a glance of severity, to which the latter replied by an obsequious gesture of incredulity. 'Well, duke, this does not correspond with what you just now said.'

"'I have lived during other crises,' exclaimed Lucien, with warmth; 'and under circumstances no less difficult than the present. It is in temporizing that the danger consists. If the Chamber be not willing to second the emperor, His Majesty can dispense with its feeble assistance. The defence of the country is the first law of the state. If the Chamber do not unite with the emperor to save France, he most save her by his single efforts. He must declare himself a dictator; he must declare the whole of France in a state of siege; and he must summon all true Frenchmen to arms.'

"Carnot earnestly supported Lucien. 'I surrender my individual opinion,' said he, 'to the necessity of circumstances; and I declare that I consider it indispensable that, during the present crisis, the sovereign should be invested with absolute power.'

"'The nation,' said the emperor, in a voice of thunder, 'did not elect the deputies to overthrow me, but to support me. Woe to them if the presence of the enemy on the French soil do not arouse their energy and patriotism! . . . Whatever course they may adopt, I shall always be supported by the people and the army. Their fate, their very existence, depends on my will. Were I to pronounce their doom, they would all be sacrificed. They are playing an artful game. No matter! I have no need to resort to stratagem. I have right on my side. The patriotism of the people, their antipathy to the Bourbons, who are kept in reserve for them, their attachment to my person—all these circumstances still afford immense resources if we know bow to profit by them.'

"He successively brought under consideration the means of repairing the disasters of Waterloo. He drew a bold picture of the misfortunes which threatened France, and concluded by developing an admirable plan of defence and attack for opposing the invasion of the enemy. All eyes were fixed upon him: all attention was concentrated on the workings of that stupendous mind, the energy of which was unimpaired by the reverses and difficulties rising up on every side.

"The various shades of opinion which had prevailed among the members of the council at length blended into one, and all united in approving the plans of the emperor. Measures were adopted for facilitating their immediate execution. It was resolved that the ministers should proceed in a body to the Chambers, and make an official communication, or that they should adopt a resolution consistent with the urgency of circumstances.

"I am betraying state secrets," said the duke, smiling; "I have unfolded to you this scene in the council in order to give you a true idea of the terrible position of Napoleon, and the motives which forced on the second abdication. Many persons pronounce this abdication to have been an act of weakness. Thus it is that history is written from conjecture.

"The council was interrupted by a message from the Chamber of Representatives. I will spare you the literal tenour of the ultimatum addressed to the emperor. The Chamber declared itself permanent, designated as high treason any attempt to dissolve it, and declared to be treasonable any encroachment on the rights of the representatives, &c.

"The ministers of the war department, of foreign affairs, and the interior, were requested to proceed immediately to the assembly.

"The emperor turned pale with anger. He rose, and striking his hand forcibly on the table, exclaimed, in a tone of indignation—'I ought to have dismissed these men before my departure. I foresaw this. These factious firebrands will ruin France. I can measure the full extent of the evil. They are in open rebellion against intimate authority. I must reflect on what is to be done.' He dissolved the sitting.

"I never beheld anything more hideous than the sardonic expression which was at that moment depicted in the countenance of Fouché

"I was roused to the utmost degree of indignation. I declared, that for my own part, convinced as I was of the uselessness of seeking to convince people who were resolved not to be convinced, I would not obey the summons of the Representatives, and that I did not acknowledge their right to call me to their bar.

"The emperor, who was exceedingly indignant, sent Regnault with a message to the Chamber of Deputies. Carnot was dispatched with a similar communication to the Chamber of Peers. The latter was listened to with courtesy and attention; but in the Chamber of Deputies Regnault could not obtain even silence. He was refused a hearing; and a. second message imperatively commanded those ministers who had been specified in the first to appear immediately in the Chamber.

"I need not," pursued the Duke de Vicenza, "carry you through the long train of torments and disgusts which embittered the close of my political career. The numerous memoirs of the period exhibit faithful pictures of the inconsistency, the turbulence, and the deplorable inability, of the representative powers.

"Events hurried on: we counted not days, but hours and minutes. The abdication was wrested from Napoleon. For the second time he resigned the throne in favour of his son. This concession has shared the fate of all concessions made by sovereign authority to factious exigency: it bas remedied no evil; it has not saved France from becoming the prey of conflicting parties, nor from being ruined by a feeble government. In short, the emperor's abdication left the field open to all sorts of political speculations.

"The republicans insisted on the establishment of a feudal government; the imperialists, who had with them the voice of the nation, urged the claims of Napoleon II. and the Regency; whilst another party, composed of the most furious speakers in the assembly, was secretly labouring to place the Duke of Orleans on the throne. Others were for the Prince of Orange. Doubtless I must seem to be relating the occurrences of a romance; but, to our everlasting shame, these occurrences must find a place in the pages of French history. But amongst all the projects that were set afloat, it is easy to distinguish those which were projected by honest men and dupes from the machinations of unprincipled intriguers, who are ever ready to barter the interests of their country.

"Whilst parties were thus contending one with another, in order to obtain the sovereign of their choice, one man succeeded in baffling them all, and placing the exiled family on the throne. He had maintained constant correspondence with Ghent; his conditions were agreed to, and his regicide vote of '93 received the baptism of the amnesty. In return for the sovereignty of France, which he surrendered to the Bourbons, the latter presented to astonished Europe the inconceivable spectacle of Fouché the regicide, becoming a minister in the council of the brother of Louis XVI.

"I was with the emperor when the deputation from the Chamber of Deputies came to express the respect and gratitude with which the Chamber received the sacrifice he had made to the independence and happiness of the French people.

"The emperor at first received the deputation with dignified coolness; but inspired by his natural feelings, he delivered an answer replete with sound arguments and lofty ideas. His earnest prayers and recommendations for the national prosperity and glory moved all present.

Lanjuinais himself with difficulty repressed his emotion, and no doubt he and some others felt compunctious visitings.

"After the departure of the deputation, Regnault observed that he esteemed himself happy in having prevailed on the Chamber to adopt this respectful measure.

"'Ah!' exclaimed the emperor, in a tone of mingled anger and disdain, 'then this is your work?'

"'Yes, Sire.'

"'Well then, you ought to have remembered that the title of emperor cannot be forfeited ;' and he turned his back on Lanjuinais.

"'The emperor had good reason for treating him in this way. In the address, the Chamber had substituted for the title of emperor the denomination *General Bonaparte*. This was an act of insolence which ought not to have been permitted by one of the emperor's ministers of state, the more especially as the acknowledgment of Napoleon's right to abdicate was a formal acknowledgment of his sovereign dignity. Such conduct is truly contemptible!

"The painful restraint which the emperor imposed on himself, for the sake of appearing calm in public, was thrown aside in his intercourse with persons with whom he was intimate. He then seemed to be profoundly wretched. He felt unspeakable mortification in attributing to the French people the outrages which had been inflicted on him. 'Caulincourt,' said he to me, 'this last experience of mankind has irrevocably banished from me those illusions which help to counteract the cares of sovereignty. I have no longer any faith in patriotism: it is a mere empty word, expressing a noble idea. The love of country is the love of one's self, of one's position, of one's personal interest . . Interest! that miserable motive is now paramount over every other in France.

"'There is no longer faith or integrity in the bond which unites the nation to its sovereign. France is verging towards her decline . . . The future is pregnant with disasters . . . Kings are treading on volcanised ground . . . The Bourbons have stripped from the crown the halo with which I sought to encircle it . . . How short-sighted . . . They cannot perceive that by disavowing our glory, and our conquests—by depreciating the great and brilliant works which have elevated the throne, they are destroying its illusions. I have elevated, not degraded royalty. I have made it great and powerful—I have presented it under a new and favourable aspect, to a people to whom it had become obnoxious—I had collected round the national throne everything that could fix popular admiration. My successors will not feel the value of these attractions. They will imprudently strip off the velvet and gold, and show that the throne is only a few deal planks.'

"Ah! thought I, struck with these prophetic words, the glorious days of France are past. The sovereign who may venture to seat himself on Napoleon's throne, may possibly reign, but he will never govern,"

CHAPTER 25

The Duke's Visit to the Elysèe

"The representatives who were in open rebellion launched into the most furious declamations. In vain did Lucien, Labédoyére, Boulay de la Meurthe, Segur, and all the friends of the emperor, advocate the inheritance of Napoleon II. in virtue of the abdication. Several advocates, among whom was M. Dupin, made themselves conspicuous by their bitter hostility to the Imperial cause, and their exertions in favour of a heterogeneous system of government, which was neither republic nor empire. The time of the Chambers was wasted in idle harangues, which were frequently interrupted by violent murmurs. But the brand of discord was lighted, and the enemies of the emperor attained their object.

"Fouché, who was president of the provisional government, of which I was likewise a member, was regent *de facto*. He was the central point of every intrigue; and by a thousand hidden springs he controlled the deliberations of the assembly. When urged to explain his views and intentions, Fouché replied that he had never disavowed the claims of Napoleon II.; but that prince, not having yet been acknowledged by any of the Powers, we could not treat with them in his name. It was therefore requisite, he said, to adopt Deputy Dupin's suggestion, and to stipulate provisionally in the name of the nation, so as to afford the enemy no pretence for rejecting the negotiators selected by the Chamber.

"Fouché's reply was dictated by the most artful Machiavelism and perfidy. The throne was thus declared vacant, and was at the full and entire disposal of the Allied Powers, who were advancing by forced marches on Paris. We exerted our utmost efforts to show the fatal consequences of this measure; but the violent declamations of our antagonists prevailed, and it was found more convenient to adopt the opinion expressed by Fouché than to oppose it.

"During this usurped reign of the Chambers, the feeling that pervaded the Parisian population was remarkable. Among masses of people there usually prevails a degree of good sense which enables them, with inconceivable sagacity, to estimate the ability of those who are appointed to rule them. The legislative authority, proceeding, as it did, without object or unity, was watched with painful impatience, and it was clearly understood that no benefit could accrue from the fiery harangues in the Chambers. The enemy was now within ten leagues of Paris.

"The emperor, who was a prisoner in the Elysèe, excited the sympathy of the populace, whose menacing aspect diffused terror through the capital. Bands of federalists paraded the streets, uttering threats against the representatives. An armed force, under the command of Fouché, surrounded the Chamber, and protected its deliberations, whilst the approaches to the Elysèe were filled by crowds, who mingled menaces with shouts of '*Vive l'Empereur!*' The state of Paris was most alarming.

"The palace, which was invested on the outside by turbulent mobs, was in the interior a vast solitude. It was deserted by men devoid of honour and faith, those who crouch to good fortune and fly from adversity. The guard—the faithful Imperial guard—no longer surrounded Napoleon. Happy were they who were sleeping their last sleep on the field of Waterloo. The ill-starred men who survived that great disaster, soon knew not where to hide their proscribed heads, or how to conceal the insignia of their immortal glory. Alas! is it to be wondered at that feelings of hatred still lurk in those broken hearts!

"Some wrecks of those heroes who had been forgotten in the hecatombs of Mont St.-Jean, wandered to Paris, and from thence to the Elysèe. There they were without commanders, without orders . . . . but no matter, they were there. A single sentinel, in a tattered uniform, guarded the door of the hero who so lately had legions enrolled under his banners. How many unheard-of pangs accompanied the last convulsions of Napoleon's political existence!

"His position at the Elysèe is unexampled in history. He might, had he been so inclined, have annihilated the traitors by a single word. The crowds who surrounded him would, on the slightest signal, have overthrown any obstacle that stood between Napoleon and the nation. But the emperor would never have consented to excite scenes of carnage. He well knew the terrific nature of popular justice.

"I proceeded to the Elysèe to render him an account of what was passing in the Chamber of Deputies. I experienced no little difficulty in gaining access to the palace. I was obliged once or twice to harangue the crowd, in order to obtain room for my carriage to pass along, and though I knew the people to be all friendly to the emperor, yet the fury depicted in their countenances not a little alarmed me.

"I found the emperor very impatient to know what had been done in Paris. The shouts of the populace were distinctly heard within the walls of the palace.

"'This is dreadful,' said he to me, as I entered. 'The mob may be led to the commission of some excess; and I shall be accused of being the cause. These mistaken people wish to serve me, and yet they are doing all they can to injure me. What effect do these demonstrations produce in Paris?'

"Paris, replied I, is in a state of stupor. Many families have fled. Almost all the best houses are empty. As I drove through the streets I met scarcely one respectably-dressed man. Some riots are apprehended tonight.

"'This is deplorable!—most deplorable.—Let us go into the garden,' pursued he. 'The heat is suffocating here.'

"The sun was setting. We walked into that part of the grounds, called the *jardin-Anglais*, to escape the observation of the crowd, who formed a cordon round the palace.

"'Well,' said the emperor, 'let me know what has been done in the Chambers?'

"I told him the particulars, which I have just detailed to you.

"'All is lost!' he exclaimed. 'They seem not to be aware that by declaring the throne to be vacant they surrender it to the first claimant. The Allies will not now treat; they will dictate their conditions, and they must be accepted. . . . All this has been arranged beforehand. Fouché is a base intriguer, and he has artfully laid his plans. The majority of the Chamber is hostile to the Bourbons; and yet there is no doubt the Bourbons will be brought back through their refusal to proclaim Napoleon II. To overthrow an established government, supported by the constituted authorities, by the army, by the citizen guards, and by the populace, is a very different affair from finding a government in a state of dissolution, distracted by factions, and a prey to anarchy. To abandon the rights of my son, is to smooth the path for the Allies. France is at the mercy of her foreign enemies. She will pay dearly for the inability of her representatives.'

"At the moment we were interrupted by a great noise, which seemed to proceed from the direction of the Champs-Elysèe. We first heard acclamations and shouts of '*Vive l'Empereur!*' and then loud and tumultuous bravos.

"The following episode, which intervened amidst the great political scenes of the time, revealed a very important fact, and furnished us with a key to many others. We at length discovered secret causes which had heretofore been hidden from us. We found an explanation of the circumstances which had brought about our disasters at Waterloo, and the fabulous rapidity of events which baffled all foresight

"The sound of voices in the garden arrested our attention. We stopped, and through the trees we perceived, between two grenadiers, an elegantly-dressed lady. She looked pale and terrified, and she directed her steps towards the palace. 'Who is that?' inquired the emperor, with astonishment.

"Where are you going? said I, advancing towards the guards. Whom do you want, madam?

"Alarm seemed almost to have bereft the lady of her senses. I repeated my question, and at length, in a very sweetly-toned voice, she uttered the following words, which were interrupted by torrents of tears:—'Protect me, sir, I conjure you. I wish to see the emperor. I must speak with him personally!'

"'That may be all very true,' interrupted one of the old grenadiers; 'but that is no reason why you should have darted, like a bullet, over the walls;' then, scanning the lady from head to foot, he added—'This manoeuvre seems to me rather suspicious. She may be an assassin in disguise for anything we know. We have seen such things in Egypt.'

"On hearing this I could scarcely refrain from smiling. The poor lady certainly looked like anything but an assassin.

"'Sir,' said she, turning to me, 'I entreat that you will obtain for me an interview with the emperor.'

"That is impossible, madam; bat permit me to inquire how you gamed access to this garden?

"'How! how!' she repeated; and her looks expressed great alarm. 'A terrific turbulent crowd raised me to the top of the terrace, and from thence I threw myself down into the garden. Had it been an abyss I would not have hesitated to plunge into it to escape from my fearful protectors.

"'After braving a thousand dangers, I reached the gate of the Elysèe. The porter refused me admittance, and then, almost distracted by disappointment, I exclaimed that I must see the emperor;—that I wished to impart to him a communication from my husband, who is a captain in the Imperial guards. I mentioned that I had about me papers of the utmost importance to the emperor's safety. In short, I scarcely knew what I said, I was so terrified when I beheld the furious crowd that surrounded me. Some persons among the mob cried out—"She is a good patriot. We will protect her. We will try to get her into the palace. She says she has papers which are important to the emperor." These men, whose looks filled me with alarm, then led me from the Champs-Elysèe, and we passed through the crowd, who opened a passage for us as if by enchantment. On' arriving in front of the palace they raised me up on their shoulders, and on recovering from the bewilderment into which this scene had thrown me, I found myself on the terrace wall. These two brave men,' said she, turning her eyes towards the grenadiers, 'hastened to me and conducted me hither.'

"The emperor who, concealed behind the trees, had heard the lady's story, now suddenly presented himself, and said, in a very kind tone—'What have you to say to me, madam?'

"'Sire! Ah, Sire!' she exclaimed, with increased trepidation, and with trembling hands she drew some papers from her bosom.

"'Compose yourself, madam,' said the emperor; 'let me know what you wish to communicate to me.'

"She presented the papers to the emperor, who took them from her, and perused them attentively. I observed that his countenance betrayed an expression of strong indignation; and when he had finished reading he convulsively squeezed the papers in his hands. His agitation was very great, but after the lapse of a few moments, he said, addressing himself to the lady—'Your husband, madam, has done his duty. It is no longer in my power to recompense fidelity, but—'

"'Sire,' interrupted the lady, earnestly, 'the only recompense my husband wishes is an opportunity of shedding his blood for your Majesty.'

"'Tell him, madam, that I would most willingly give mine to redeem the misfortunes of my brave companions in arms. *Adieu*, madam, you have performed your mission courageously, and I thank you.'

"'Sire, what is to be done with the man? Will not your majesty order him to undergo a legal examination.'

"'Restore him to liberty, madam. Rid yourselves of him. It is too late to obtain justice!'

"I was struck with the graceful and elegant figure of the lady, whose personal appearance was far from denoting the courage and heroism of which her conduct afforded proofs. The delicate woman had braved a thousand dangers in the fulfilment of a duty, and I reflected with 'feelings of indignation on the many men who at that moment forgot their duty and their country.

"The lady appeared confused, and looking fearfully around her, she seemed to ask pardon for the breach of etiquette which she had unwillingly committed. I could perceive that overexcited feeling had borne her up, and that she had hitherto disregarded the dangers she had encountered in the attainment of her object; but now her heart failed her, and she had not courage to venture again to pass through the crowd. My carriage was standing in the court yard. I offered her the use of it, which she accepted, and she was driven home unmolested.

"Meanwhile the emperor had left the garden and retired to his cabinet. When I rejoined him he was walking about, with his arms crossed on his bosom. He was absorbed in reflection, and he did not perceive my entrance. I was of course very curious to know the contents of the papers which had been delivered in so mysterious a way; but I made it a rule never to interrogate the emperor. He seated himself at his desk, and been to peruse the papers a second time. '*Malediction!*' he exclaimed. 'Look, Caulincourt; read this. Such turpitude would suffice to make one hate the very name of man, if some rare exceptions did not plead the cause of human nature!'

"I will now," pursued the duke, "briefly relate to you the whole of this mysterious adventure!

"A captain in the guards named Délort, who had been wounded in the Battle of Mont Saint-Jean, succeeded in gaining Charleroy. His wound was not so dangerous as to prevent him from continuing his route. A friend who resided at Charleroy, lent him his carriage, and at considerable expense, two strong horses were procured to convey him to Paris. A sergeant of his regiment, who had likewise been wounded, accompanied him. On arriving at Amiens, the captain alighted at a hotel, for the purpose of taking a little rest. When he was about to resume his journey, a man of respectable appearance stepped up to him. This person represented himself as being charged with an important mission to the government; and he stated that, having reached Amiens with considerable difficulty, he found himself absolutely without out the means of continuing his journey.

"He begged the captain would allow him a seat in his carriage, and offered to refund any expenses on reaching home. M. Délort granted the place, and refused the payment, and the carriage immediately started for Paris. In the course of conversation, Captain Délort discovered that his new companion was singularly well acquainted with passing events. He spoke of the Battle of Waterloo, estimated the amount of the Allied forces, and repeatedly corrected errors committed by the captain, in his statement of the amount of French troops engaged in the battle. He decidedly declared that the cause of Napoleon was lost, and that before the lapse of a week, the Allies would be under the walls of Paris.

"Captain Délort puzzled himself in trying to guess who this person could possibly be. He was not a military man, and yet he was accurately acquainted with everything connected with the army. Some remarks which fell from him awakened the captain's suspicion; and at length be came to the conclusion that his new acquaintance was neither more nor less than a spy.

"At the different places at which they stopped on the road, the captain communicated to his sergeant his suspicions, and they arranged together a plan for cutting short the mischievous proceedings of their travelling companion.

"Captain Délort possessed a country house at Saint-Ouen, where his wife was at that time residing. The house was situated on the road to Paris, and Délort naturally gave directions for being set down at his own house. On reaching home, he begged that the stranger would step in and accept of some refreshment. As soon as the door was closed, he made a military capture of the man and his portmanteau. On examining the latter, he found unquestionable proofs that the man was a spy in the pay of the police. The miserable traitor had set out from Paris with the ostensible mission of proceeding to Belgium to obtain information relating to the forces and movements of the enemy; but his real mission was to convey to the enemy the most accurate information respecting our forces and movements.

"This discovery roused the indignation of Captain Délort and the sergeant; and their first resolution was to inflict summary justice on the villain who had fallen into their hands. However, on reflection. Captain Délort thought it would be more advisable to confine him securely in a cellar. The next thing to be done was to find some prompt mode of transmitting to the emperor the written proofs of the treason of the ministers who had been entrusted with the government during his absence. The captain's wound prevented him from moving;

and he could not sufficiently rely on the intelligence of his sergeant, who moreover could not hope to gain access to the emperor personally. The papers could not be entrusted to any intermediary hands, for the emperor was known to be surrounded by traitors.

"Madame Délort was the daughter of a colonel who was killed on the field of battle. She had been educated at the Maison d'Evouen, and her attachment to the emperor amounted to idolatry. She offered to undertake the difficult mission. Proud of the confidence of her husband, and fully aware of the importance of the communication with which she was entrusted, this courageous woman set out from Paris, resolved to surmount every difficulty which might impede her attempts to gain access to the emperor. It was not till she approached the Elysèe that her courage began to fail her. She felt alarmed at the sight of the vast multitude of people. She now perceived that she had not ordinary difficulties to surmount; but that she must brave real dangers. For a moment she hesitated; but the safety of Napoleon, perhaps of France, depended on her resolution. She raised a supplicating look to heaven, praying for support, and courageously made her way into the thick of the crowd.

"Madame Délort," continued the duke, "was not precisely handsome, but when she suddenly presented herself in the garden of the Elysèe, I thought her extremely interesting. But the truth is, I have but a faint recollection of her, for the whole scene did not last half an hour.

"Every ten minutes the emperor received news of what was passing in the Chamber. The storm was rapidly gathering, and at length the thunderbolt broke.

"It was not the insolent insinuations of the representatives which induced the emperor to quit the capital, where he was an object of alarm to intriguers. He was weary of mankind; but he despised them too much to fear them. He yielded, not to fear, but to disgust, excited by perfidy and baseness. He would not permit blood to be shed in Paris for the triumph of his cause.

"At noon, on the 25th, the emperor left the Elysèe for Malmaison. 'Remain where you are, Caulincourt,' said he, on taking leave of me. 'Do whatever you can to prevent mischief. Carnot will second you. He is an honest man. For me, all is at an end. Strive to serve France, and you will still be serving me. Courage, Caulincourt. If you and other honourable men decline to take an active part in affairs, that traitor, Fouché, will sell France to foreigners.'

"All is over. All is consummated, said I, totally dispirited. I will remain. Sire; but only because I hope for the possibility of being yet useful to your Majesty."

CHAPTER 26

Death of the Duke de Vicenza

"The government committee, of which the Duke of Otranto was president, held its sittings at the Tuileries. It would be impossible to describe the misery I suffered during the last days of the crisis. I was not now, as in 1814, supported in the painful conflict by the consciousness of being useful to the emperor. Now, all I could do was to obtain some little mitigation of the vexations to which he was exposed. I was like a sentinel stationed to watch the approach of danger, and to use my efforts to avert it.

"The emperor's removal to Malmaison gave Fouché some uneasiness. He communicated his fears to the representatives, and it was consequently determined that General Becker should accompany the emperor to the Isle d'Aix, and to remain with him till his embarkation. The general was immediately dispatched to Malmaison, to watch the movements of the prisoner. Napoleon perceived the object of the general's visit; but he felt that it would be beneath his dignity to express, by words, his contempt of the mean conduct practised towards him. He took no notice of it. It must be observed, too, that General Becker behaved with perfect propriety and respect. The emperor had no reason to complain of him.

"In my visits to Malmaison the emperor did not manifest, in his conversation, any of these violent ebullitions of feeling which were of such frequent occurrence at Fontainebleau. All that could rouse the indignation of a lofty spirit, all that could lacerate a mortal wound, was studiously put into practice, and this treatment had wrought the wished-for effect—that of impairing his enemy. His mental suffering was extreme. 'My removal to this place,' said he, 'is an additional annoyance to me. Every object that presents itself to my eyes revives some distressing recollection. This Malmaison was the first considerable property that I became possessed of. The money with which I purchased it was my own earning. It was long the abode of happiness; but she who was its chief ornament is now no more;—my misfortunes killed her. Ten years ago I little foresaw that I should one day take refuge here to avoid my persecutors. And who are these persecutors? Men whom I have loaded with favours; men whom I have raised from humble to exalted stations. I made myself what I was; but they are only what I made them. What recollections I shall carry with me from France.'

"I impressed upon him the necessity of coming to a prompt determination as to the residence which he wished to make choice of. I was in a state of great anxiety. Malmaison was surrounded by the enemy. Blucher was advancing; and some detachments of his force had arrived at Saint-Germain. What was to be the fate of the emperor?

"He spoke of England, and the United States; but he had made no decided choice. I ventured to throw out a hint, which he immediately understood.

"'No,' said he, emphatically, 'that cannot be. Circumstances have occurred between Alexander and me which render it impossible for me to make any such proposition to him.'

"Alas!" continued the duke; "the Niemen, Tilsit, and other recollections of friendly intercourse with Alexander, were still fresh in the memory of Napoleon. How bitter must have been the regrets which they excited.

"However, it was necessary for his own safety that he should quit France. Friends and enemies, from different motives, regarded his speedy departure as indispensable. Decres and Boulay de la Meurthe arrived at Malmaison. We prevailed on the emperor to fix his departure for the following day.

"I returned to Paris, to settle the preliminary arrangements. I was just about to return to Malmaison when General Becker arrived with a letter from the emperor to the government committee. Becker stated, that in the morning the emperor heard the distant roaring of the cannon, and, starting up as if electrified by the sound, he exclaimed:— 'Let the committee restore to me the command of the army, and I swear, on the faith of a soldier and a citizen, to depart as soon as I shall have delivered the capital. All I wish is to defeat the enemy, and force him to consent to negotiations which will secure the interests of France. I do not wish to repossess sovereign power—heaven forbid that I should. I wish only to fight in the cause of France.'

"Napoleon's letter, of which Becker was the bearer, contained a repetition of this noble declaration. The Duke of Otranto for a moment felt alarmed; but his characteristic cunning came to his aid, and he said, in his sharp discordant voice, 'Surely, *he* is jesting.'

"Carnot and I made some remark favourable to Napoleon's proposition; and yet it must be confessed that many obstacles stood in the way of its execution. Fouché grew warm; and a vehement discussion ensued. The majority was hostile to the measure, which, I repeat, appeared likely to be attended with great inconveniences in the then critical position of affairs; for we did not possess a sufficient number of troops to make head against the overwhelming forces which were pouring in upon us. No time was to be lost!

"Becker conveyed to Malmaison the determination of the council. The emperor then determined to depart, and he sent Flahant to arrange with the committee the period of his departure, and the place of his embarkation. The Prince of Eckmuhl , who was present, suspected that this new message was merely a subterfuge to gain time. He made some remarks to the emperor, couched in terms the most disrespectful. Davoust, who was overwhelmed with the Emperor's bounty (he possessed an income of 1,800,000 *livres per annum*)—Davoust carried his insolence so far as to threaten *to have Napoleon arrested*, or to *arrest him himself!* This infamous conduct is sufficiently well authenticated. But Davoust has already paid the penalty due to his turpitude.

"The emperor's departure was at length irrevocably fixed for the 29th of June. He proceeded to Rochefort, where two frigates were to be in readiness to convey him to the United States of America. There he had determined to fix his future residence. He seemed now to recover some degree of mental tranquillity; as he always did whenever he succeeded in prevailing on himself to yield to necessity. Only those who have closely watched the working of Napoleon's vigorous mind can conceive the violence he must have imposed upon himself when he surrendered his own will to that of others. Napoleon possessed a consciousness of his personal superiority, and conquered as he was by the force of events, be felt that nature bad created him to fill the foremost rank among men.

"At the period to which I am here referring, Napoleon proved himself to be what he had been at all times, and under all circumstances—namely, superior to his condition. Though internally racked by mental torture, yet be had sufficient self-command to conceal his sufferings, and to maintain a dignity which awed even his persecutors.

With coolness and presence of mind he made the necessary preparations for his journey. On the day preceding his departure from Malmaison, he sent for Lafitte the banker, and he conversed with him with the most perfect composure on the state of public affairs. He lodged in Lafitte's hands a deposit of eight hundred thousand *francs* in specie, and about three millions in bonds and *rentes*. He would not accept any acknowledgment of the receipt of these vast sums, though M. Lafitte earnestly entreated him to do so. When speaking to me on the subject of these arrangements, the emperor said:—'I would with equal readiness have entrusted the finances of the empire to M. Lafitte. I know he is not favourable to my government; but I also know him to be an honest man.' This was a high eulogy on the banker, in the mouth of Napoleon, who entertained a most decided prejudice against what he termed *maltotiers*.

"On the morning of the 29th, the day fixed for the emperor's departure, I proceeded to Malmaison. That charming retreat, which in the month of June was in its full beauty, presented a painful contrast to the grief depicted in the countenances of its inmates. Queen Hortense and a few faithful friends, who had not forsaken the illustrious exile, were there. As we gazed around on the smiling gardens and splendid apartments, we all felt how unavailing are the enjoyments of luxury as a solace to the wounded spirit. We felt how true it is that there is nothing positive but misfortune,

"When I arrived at Malmaison the emperor was alone in his cabinet. I found him seated at his writing table, his head resting on one hand, whilst with the other he was writing. His pen glided rapidly over the paper, which was thrust to a distance from him. His attitude was indicative of dejection; and his whole appearance betrayed the efforts he had made to conceal the grief which inwardly preyed upon him. It was evident that he suffered the utmost extreme of mental misery. I shuddered as I read the anguish depicted in his looks. His glory and his dignity were insulted—his feelings and affections were violated! He was now sinking under the lassitude consequent on the efforts he had made to conceal his real emotions. He summoned all his energy to struggle against his pitiless destiny, and to subdue the irritation continually created by the circumstances of his position.

"As I entered the cabinet, he raised his head, laid down his pen, and holding out his hand, though without changing his attitude, he said—'Well, Caulincourt! this is truly draining the cup of misfortune to the dregs. I wished to defer my departure only for the sake of fighting at the head of the array. I wished only to contribute my aid in repelling the enemy. I have had enough of sovereignty. I want no more of it.—I want no more of it.—(He repeated these words with marked vehemence.)—I am no longer a sovereign, but I am still a soldier! When I heard the cannon roar—when I reflected that my troops were without a leader—that they were to endure the humiliation of a defeat without having fought—my blood boiled with indignation. All I wished for was a glorious death amidst my brave troops. But my co-operation would have defeated the schemes of traitors. France has been sold. She has been surrendered up without a blow being struck in her defence. Thirty-two millions of men have been made to bow their heads to an arrogant conqueror, without disputing the victory. Such a spectacle as France now presents is not to be found in the history of any other nation. What has France become in the hands of the imbecile government which has ruled her for the last fifteen months? Is she any longer the nation unequalled in the world?'

"The emperor rose and paced up and down the apartment. His rapid utterance and animated gestures betrayed the emotion which agitated him. I listened to him, as I always did, with deep interest. On this occasion he seemed only to give expression to my own feelings.

"'In 1814,' resumed he, 'honest men might justly say, all is lost except honour—except national dignity. Let them now bow down their heads with mortification; for now all—all is lost! .... And that villain Fouché imagines that I would resume the sovereignty in the degradation to which it is now reduced! Never, never! The place that is assigned to the Sovereign is no longer tenable. I am disgusted alike with men and things, and I am anxious only to enjoy repose. I am utterly indifferent about my future fate—and I endure life, without attaching myself to it by any alluring chimeras. I carry with me from France recollections which will constitute at once the charm and the torment of the remainder of my days. A bitter and incurable regret must ever be connected with this last phasis of my singular career. Alas! what will become of the army—my brave, my unparalleled army!

"'The re-action will be terrible, Caulincourt. The army will be doomed to expiate its fidelity to my cause—its heroic resistance at Waterloo. Waterloo!—What horrible recollections are connected with that name! Oh! if you had seen that handful of heroes, closely pressed one upon another, resisting immense masses of the enemy, not to defend their lives, but to meet death on the field of battle, where they could not conquer! The English stood amazed at sight of this desperate heroism; and weary of the carnage, they implored the martyrs to surrender. This merciful summons was answered by the sublime cry:—"*Le garde meur et ne se rend pas.*" The Imperial guard has immortalized the French people and the empire !' "He paused, apparently overcome by the recollections of these gigantic scenes. How well I understood the incessant pre-occupation of Napoleon respecting the future fate of his army. Deceived, forsaken, betrayed by all who had shared his prosperity, he naturally transferred all his affection, and attached all his regret, to those devoted friends of his misfortune. Two months after, these heroic troops received the appellation of Brigands of the Loire!

"'And you,' pursued he, gazing at me with a melancholy expression; 'all you who are here will be pursued and persecuted. Compromised as you are for my cause, what will become of you! Your antagonists in the late deplorable conflict you sustained will become your persecutors.'

"Sire, I replied, your friends will suffer only through your misfortunes. Persecution will be felt lightly by them, if it spare you. A man who feels the consciousness of having faithfully served his country, and having supported a noble cause, can view persecution with indifference and contempt. That conviction brings with it a feeling of self-approbation, of which persecution cannot deprive its victims.

"'All is over, Caulincourt. We are now about to part. In a few days hence, I must quit France for ever, I will fix my abode in the United States. In the course of some little time, the spot which I shall inhabit will be in a condition to receive the glorious wrecks of the army. All my old companions in arms will find an asylum with me. Who knows but that I may one day or other have an *hospital des invalids* in the United States, for my veteran guards.'

"Suddenly, the galloping of horses was heard in the courtyard. The emperor advanced to the window, and heaved a deep sigh. He seemed greatly agitated. I was almost distracted at the thought of parting with him for ever. I moved towards the door, and, as it were unconsciously, turned back again. The emperor advanced a few paces to meet me. He fixed upon me a look which no words can express. I saw the tears start into his eyes. How cruelly painful was that moment!

"I will not attempt to describe my feelings on taking my last farewell of the emperor. I felt that he was about to enter upon an endless exile. I rushed from the cabinet, almost in a delirium of despair. There is something which utterly prostrates the mental energies, in the consciousness that misfortunes are irreparable—when we find ourselves compelled to bid farewell to hope.

"I have told you all I have to relate of the terrific interval of the *hundred days*, I need not detail anything which has subsequently occurred to me, for since then my prosaic life has been utterly devoid of interest. Since that period of trial, I have been insensible to persecution, and I have resented injuries only by cold contempt. The quiet retirement of my present existence is congenial with the state of my mind. Feeling no interest in the events that are passing in the world, I turn for recreation to the poetry of my recollections, those treasures which have escaped from the wreck of my sympathies. There is one regret which presses more heavily than all the rest on my heart, which is, that I cannot live long enough to complete the work of conscience and justice, which I am anxious to bequeath to France. By employing the few hours which I can snatch from death in portraying the hero whom faction hurled from the throne, I feel that I am discharging a sacred duty to my country. France will one day or other know her friends from her enemies, and usurped reputations will fall before inexorable truth,

"The events of the empire furnish the most brilliant pages of French history; but they are not the history of Napoleon. His wonderful character can only be accurately portrayed by those who had the opportunity of observing him in the relations of private life; they only can paint the thousand traits which characterized his extraordinary mind. Napoleon was more than a hero, more than an emperor. A comparison between him and any other man, or any other sovereign, is impossible. His death has left a void in human nature which will probably never be filled up. Future generations will bow with respect to the age on which the glory of Napoleon Bonaparte shed its lustre. For centuries to come French hearts will glow with pride at the mention of his exploits: to his name alone is attached inexhaustible admiration, imperishable remembrance."

★★★★★★

The duke paused. With what eager interest I listened to these last outpourings of his ardent and impassioned soul.

"Duke," said I, "I shall carry with me from Plombières a rich treasure of recollections, for my days of suffering and retirement, I have read with earnest interest all the histories of the emperor's reign; but now, methinks, for the first time I know Napoleon. I can never sufficiently express my thanks for the gratification your kindness has conferred on me. The details which I have heard you narrate will henceforth be the subject of my eternal meditations."

Even whilst I trace these lines I am transported in imagination to the little drawing-room at Plombières. There I fancy I can still behold the Duke de Vicenza. I see his pale countenance, his attenuated form. The melancholy tones of his voice still vibrate in my ear: that voice which, alas! death has now rendered mute.

We took leave of the duke at Plombières, in October, 1826; and in February, 1827, he was consigned to the tomb!

I leave to abler pens than mine the honour of inscribing a fitting eulogy on a man, whose many noble qualities must claim the admiration, not only of France, but of Europe. The foregoing pages contain merely a faithful record of his conversations: this record is a humble tribute deposited on a national tomb.

Appendix

DETAILS RELATING TO THE DEATH OF THE DUKE D'ENGHIEN.

The reader may find it interesting to peruse the following statement of the Duke de Rovigo, in conjunction with that given by the Duke de Vicenza:—(See chap. 5.)

"The catastrophe of the Duke d'Enghien was yet unexplained: nothing was certain but the duke's melancholy death, when, in 1823, I published an abstract of my memoirs, in which I explained the cause of that event. In this publication, I had two objects in view. The first certainly was to repel the base insinuations which were cast upon me, when, during my imprisonment at Malta, I was supposed to be lost beyond redemption: the second was to defend the memory of the emperor, to whom I had wholly devoted my existence; for I accept this reproach as an honour conferred on me. My only wish was to unfold the truth; but that which was merely the elucidation of an historical fact has suddenly become a personal question. Adversaries, whom I had never even thought of, rose up against me. Of these, General Hullin, who had hitherto been on as friendly a footing with me as I had with him, and whom I had informed of my publication before it appeared, was the first to present himself.

"He was soon followed by two others. One naturally anxious to repel in anticipation a portion of the blame which a profound investigation of the affair could not fail to cast upon him, published a letter, which, among many offensive things to which I did not condescend to reply, contained false assertions, which cannot with propriety remain unanswered.

"The other only *wrote that he would not write*: he declared that he had transmitted a letter to the king. I certainly was not aware that I was so far honoured as to be the object of his attention, until I received a letter prohibiting my appearance in a place to which I had

287

always had free access in the days of our glory.

"I was doubtless bound to respect the will of the sovereign, and to submit to it; but I regarded it only in the light of a decision wrested by surprise from his mistaken equity. Besides, it was not before him that this cause was to be tried; and the judgments of a king are not without appeal, when the reputation and honour of a citizen are concerned.

"It is public opinion, tested by public discussion, that judges in the last instance. To this I might immediately have had recourse; and some of my friends have blamed me for not doing so. I considered, however, that delay was more advisable; and it was not without well-founded motives that I came to this determination.

"Like all political publications, mine had its inconveniences and advantages. It drew public attention to transactions which some persons had good reason to wish for ever buried in oblivion: it compromised some personal interests; it disturbed securities which were believed to be well secured; and committed the unpardonable offence of alarming certain Parisian saloons. But, on the other hand, it brought to light important facts; it resuscitated incontrovertible documents which had escaped the search of those who would willingly have destroyed them; and it excited a polemical discussion from which history cannot fail to profit, and by which truth must unavoidably be elicited. It became me then to wait, that I, as well as others, might be benefited by these new lights.

"Besides, at the point to which the question had been brought, was it proper to reply by a pamphlet to pamphlets, or to oppose a justificatory memorial to vague or false assertions? I know not whether such a contest would have convinced my adversaries, but it certainly was not in my opinion worthy of me, I owed it to my honour to make a more noble and more complete defence. I owed it also to my children, to whom I have to transmit a name, the lustre of which is proved by titles which cannot be disputed. I therefore resolved to publish my *Memoirs*—that is, to submit my whole life to public examination.

"Let my adversaries thus descend into the arena with me, and take up this new kind of gauntlet. A fine opportunity is afforded them for doing homage to the memory of him who loaded them with benefits, and for explaining events much more serious, and of much higher historical importance, than the question which has awakened their inquietudes or disconcerted their views.

"A day will come when public opinion will judge, without reserve and without partiality, all who have acted a part in the great drama of the empire. The course of nature puts a period to personal influences; the petty animosities and gossiping traditions of drawing-rooms sink into oblivion. Men then decide on documents—and to that decision I submit mine.

"I wish, but I doubt, that my adversaries would follow this example.

"Among the works which have appeared since 1823, I must particularly mention:—

"1. Examination of the proceedings of the court-martial instituted to try the Duke d'Enghien.

"2. A justificatory *Memorial* published by the Duke de Vicenza.

"3. Some letters published by the Duke de Dalberg, minister from the Court of Baden to the French Government, in the year XII. (1804.)

"4. An important note from the Baron de Massias, then French Minister at the Court of Baden.

"5. Minutes made on the exhumation of the Duke d'Enghien, in 1816.

"6. A Deposition of the Sieur Anfort, brigadier of *gendarmerie* at Vincennes, preserved and separately published, in 1822, by a writer who styles himself a Bourgeois de Paris.

"Such are the documents which ought to be referred to for the solution of a question which it is in vain attempted to render personal, and which belongs wholly to history.

★★★★★★

"I shall not repeat here what I have already stated in reference to the circumstances which transpired on the trial of Georges, and which would lead to the conclusion that the mysterious personage whom certain subaltern agents alluded to, was the Duke d'Enghien. What I have written gives on this subject every desirable explanation. I have nothing to add.

"But what I did not state, and what, for the elucidation of other important circumstances which require investigation, must not now be omitted, is, that at the time of that trial the Duke de Dalberg was the envoy from the Elector of Baden to the French republic: though descended from a princely German family, he was then only a baron. He was nephew of the last Elector of Mentz, who had not yet become Primate of Germany. Thus, in 1804, Baron Dalberg was from relationship, and as feudatory of the German empire, connected with the ambassador of the chief of that empire. His transactions most naturally have been intimately combined with those of that ambassador; unless it be supposed, contrary to all probability, that the court of Baden had instructed the baron to sacrifice the general interests of Germany for the sake of favouring the extension of the French republic.

"Be this as it may, Baron Dalberg, in his apologetic letter, declares that 'M. de Talleyrand, during his ministry, had constantly endeavoured to moderate the violent passions of Bonaparte.'

"Had, then. Baron Dalberg private communications with M. de Talleyrand? It certainly could not be in any intercourse between them, as minister with minister, that he was informed by Talleyrand of the efforts which be might or might not have made to calm the violence of the First Consul's passions.

"Baron Dalberg, Indeed, dates this confidence only from the war of 1806; but I will soon fix its real date.

"In the first place, I would ask how it happened that, according to these premises. Baron Dalberg left a country, where his birth ensured him the highest consideration, to come to France and connect himself with a republican system against which all Europe had risen? How came he to renounce the high honour of being proclaimed at every coronation of the German emperors, when the emperor himself used to ask aloud, in the presence of the nobility of Germany assembled in the church at Frankfort, 'Is there a Dalberg here?'

"It may be readily conceived that the First Consul, on becoming emperor, had to reward greet services in war; and there is nothing extraordinary in the political fortunes of men who astonished the world by their talents and their achievements.

"It was the same in the civil administration, where great talents and efforts, supported by patriotic zeal, substituted a code of laws for the anarchy which desolated society, a system of finance for the waste of the republic, and restored order and economy in every branch of the government

"All these superior men naturally became the objects of particular attention, and the causes of their elevation were perfectly honourable.

"But when Baron Dalberg joined our fortunes, he had neither incurred the danger of our battles nor shared the labours of our administration. What, then, were the *potent* services which he could have rendered us, and which warranted his sudden entrance into the service of France as Duke de Dalberg, instead of Baron—the title he had borne in Germany—and being, in the course of *a few months*, endowed with the sum of four millions, and with the appointments of counsellor of state and senator?—*None*. It must, then, be presumed, that *officious* services already performed, but not publicly known, drew upon Baron Dalberg all these accumulated favours.

"The Emperor Napoleon was not ungrateful; but he was not in the habit of rewarding services before they were performed. Why, then, has not Baron Dalberg himself explained his private services? I can supply what his modesty has omitted. He knows this well; for he admitted me sufficiently into his confidence. His zeal to bring about the marriage of the grandson of his elector with Mademoiselle Stéphanie de Beuharnois—the choice which was made of Cardinal Fesch to succeed to the primateship of Germany in preference to a German ecclesiastical prince—the good offices and the particular relations of Baron Dalberg when a member of the diplomatic body at Warsaw, in 1806—the eagerness of M. de Talleyrand to summon him to Tilsit, in order that he might mingle with the foreign diplomatists, though the emperor ordered me to prevent his arrival at Tilsit, when I was governor of old Prussia, at Konigsberg—the *officious* part which he acted at Erfurt, and even the anecdote which forced him to enter the service of France—are all known to me.

"But this is not the place to break the prudent silence which the Duke de Dalberg thinks proper to maintain with reference to these circumstances. An explanation of all these facts, and others not less characteristic, will perhaps find a place in contemporary *Memoirs*. What I have now said is sufficient to show that Baron Dalberg never thought that, while engaged in an *official* correspondence arising out of his ostensible functions, he was not also at liberty to maintain officious communications.

"Let us now examine the conduct of Baron Dalberg, the minister representing that venerable and respected prince, the Elector of Baden, at the period of the catastrophe of the Duke d'Enghien, and we shall see whether he was not at once the official agent of his sovereign, and the officious agent of a French minister.

"The affair of Georges then occupied the attention of the French government. Our diplomatic agents were making investigations in all directions. Baron Dalberg had, doubtless, given official information of this affair to his sovereign; for in his letter to M. de Talleyrand, dated 13th November, 1823, he acknowledges, 'that he had received orders to inquire whether there was any complaint against the emigrants who resided in the electorate, and whether their abode there excited any dissatisfaction.'

"Could the *pretended* distance at which Baron Dalberg kept himself from the French Ministry have made him the dupe of M. de Talleyrand's assertion, and could he really believe that he might transmit to his court, as sincere, this reply of the minister of foreign affairs for the Republic—"That he did not think the government of Baden should be more severe than the French Government; that he was not aware of any complaint on the subject, and that the emigrants must be left unmolested?" Or did Baron Dalberg transmit this reply merely in discharge of his *official* duties, and in opposition to other positive opinions? It is not to be expected that Baron Dalberg will make an honest confession on this point: we must therefore seek the truth in comparisons, which are likely to lead to it.

"Baron Dalberg had scarcely transmitted M. de Talleyrand's letter to the court of his Sovereign, when the territory of Baden was violated. Previous to this violation, a privy-council had been assembled on the 10th of March, composed of the three consuls, the grand-judge, the minister for foreign affairs, and M. Fouché.

In this council, a report was read on the foreign ramifications of Georges' conspiracy. The evidence of these ramifications rested on the reports of the Sieur Mehée. From these reports it was inferred, that it could be no other than the Duke d'Enghien who was to head the insurrection after the blow should be struck. This opinion was held to coincide with the declarations of the subordinate confederates of Georges; and the report terminated with the proposition for carrying off the Duke d'Enghien, and *getting rid of him.*

"A diplomatist like Baron Dalberg could not be ignorant of the assembling of this council. According to his own confession he knew, on the 12th of March, of the departure of General Caulincourt, who, he says, it was suspected had orders for the arrest of Dumouriez on the territory of Baden.

"I was at Rouen on the 12th of March; and I learned through the ordinary channels the departure of General Caulincourt and of General Ordener.

"Baron Dalberg was the advanced sentinel of the court of Baden. He had hitherto had no guarantee for the safety of the emigrants to whom his sovereign granted an asylum but the law of nations, and the assurances of the minister for foreign affairs. If the French government, in the very face of Baron Dalberg, violated that law, and acted in opposition to those assurances, it was the incumbent duty of the minister of Baden, who knew that the Duke d'Enghien and other emigrants resided at Ettenheim, to make immediate communications to his court. The emigrants were especially compromised by the depositions of the agents of Georges. Not a single individual in Paris was ignorant of this fact: for the first proceedings on the trial took place publicly in the Temple.

"Thus, on learning the fact of the holding of the council on the 10th, and the departure of M. Caulincourt, which took place on the 11th, Baron Dalberg, if he had not voluntarily allowed himself to be misled by the minister for foreign affairs ought immediately to have dispatched couriers to his Sovereign, to rouse him from the false security into which he had been plunged some days before, by the transmission of the reply of the minister for foreign affairs. From that moment there could exist no doubt that the territory of the electorate would be violated; and from that moment Baron Dalberg might have appreciated the just value of the assurances he had received from the minister for foreign affairs.

"An *estafette* may go from Paris to Carlsruhe in forty hours: to this I have myself been many times a witness. A courier dispatched by Baron Dalberg even on the 12th, would have reached Carlsruhe, or rather Ettenheim (where he might have been directed to the *grand-bailli* of the place), in the course of the 14th, and in sufficient time for warning to have been given to the prince, who was not arrested until the 15th: yet Baron Dalberg remained inactive. Surely there is no injustice in affirming that this inactivity was not in unison with his official duties.

"But what are we to think, when we find that it was only on the 20th of March, the day on which the Duke d'Enghien arrived in Paris, that Baron Dalberg wrote to the court of Baden to announce the departure of M. Caulincourt, and the object of his journey; that it was not until the 21st, when all Paris knew that the prince had perished at six o'clock on that very morning, that he again wrote to Baden, stating, that the Duke d'Enghien *had arrived, escorted by fifty gendarmes,* and 'that everybody was inquiring what was intended to be done with him?'

"The courier then left Paris at four in the afternoon: and at that hour, on the 21st of March, Baron Dalberg writes, that the above question was asked with reference to the Duke d'Enghien!

"Finally, it was not until the 22nd of March, *when the Moniteur published the lenience of death, that, in a postscript to a letter of the same day,* the minister of Baden informed his court that the unfortunate prince was no more.

"All these circumstances are now revealed by the correspondence of Baron Dalberg. Nothing but the publication of the *Moniteur* would have forced him to mention the catastrophe. Thus far his official duties had not been forgotten; they might, according to his combinations, yield to his officious duties . . . . But let us proceed.

"The Duke d'Enghien was arrested at Ettenheim at five in the morning of the 15th of March. This news must immediately have been conveyed to Carlsruhe. The letter of the 11th, of which M. de Caulincourt was the bearer, written by M. de Talleyrand to the Baden minister for foreign affairs, was transmitted on the 15th. This is proved by the decree published by the Elector of Baden on the 16th, in which the arrests of the preceding day are alluded to.

"It is impossible that an event of this importance could take place without the court of Carlsruhe writing on the same day, or at latest on the 16th, to its minister at Paris, to remonstrate against this violation of territory, or at]east to attest the peaceable and inoffensive conduct of the Duke d'Enghien, and to intercede in his behalf. The spirited M. de Massias, the French minister at the court of Baden, himself wrote to the minister for foreign affairs; and he could only have done so on the communications made to him the same day by the Baden minister. M. de Massias did not fear to affirm, that, during his residence in the electorate, the conduct of the Duke d'Enghien had been *moderate and innocent.*

"The dispatches of M. de Massias to the minister for foreign affairs, and those of the minister of Baden to Baron Dalberg, ought therefore to have been received in Paris at the latest on the 18th or 19th of March; but certainly before the arrival of the Duke d'Enghien, who did not reach Vincennes till the 20th, at six in the evening.

"Baron Dalberg himself admits, in his letter of the 20th of March, 'that on Thursday the 15th he knew positively the order of which M. Caulincourt was the bearer;' that is to say, he was informed that M. de Talleyrand had written to his court, slating that General Ordener was directed to arrest the Duke d'Enghien and General Dumouriez.

"But on learning the object of this expedition, why did not Baron Dalberg Immediately repair to the minister for foreign affairs? Why did he not instantly assemble the diplomatic body to intercede for the Duke d'Enghien? Had Baron Dalberg taken these measures, they certainly could not have failed in their object; if, as he affirms in his letter of the 13th of November, 1823, the minister for foreign affairs was of opinion that the emigrants ought to remain unmolested in the electorate; or if, according to the letter he addressed to the court of Baden» on the 22nd March, 1804, 'M. de Talleyrand himself seemed, until the last moment, to be ignorant of the resolution that was adopted.'

"Nevertheless, the First Consul, who, as every circumstance proves, entertained no private resentment against the Duke d'Enghien, except indeed that which might have been excited by the report on which be ordered the arrest of the prince, might have suspended the sentence. Communications between Baron Dalberg and other members of the diplomatic body, and the minister for foreign affairs—had the latter been as favourably disposed as Baron Dalberg pretends he was—might have produced this result; especially as such communications would have induced the ministers to lay before the First Consul the letter of Baron Massias, which was concealed from him, as I shall soon have occasion to show, and all would have terminated by explanations in favour of the Duke d'Enghien.

"Instead of pursuing this course, Baron Dalberg remained passive until after the catastrophe. It was not until the 22nd of March that he wrote to the court of Baden: 'I cannot, in the very difficult and delicate situation in which I stand, do anything else than explain to the ministers of the courts with which we are most intimately related, the circumstances, such as they are.'

"This was the language which Baron Dalberg held on the 22nd, when the prince was no more; but were these also his sentiments on the 15th?

"But what need was there of express orders, when, on the 20th of March, and consequently before the trial of the Duke d'Enghien, Baron Dalberg wrote that he was informed of arrests having taken place at Ettenheim? And when he knew that the honour of the respectable Elector of Baden was offended, the territory of his electorate violated, the law of nations disregarded, and a prince of the house of Bourbon, at a critical moment, arrested—were there not in these circumstances sufficient motives to give a generous impulse to Baron Dalberg, had he been entirely devoted to his duty as minister of the court of Baden? Besides, how could Baron Dalberg, a man of high monarchical principles, as he would have himself believed to be, allow those principles to yield, on so very important an occasion, to the childish considerations stated in his dispatch of the 20th of March?

"The conjectures which must unavoidably be deduced from the

conduct of Baron Dalberg, acquire additional force from the consideration that he knew, on the 20th of March, what degree of reliance he ought to place on a minister who was contemplating the arrests at Ettenheim, at the very moment when he was giving assurances that the emigrants residing in the electorate should not be molested.

"It even appears that Baron Dalberg, on writing at this period to his court, pronounced an official judgment on the conduct of this minister which was far from being favourable.

"In fact, there appears in a letter written on the 12th Nov. 1823, by Baron Berstett, minister for foreign affairs at Carlsruhe, to Baron Dalberg, permitting him to publish some parts of his diplomatic correspondence, the statement that Baron Dalberg would find, in No. 27, dated March 27, 1804, 'that, at the fatal epoch, he (Baron Dalberg) had not yet reason to be proud of the confidence of the minister fur foreign affairs at Paris.'

"I need not stop to consider what are the causes which afterwards obtained for Baron Dalberg the confidence of the minister for foreign affairs; but I must remark, that Baron Dalberg has taken care not to publish this letter. No. 27. The reason of this reserve may be easily divined. The *official* judgment, then pronounced by Dalberg on the minister for foreign affairs, would form too revolting a contrast with the *officious* judgment contained in his letter of the 13th of November, 1823, in which he states, 'that it is well known that, during his ministry, M. de Talleyrand never ceased to moderate the violent passions of Bonaparte.'

"But what Baron Dalberg did not wish to say, doubtless because since that time he had obtained the confidence of M. de Talleyrand, may be easily conjectured from Baron Berstett's letter.

"Be this as it may, it is easy to estimate at its true value Baron Dalberg's recent apology for the conduct of the minister for foreign affairs, respecting the catastrophe of the Duke d'Enghien. It will also readily be conceived, that the most favourable judgment which can be formed of Baron Dalberg's conduct is, that though he knew every thing which was going on, his scruples had been satisfied by being told that the Duke d'Enghien would only be detained as a hostage; and that this was told him because it was foreseen that Baron Dalberg must transmit some statement on the subject to his court; and that, on finding himself placed between the fear of compromising his government, and of compromising himself in his relations with France, on which he probably had already founded projects for the future, he would quietly allow the affair to take its course; being persuaded that his court would easily exculpate itself as to an event which, in the absence of previous information, it could not prevent.

"But if Baron Dalberg was only the dupe of those who contrived this plot—if his diplomatic self-love induced him at that epoch to disguise from his court a part of the mystification which was practised upon him, instead of acknowledging his fatal mistake, the odium of the atrocity does not fall with the less weight on those who planned and effected its accomplishment.

"Who were those machinators? I conceive that I have sufficiently indicated them, and that I have supported my assertions by circumstances and comparisons of dates which carry with them at once the stamp of truth and of authenticity. M. de Talleyrand has referred for his justification to his letter to the king, the contents of which are not known; to the attestations which Baron Dalberg and himself have reciprocally given for each other in their own cause, and which they affect to regard as the public opinion; and finally, to General Hullin's memorial, which does not say one word about the circumstances personally implicating M. de Talleyrand. I might acknowledge all the part of the catastrophe of the Duke d'Enghien attributed to me in that memorial, or rather that with which General Hullin must himself remain charged, and still the part assigned to M. de Talleyrand would not be changed.

"My accusation then remains complete against him. Nether the cautious silence which he observes, nor his secret intrigues affect it.

"When I preferred this accusation against him, what were, it may be asked, my antecedent relations with M. de Talleyrand? On this it is proper to say a few words.

"At the period when I was promoted to the ministry, Talleyrand was in a deplorable situation, both as to his pecuniary end political circumstances. Many avoided him, believing thereby to pay their court to superior power. I was not one of the number.

"It is to me he was indebted for payment of the rent of his *château* of Valençay, which was occupied by the Spanish princes. This, doubtless, was only an act of justice; but in fact, from motives which I do not pretend to judge, the payment had been withheld from M. de Talleyrand, and he solicited it in vain. Had it not been for my interference, the state of things would have long continued; but my applications procured him payment of the rent of his *château*, at the rate of 75,000 *francs per annum*.

"It was I also who ventured to speak to the emperor respecting threats of prosecution by some of M. de Talleyrand's creditors. In consequence of what I said, the emperor was induced to purchase the Hotel de Valentinois, completely furnished, which belonged to M. de Talleyrand, and for which be gave him the sum of 2,100,000 *francs*. For this he was indebted to me: and besides that, he was not obliged to bring back the articles which he had already moved to furnish his present hotel.

"Again, it was I who, during four years, suspended the effect of certain disagreeable manoeuvres, which could not have failed to reach him; and I went so far in my services as to throw an obstacle in the way of the unexpected return of a member of his family from Berne to Paris; an event which, at that moment, would have placed him in a most embarrassing situation.

"Such was my perseverance in reconciling the emperor, whom this affair had greatly displeased, that, in 1812, when he departed for the Russian campaign, he was inclined to take M. de Talleyrand with him.

"If, from the conduct of M. de Talleyrand towards his benefac.tor, I turn to that which he has held with regard to me, it is there proved that, in return for my good offices, I owe to him my being placed on the most fatal of the two lists of proscription.

"It is impossible to mistake the secret object of this testimony of his gratitude. My crime was the being able to show what his part had been in the affair of the Duke d'Enghien. This explains M. de Talleyrand's efforts to obtain my removal from Malta in 1815; and why, during the whole period of my imprisonment, I could look to no security until after he left the department of foreign affairs. In 1815, it was intended to bring me before a court-martial at Toulon or Marseilles; I have evidence of this fact before me. I should, as a matter of course, have been condemned and executed: after which, M. de Talleyrand would have boasted to my family of his efforts to save me. It is a maxim with M. de Talleyrand, that a man who can speak only ceases to be an object of fear when he is no more.

"After what has now been said, few will be surprised at the pains I in my turn take to leave to M. de Talleyrand the share which duly belongs to him in a catastrophe in which I took no part for which I can with justice be reproached.

"What further encourages my efforts in this respect is, my perfect conviction that the emperor Napoleon did not act on the impulse of his own mind when he ordered the arrest of the Duke d'Enghien. My opinion is fully confirmed by the works written at St. Helena. The authenticity of these works is unquestionably augmented by the circumstance of the authors, who composed them without communication with each other, being unanimous on this point.

"The Emperor Napoleon, whose words and even autograph notes these works record, had no motive for blaming or accusing any one person more than another. He knew that what he was writing was to come under the severe scrutiny of history, and to its judgment he looked forward with respect. He besides expressed himself in a way which proves that he had no wish to rid himself of any part of the transaction which could reasonably be attributed to him.

"The emperor ought then to be believed, when he himself wrote that 'the death of the Duke d'Enghien must be ascribed to those who laboured by reports and conjectures to represent him as the chief of a conspiracy;' and when, in familiar intimacy with his faithful followers at St. Helena, he added—'that he had been suddenly urged,' that his opinion had been taken as it were by surprise, his measures precipitated, and their result secured beforehand. I was alone one day,' he says; 'I was still at the table where I had just dined, and was finishing my coffee: I was hastily told of a new conspiracy. I was vehemently reminded that a period ought to be put to such horrible attempts; that it was full time to give a lesson to those who were in the daily habit of plotting against my life; *that there was no way of putting an end to the business but by shedding the blood of one of them*; that the Duke d'Enghien ought to be the victim, since he might be taken in the fact, as forming part of the existing conspiracy.

"I did not rightly know who the Duke d'Enghien was. The revolution came upon me when I was very young, and I had never been at court. I did not even know where the duke was. *All these points were explained to me.* If it be so, I said, he must be seized; and the necessary orders were given in consequence. Everything had been provided beforehand; *the papers were prepared, and there was nothing to do but to sign them;* and the fate of the prince was already decided.'

"Mr. O'Meara's veracity cannot be suspected when, agreeing in his work with the other publications from St. Helena, he affirms, that having asked Napoleon whether it was true a letter written to him by the Duke d'Enghien had been received by M. de Talleyrand, and not delivered until two days after, the emperor replied—'After the prince's arrival at Strasburg, he wrote me a letter; that letter was delivered to

T—— who kept it until after the execution.'

"But who, then, were those who, by *reports* and *conjectures*, represented the Duke d'Enghien as chief of a conspiracy? Who was at that time in a situation to induce the First Consul to compromise himself by shedding the blood of a Bourbon? Who could it be that had foreseen everything; who had in anticipation *prepared the papers*, which were *instantaneously presented for the First Consul's signature*, and which decided the fate of the prince?

"The minister for foreign affairs under the Directory shall now himself declare what interest he had in making the First Consul compromise himself. The functions and the personal transactions of that minister under the First Consul will also show whether it was he who prepared the reports and the papers which determined the fatal measure.

"In a pamphlet which was published in the year V., and which was addressed by Citizen Talleyrand to his fellow-citizens, he thus expresses himself:—

I should be unworthy to have served the noble cause of liberty, if I dared regard as a sacrifice what I then did (1789) for its triumph. But I may at least express my surprise, that after having so many just claims on the implacable hatred of the heretofore clergy and nobility, I should draw upon myself the same hatred from those who style themselves the vehement enemies of the nobility and clergy. (*Eclaircissemens donnés par le citoyen Talleyrand à ses concitoyens*).

"The man whose former conduct authorized such language, could not, without fear, see the French republic ready to expire in the year XII. in the person of the First Consul, without wishing to place that personage in a situation which would render it impossible for him ever to become a Monck... Citizen Talleyrand in his foresight might not repel the idea of one day becoming Prince of Benevento under a new dynasty: but, priding himself in the advantage of having merited the implacable hatred of the clergy, from whom he was a renegade, and of the nobility, to whom he was a traitor, he must doubtless have shuddered at the very thought of their return under the banner of the Bourbons.

"M. de Talleyrand has unfortunately learned , in the course of his political life that rule by which certain men make interest the sole motive of their actions. This may explain the motive he had to be one of those who endeavoured, 'by *reports* and *conjectures*, to represent the Duke d'Enghien as the chief of a conspiracy; to take the judgment of the First Consul by surprise; and to advise him to finish the business by steeping his hands in the blood of a Bourbon.'

"His terror at the bare idea of the possible return of the Bourbons was perhaps peculiarly strong at this time, as when the conspiracy of George was detected, the First Consul had not disclosed his project of ascending the throne. On the contrary, it is alleged that he formally refused the title of King of France, which was offered to him during the negotiations at Amiens, in compensation for sacrifices of conquered territory, which it was wished to prevail on him to make.

"The official transactions of the minister for foreign affairs, and his general conduct, add greatly to the evidence by which the truth of the facts stated has been demonstrated. The minister for foreign affairs was the only person who could answer the questions which the First Consul declared he had asked respecting the Duke d'Enghien, of whose name even he was ignorant, when that prince was pointed out to him as the chief of a conspiracy. He alone corresponded with foreign cabinets, and with our ministers at foreign courts. To him only belonged the duty of watching the proceedings of the emigrants. Of this, proof may be found in the diplomatic note which he addressed, on the 11th of Mardi, to Baron Edelsheim, minister of state at Carlsruhe, of which M. de Caulincourt was the bearer. In this note, which officially announces the order given for the arrest of the Duke d'Enghien, M. de Talleyrand admits that he had previously transmitted another note, which contained a demand for the arrest of the committee of French emigrants at Offenburg.

"The nature of M. de Talleyrand's functions sufficiently explain why the arrest of the Duke d'Enghien was decreed and ordered on his report in the privy-council, which preceded the departure of General Ordener.

"It could not have taken place an the report of any of the three consuls; for it was clearly foreign to their functions. M. Fouché, who was admitted to the council, was not then in office, and was only called as an assistant in the deliberations, and because he was considered to be greatly interested in the adoption of the proposed measure. It is, however, but just to state, that it was warmly opposed by the Consul Cambaceres. He recommended that instead of forcibly seizing the Duke d'Enghien, as the report proposed, the measure should at least be postponed until the prince entered the French territory. It was on this occasion that Cambaceres was asked, how long it was since he had been so sparing of Bourbon blood.

"This information was communicated to me by the Duke de Cambaceres; who, besides, assured me that he had recorded the facts in his *Memoirs*.

"It, however, may be asked, whether it be true, that when M. de Talleyrand instigated the arrest of the Duke d'Enghien, before that of Pichegru had explained the fatal mistake respecting the real head of the conspiracy, he participated in the common error, or rather whether such error ever existed on his part. His anterior correspondence with the French minister at Baden had given him such positive information on the Duke d'Enghien's mode of living, that it was not possible for him to believe that the Duke d'Enghien could be the mysterious personage spoken of in the examinations preliminary to the trial of George.

"If such was M. de Talleyrand's belief, still it most be asked, why did he not put in the balance against it, in the privy-council of the 10th March, the previous reports of M. de Massias? Why so much zeal in accusing the Duke d'Enghien? In a case of doubt, to abstain from proposing a forcible removal was an indispensable duty.

"I have been informed that M. de Talleyrand presented to the king an attested declaration of the Princess de Rohan, from which it appears that the Duke d'Enghien was warned to go out of the way some days before he was arrested. He also pretends that he sent this information by a courier; who, according to his statement, broke a leg at Saverne. This, however, is nothing but a fable; for such a fact could at any time be proved, and yet no proof whatever is offered of it. It is not at all probable that he sent a courier; but had he wished to do so, there were many persons in his family who would have gladly undertaken the mission, and the messenger would now be ready to declare himself.

"But the degree of credit due to this attested declaration of the Princess de Rohan's may be easily appreciated. M. de Talleyrand only obtained it at Paris after the restoration; and for the possession of it he has to thank the urgent applications made to the Princess de Rohan-Rochefort by Madame Aimée de Coigny, formerly Duchess de Fleury.

"The truth is, that M. de Talleyrand never sent. The information which was conveyed to the Duke d'Enghien, and to which Madame Rohan-Rochefort bore witness, without specifying whence it came, proceeded from another source. The King of Sweden, who was then at Carlsruhe, and the Elector himself, warned the prince of the danger he might incur, and advised him to depart. Baron Dalberg, a witness whom M. de Talleyrand will not certainly refuse, admits this in his letter of the 13th of November, 1823. The warning thus conveyed to the prince was the consequence of the diplomatic note sent by M. de Talleyrand to Carlsruhe, previously to the 10th of March, in which he demanded the arrest of the committee of French emigrants at Offenburg. The Duke d'Enghien did not immediately depart, and his delay proved fatal. The whole of M. de Talleyrand's conduct controverts the idea that he ever wished to save the Duke d'Enghien; and, certainly, if the prince had received from Paris any intimation confirming that which was given him by the King of Sweden, it cannot be doubted that he would have quitted Ettenheim without delay.

"Let us now hear what M. de Massias says, in a note which he thought it necessary to publish on this subject

Some days after the catastrophe, I received a letter from the minister for foreign affairs, directing me to go to Aix-la-Chapelle, where I should find the Emperor Napoleon, to whom I had to render an account of my conduct. On my arrival, I called on General Lannes, with whom I had served in the wars of Spain and Italy, and to whose friendship I was indebted for the post I held, and for all my future prospects. He informed me that I was accused of having married the near relation of a dangerous intriguer, and of having contrived the conspiracy of the Duke d'Enghien.

On leaving General Lannes, I went to the minister for foreign affairs, to whom I repeated that which I had mentioned to him in my correspondence,—*viz., that the conduct of the prince was peaceable and innocent, and that my wife was no relation of the Baroness de Reich; a fact, of which he was assured by an authentic certificate which I had sent him.* He told me that all would be arranged.

The emperor began by asking news of the grand-duke and his family; and, having heard my reply, without any further observations, he said, "How could you, M. de Massias, whom I have treated with kindness, join in the miserable intrigues of the enemies of France?"

I knew his address; and I was aware that if I entered immediately on my justification, he would seize and draw inferences from certain circumstances, on which I should not be able to give categorical explanations: I therefore determined to manifest astonishment, and to appear not to understand what he meant.'

'Ah!' he exclaimed, with a gesticulation and a start back; 'one might almost believe that he does not know what I am talking about.'

(The same astonishment and the same appearance of ignorance on my part.)

'How!' continued he, emphatically, but not angrily; 'have you not married a near relative of that wretched intriguer, the Baroness de Reich?'—Sire, said I, this gentleman (pointing to the minister) has unworthily deceived your Majesty. He was informed by me that my wife was no relation of Baroness de Reich. Of this fact I sent him an authentic certificate. On hearing this, the emperor smiled and stepped back, and then paced up and down his closet, still looking at us. He afterwards stepped up to me, and said, in a softened tone, 'You, nevertheless, permitted meetings of emigrants at Offenburg?'—I rendered a faithful account of all that had taken place during my mission.

'How could I,' said I, 'think of persecuting a few unfortunate men, while, with your permission, they were crossing the Rhine by hundreds and thousands? I was merely acting in the spirit of your government.'—'You might, however,' resumed the emperor, 'have prevented the plots which the Duke d'Enghien was organising at Ettenheim?'—'Sire, I am too old to learn to utter falsehoods. Your Majesty has also been deceived on this point.'—'Do you think, then,' said he, with vehemence, 'that if the conspiracy of George and Pichegru had succeeded, the prince would not have crossed the Rhine, and posted to Paris?' I hung down my head, and said nothing. Then, assuming a careless air, he spoke to me of Carlsruhe, and some other subjects of little interest, after which he dismissed me.'

★★★★★★

Note:—"On the following day," adds M. de Massias, "there was public and solemn distribution of crosses of the Legion of Honour, which the emperor had then newly instituted. According to the regulations, I was entitled to one, both on account of my post of *chargé d'affaires*, and my rank as a colonel in the army,

"The honour was, however, conferred on all my colleagues who were present, and I was the only person who did not receive one. General Lannes, whom I saw in the morning, told me, that the emperor was perfectly satisfied with my courage and honourable conduct, but that he wished to punish my want of respect to my superior.

"I returned to Carlsruhe; and in about a month or two afterwards, one of his Majesty's chamberlains called on me. This was the Count de Beaumont, who delivered to me a letter from Duroc, the grand-marshal of the place. This letter informed me that the emperor would shortly send to Carlsruhe his adopted daughter, Princess Stephanie, wife of the Grand-Duke of Baden, whom he intended to confide to my care; and that in everything concerning her, I was not to correspond with the minister for foreign affairs, but directly with the emperor himself.

"About a year after the arrival of the princess, the emperor appointed me resident-consul-general at Dantzick. I had scarcely held this new situation a week, when I was appointed *intendant* of the city; a post to which great emoluments are attached.

"On my return to France, which my health obliged me to revisit, on leave of absence, the emperor created me a baron, with authority to institute a majorate for my family."

★★★★★★

"M. de Talleyrand then deceived the emperor, in not rendering him a faithful account of the tenor of the correspondence of M. de Massias;—he deceived M. de Massias himself whom he misrepresented to the emperor;—he deceived the Elector of Baden, by assuring him, through Baron Dalberg (whom he was, doubtless, at the same time deceiving), that the emigrants residing in the electorate would not be molested, while he was preparing his diplomatic note of the 11th of March, which was not to be transmitted to the Baden minister of state until after the arrest of the Duke d'Enghien!

"M. de Massias thus continues:—'As soon as I learned that the prince had been arrested, and removed to the citadel of Strasburg, I wrote, without loss of time, to the minister for foreign affairs, to inform him that, during his residence in the electorate (*of which my former dispatches had apprised him*), the conduct of the prince had been moderate and blameless. *My letter must be in the archives*; it is the only one in which I ever introduced a Latin quotation. To give additional force to my ideas, and greater weight to my assertion, I borrowed these words from Tacitus—'*Nec beneficio nee ijuriâ cognitus*; which perfectly explained the situation in which I stood with reference to the august personage, whom the cause of truth alone led me to defend.'

"But this letter, which could only have been written on the 15th of March, must have reached Paris on the 18th at latest; and it was not until that very day that the prince quitted the citadel of Strasburg.

"Let M. de Talleyrand inform us what efforts he employed in the interval between the 18th and 20th, to substantiate the clear evidence of an honest man, which must have dispelled, or at least have diminished, the alarms which had been excited in the mind of the First Consul.

"The evidence of M. de Massias is positive. Had it been viewed solely with the object of elucidating the truth, it could not in any way have squared with the portrait of the individual who was supposed to be at the head of the conspiracy. Three previous days ought to have sufficed for M. de Talleyrand to endeavour to undeceive the First Consul, and to prevent the great catastrophe. How did he employ this valuable time? What said he? What did he to corroborate the letter of M. de Massias, and to get it introduced as a defensive document on the trial? The sentence shows that the documents for and against the prisoner amounted to one only; and it may be easily guessed that this one was not the letter of M. de Massias.

"Let M. de Talleyrand answer this.

"This letter, and other documents relative to the fatal event, have disappeared from the archives of the department of foreign affairs, at the head of which M. de Talleyrand has successively been during the Republic, the Directory, the Consulate, the Empire, and the Kingdom.

★★★★★★

It is possible that this letter is the same to which, the Emperor Napoleon alluded, in replying to Mr. O'Meara, when he complained that it had not been delivered to him until after the death of the prince. From the declarations of persons attached to the emperor's cabinet, it appears that they had no knowledge of any letter of the Duke d'Enghien's.

★★★★★★

"Let us proceed.

"On the morning of the 29th *Ventose* (20th of March), the day on which the sentence was pronounced, I saw M. de Talleyrand at Malmaison. By a singular coincidence, it was shortly after this that orders were given for the removal of the prince to Vincennes. In the afternoon he called on the governor of Paris. His duty might have required his attendance on the First Consul; but he, a minister, and the reports of the privy-council which had determined the arrest of the Duke d'Enghien, what business could he have with the general who was appointed to nominate the prince's judges, and to direct them to bring him before their tribunal? If the letter of the First Consul, of which I was the bearer to the governor of Paris, said all, as it may be supposed it did, what was the object of M. Talleyrand's extraordinary visit? Did he go to add his own comments to the letter, or to transmit the last instructions, the last commands, of the First Consul? . . . It must be observed) that the decree of the government of the same day, which directed that the Duke d'Enghien should be brought before a court-martial, certainly authorised the governor of Paris to nominate the court; but that it should be *immediately* summoned by order of the governor, who selected its members, is not in the decree.

"M. de Talleyrand, like Count Hullin, may justly exclaim, 'How unfortunate I am!' He did everything to bring about the catastrophe, and nothing to prevent it. After the event he was so unlucky as to be the individual on whom devolved the task of announcing and justifying the death of the Duke d'Enghien to the foreign powers. If he acted against his inclination, it may truly be said that he has drained the cup of bitterness to the very dregs. But what is to be thought of the fate of the victim?

"Will it now be said that I have done wrong in endeavouring to exculpate the emperor at the expense of M. de Talleyrand,—that is to say, candidly unfolding facts of which I entertain a thorough conviction? I am aware that the Emperor Napoleon, in his testament, seems to take upon himself the whole responsibility of the catastrophe; but I know him well enough to estimate differently from many other persons the value of his own declarations. Even in his last moments, the Emperor Napoleon was less concerned by the approach of death, than he was anxious to preserve unbroken, in public opinion, the illusion attached to his power; and I am certain that, even on the brink of the grave, he would have felt highly displeased at an attempt to prove that any event of his reign took place without his authority. 'The Duke d'Enghien died because I willed it.' Such is the language of the emperor to posterity; which is as much as to say—'I being sovereign, nobody dared to conceive the thought of disposing of the life or liberty of any one whatever. I might have been misled, but no one dared for a moment to interfere with my power,'

"Penetrated with these ideas, to which all the facts I have recorded, as well as the words of the emperor himself, add considerable weight, I propose this objection to those who persist in maintaining that the emperor ordered the execution of the Duke d'Enghien, as the sultan sends the bowstring to a *vizier*.

"The emperor regretted the death of the Duke d'Enghien; but the deed was done, and he could not throw the blame of it on anyone. His inflexible character, the strong feeling of his dignity and his duty as a sovereign, would not permit him to evade the responsibility of anything that had been done, still less to screen himself by throwing blame on another.

"If matters had been managed at Vincennes, by the president of the court-martial, in such a way that M. Real had found the prince still living; if the examination had proved that he was not the mysterious person who had been seen with George, and who was sought for, I ask all who knew the First Consul, whether it is their belief that he would have suffered the Duke d'Enghien to be sacrificed. I also ask what would have become of M. de Talleyrand, if, after his terrible proposition of removing the prince and putting him out of the way, he had seen the chief of the state relinquish the prey, which he had been induced to seize as the means of protecting his life against the plots of his irreconcilable enemies.

"Another trait yet remains to be recorded, and with it I shall wind up the observations which this statement of facts has suggested. In the evening of the Duke d'Enghien's execution, M. de Talleyrand gave a masked ball, to which all the diplomatic body were invited. Nothing could exceed the dullness of this ball, which was an outrage upon public feeling. Some individuals had spirit enough to refuse the invitations; among these were, Princess Dolgoroucky and M. de Moustier, now one of his Majesty's ambassadors, who informed me of this fact.

"Such was the part which M. de Talleyrand performed in the catastrophe of the Duke d'Enghien. Let him now say whether the exchange of a few polite phrases with Baron Dalberg, and the silence he has maintained, suffice to remove the serious accusations which public opinion has affixed upon him for the share he took in that fatal event."

LEONAUR

ALSO FROM LEONAUR
AVAILABLE IN SOFTCOVER OR HARDCOVER WITH DUST JACKET

OFFICERS & GENTLEMEN *by Peter Hawker & William Graham*—Two Accounts of British Officers During the Peninsula War: Officer of Light Dragoons by Peter Hawker & Campaign in Portugal and Spain by William Graham .

THE WALCHEREN EXPEDITION *by Anonymous*—The Experiences of a British Officer of the 81st Regt. During the Campaign in the Low Countries of 1809.

LADIES OF WATERLOO *by Charlotte A. Eaton, Magdalene de Lancey & Juana Smith*—The Experiences of Three Women During the Campaign of 1815: Waterloo Days by Charlotte A. Eaton, A Week at Waterloo by Magdalene de Lancey & Juana's Story by Juana Smith.

JOURNAL OF AN OFFICER IN THE KING'S GERMAN LEGION *by John Frederick Hering*—Recollections of Campaigning During the Napoleonic Wars.

JOURNAL OF AN ARMY SURGEON IN THE PENINSULAR WAR *by Charles Boutflower*—The Recollections of a British Army Medical Man on Campaign During the Napoleonic Wars.

ON CAMPAIGN WITH MOORE AND WELLINGTON *by Anthony Hamilton*—The Experiences of a Soldier of the 43rd Regiment During the Peninsular War.

THE ROAD TO AUSTERLITZ *by R. G. Burton*—Napoleon's Campaign of 1805.

SOLDIERS OF NAPOLEON *by A. J. Doisy De Villargennes & Arthur Chuquet*—The Experiences of the Men of the French First Empire: Under the Eagles by A. J. Doisy De Villargennes & Voices of 1812 by Arthur Chuquet .

INVASION OF FRANCE, 1814 *by F. W. O. Maycock*—The Final Battles of the Napoleonic First Empire.

LEIPZIG—A CONFLICT OF TITANS *by Frederic Shoberl*—A Personal Experience of the 'Battle of the Nations' During the Napoleonic Wars, October 14th-19th, 1813.

SLASHERS *by Charles Cadell*—The Campaigns of the 28th Regiment of Foot During the Napoleonic Wars by a Serving Officer.

BATTLE IMPERIAL *by Charles William Vane*—The Campaigns in Germany & France for the Defeat of Napoleon 1813-1814.

SWIFT & BOLD *by Gibbes Rigaud*—The 60th Rifles During the Peninsula War.